THE PARANORM

A Bishop Investigates

Hugh Montefiore

D1103070

UPFRONT PUBLISHING
LEICESTERSHIRE

THE PARANORMAL: *A Bishop Investigates*
Copyright © Hugh Montefiore 2002

ISBN 1 84426 114 X

First Published 2002 by
UPFRONT PUBLISHING
Leicestershire

THE PARANORMAL
A Bishop Investigates

Contents

PART THREE
The Paranormal and Christianity

INTRODUCTION

Nearly two-thirds of the population, according to a recent poll, believe paranormal phenomena occur that science cannot explain. I count myself among them. Although in the past my main work has been in theology, I have always been interested in the paranormal, but it was not until I heard at first hand of some phenomena for which no normal explanation seemed adequate that I decided to look into the whole subject in some depth. As I shall explain in the first chapter, the phenomena with which I was confronted were two cases of what is called 'psychometry', that is to say, the alleged ability to tell the future or the past of individuals by simply handling some object that belongs to them.

The upshot of this enquiry has been that the paranormal seems to me a subject of real importance, and I find it deplorable that scientists deride it and that religion ignores it. I hope that this book might contribute to altering such negative attitudes. I shall describe the Church's lack of interest later when I consider specifically Christian paranormal experiences: here I confine myself to the negative attitude of most scientists, an attitude that seems to me unscientific. A well-known professor of science writes:

> Paranormalism could be called an abuse of the legitimate sense of poetic wonder which true science should be feeding.
>
> Dawkins, p.xi

He derides what he calls 'paranormal superstitions'. I think that the belief that science can give us a better vision of life's meaning than religion is a minority view; but nevertheless Dawkins goes on to claim that:

> In so far as religions are in decline in the West, their place seems to be taken not by science, with its clearer sighted, grander vision

of the cosmos, so much as by the paranormal and astrology.

Dawkins, p.115

I am citing Professor Dawkins because he is one of the most popular scientific writers of our day.

> Disturbed people recount their fantasies of ghosts and polter-geists. Instead of sending them off to a good psychiatrist, television producers eagerly sign them up.
>
> Dawkins, p.12

I invite him to consider the phenomena that I cite later in this book.

> Existing science will undoubtedly be overthrown, not however by casual anecdotes or performances on television, but by rigorous research, repeated, dissected and repeated again.
>
> Dawkins, p.156

Rigorous criticism, yes; but Dawkins seems ignorant of the fact that paranormal phenomena by their very nature cannot usually be reproduced to order, and therefore they are not amenable to testing by the scientific method of repetition: they often need other criteria for their evaluation. To be sure, there is some research that is being done at Edinburgh University (Morris *et al.*, 1994) in which people under 'clinical' conditions guess the identity of cards or try to pass telepathic messages to another person; and these do indeed show some positive results; but they are of limited use, because they pale into insignificance beside the wealth of alleged phenomena that can occur in real-life situations.

Most paranormal phenomena are of a different kind. It is unfair to dismiss them as worthless merely because they are anecdotal. Personal testimony and personal experience certainly need rigorous evaluation to expose fraud or delusion, but they are vital because they provide primary evidence. It is unscientific to ignore them. Yet Professor Blakemore, in his fascinating book, *The Mind Machine* (Blakemore, 1988), never even mentions the paranormal, even to deride it.

As I looked into the literature on the paranormal, I could not help comparing the situation today with that of a century or so ago when, in 1882, Professor Henry Sidgwick, in company with Cambridge friends, founded the Society for Psychical Research. In those days, scientists who were household names, like Sir Oliver Lodge, interested themselves in such work. Today the sciences have become so specialised that few are able to see the larger picture, and it is so institutionalised that even fewer still can get grants for psychical research. Francis Crick, the scientist who, with Watson, cracked the genetic code by his discovery of the double helix, told me, when we belonged to the same Cambridge college, that he had once thought of interesting himself in parapsychology but decided he would have more success in biology. How right he was!

There is today only one chair in Britain in parapsychology, in Edinburgh. Even the Peterhouse ghost does not seem to have persuaded Cambridge scientists in favour of the paranormal. The Master of one of its colleges tells me how he was laughed to scorn when he recounted to his colleagues paranormal experiences that he had shared with students on a reading party. The only odd man out is a Cambridge professor of physics, Professor Josephson, FRS, a Nobel Prize winner. In 1974, he even went to Toronto to a conference of twenty-one scientists to investigate the teenager Matthew Manning (see p.336). (The preliminary report of this conference can be found as an appendix to this book.) Professor Josephson said in an interview to the *Daily Mail*:

> We are on the verge of discoveries which may be extremely important for physics.
>
> Manning, 1974, p.11

Although he thought only in terms of physics and the ordinary methods of scientific investigation, at least he was interested. There are certainly mysterious things in physics, such as the nature of the dark matter that is said to constitute 95 per cent of the physical universe, or the quantum laws which possess acausal non-local features that make it impossible to give an accurate description of an independent and objective reality. But the psi phenomena investigated in this book suggest that paranormal mysteries are of a different kind, non-physical in nature. Incidentally, Manning was not very impressed by the scientists who investigated his paranormal powers.

> I became less enthusiastic about these experiments and more disillusioned – even cynical – about the so-called science of parapsychology. I was made continually to repeat the same experiments not because scientists did not believe me but because they did not believe the findings of their fellow scientists.
>
> Manning, 1995, p.3

He also noted a very marked abhorrence on their part of the probability of life after death.

I find that the comparative lack of psychical investigation in Britain contrasts badly with what happens in America. A trustee of the American Society for Psychical Research has pointed out the higher readings of magnetic fields in places where ghosts are alleged to appear, as high as 100 milligauss against a background of 1 or 2 milligauss. These magnetic fields may move from room to room. Portable infrared thermometers which register temperatures may show drops of 25°C and 35°C in 'cold spots', which are a well-known concomitant of the paranormal. Cosmic rays have been registered in such spots. SPIDER (Simultaneous Psychophysical Incident Electronic Recorder) activates a camera as soon as something unusual occurs. Of course, photographs allegedly of entities are dismissed by sceptics as fraudulent or the result of some fault in the development process. None of these instruments can prove the existence of psi phenomena. For example, sceptics regard changes in the electromagnetic field as the cause of hallucination rather than a concomitant of psi phenomena, while enthusiasts regard the high level as providing the 'fuel' by which entities may manifest themselves (Coghlan, p.43ff.). Nonetheless, these technical devices do show a willingness to use scientific methods of investigating the apparently paranormal.

It is entirely right to use scientific methods and techniques in order to investigate the paranormal, wherever such methods and techniques can be used; and such methods do indeed appear to show the existence of such phenomena (Radin, p.6). Professor Morris even quotes the odds at millions to one in favour (Morris, 2001, p.46)! But much of the evidence for psychic phenomena does not, by its nature, permit these methods of investigation. What then are the rigorous procedures that should be undertaken before one can properly regard alleged paranormal phenomena as genuine rather than hallucinatory, imaginary or fraudulent?

It has been suggested that the following questions should be asked:

1. Is the phenomenon best explained as coincidence?
2. Is it the result of poor observation?
3. Have the observations of the phenomenon been misinterpreted?
4. Is there a hidden natural cause of the alleged paranormal phenomenon?
5. Is the alleged phenomenon the result of self-deception?
6. Is there an as yet unknown natural cause of the phenomenon?
7. Has there been deception (or self-deception) by others?
8. Has there been a distorted impression of the phenomenon through biological or functional dysfunction?

Morris, 2000, p.110ff.

I would agree that all these questions should be asked in investigating alleged paranormal phenomena. But because few of these will have taken place in the presence of the investigator, and some may have taken place some time ago, I suggest that the following additional questions should also be asked:

1. What is the general credibility of the witness(es) to an alleged paranormal event? Was anyone else present when the phenomenon took place? How reliable in general is the testimony of the person to whom it happened? How rigorous have been the enquiries into these matters during the lifetime of the persons concerned?
2. How much time has intervened between the event and its first written account? Those whose discipline is literary criticism know that the longer an account exists in a purely oral form,

the more likely it is that changes, especially exaggerations, will take place.

3. Is the account of the event internally coherent? If there are inconsistencies, the probability is that memories have become blurred.

4. Is the phenomenon unique, or are there other similar examples of the phenomenon which are well attested?

5. How strong are the general arguments against this type of paranormal phenomenon?

6. What is the balance of probability between accepting the phenomenon as paranormal and looking for some (as yet unknown) natural explanation?

Within the constraints of a book, I have been able to give only a few of the thousands of psi phenomena that have been recorded. It is impossible to apply all the foregoing criteria when considering each psi phenomenon recounted in the pages that follow. The reader must make up his or her mind about each. More data may well be required to do this, so I have given references to sources where this may be found. It is not my intention to prove or disprove the existence of any individual phenomenon, but rather to show that it is worthy of study; but I would like to record my own conviction that in many cases they recount genuine paranormal phenomena.

PART ONE
The Paranormal in Secular Life

Chapter I
PSI PHENOMENA

I was at one time suffragan bishop to Mervyn Stockwood, Bishop of Southwark, who was interested in the paranormal. He told me that he had gone to visit the well-known medium Ena Twigg. He said that he handed her his episcopal ring, and she thereupon gave him a rundown on his life. As I was not present myself and Bishop Stockwood is now dead, this lacks any supporting evidence; but it greatly impressed me because I knew the bishop well. He was an honourable man who would never have made up such a story.

Later, someone who became a family friend was looking after my sick wife. I came to know her very well, and she told me an extraordinary story of her teens:

> When we were living in Belfast, I met an old lady. She lived in a humble cottage in Connemara, and was most reluctant to visit the city. On the rare occasions when she did, everyone was astonished at the accuracy of her predictions. Although she didn't charge any fees, everyone would give her a little something for her trouble. Holding something that belonged to you, which could be only a handkerchief, she would start as though reading from a book, and tell you your entire future. There would be nothing about the past, she would ask no questions: in fact, you couldn't speak at all during the entire session. One of my friends was called Ella, who was engaged to be married at the time. She was told that she would never marry the man whose ring she was wearing, but that she would marry a sailor. I remember how we teased Ella mercilessly, singing 'A Life on the Ocean Waves' as we danced the hornpipe up and down the room. Of course, we were all teenagers at the time. However, eventually Ella did break off her engagement. When it happened, she was heartbroken and her family became extremely worried about her. She refused to go

out anywhere. They suggested a luxury cruise, but it was no good. Eventually her father did persuade her to go for a trip on board a cargo vessel which also carried a few passengers round the Mediterranean, calling at various ports. She came back engaged to the First Officer and married him.

Then there was another friend called Julie. The old lady told her that she would run away from home and marry, as she put it, 'out of the faith', meaning someone who was not a Protestant. Pretty taboo in Ireland in those days. She was also told she would end up deaf. Julie was still at college, and she had not had any trouble with her ears. We could not take it seriously, suggesting in fun that we should buy her an ear trumpet. It was startling therefore when Julie did elope when she was still at college. She fled over the border into Eire with a much older man who was a Catholic. Moreover, a short time after, she developed ear trouble and became deaf.

The third person was Pamela. She was responsible for bringing the old lady to our house. Her husband would not let her use their house, so she came to my mother's instead. When it was Pamela's turn, the old lady told her she could tell her nothing. Her husband had been ill, and she thought it was because of him. This was not the case. In six months, Pamela was dead from a rapid form of cancer.

The old lady then told my friend about her future.

She told me that I would become ill and nearly die. This was certainly true. I did become very, very ill, and all the specialists and doctors said I would die, and I astounded them by not dying.

She told me I would have many businesses, and that none of them would have my name on it. This again came true. I had eight businesses in all, and none of them had my name on them! She told me that I would travel the world, not once, but many times back and forth. This seemed absurd at the time, but it too became true, as it happened through my businesses and when I married a Sri Lankan and used to visit his family. She told me that I would die in my own bed surrounded by people who loved me. I laughed when she said this, and she reached over and took my hand and said, 'Don't laugh. If you saw the ending of some people, like myself, you wouldn't laugh. I wish I could say my ending would be like yours.'

She said I would have a very successful business which would fail at the height of its success. She said, 'This sounds strange, but it will be no fault of yours.' She told me my life would never be ordinary, and that I would know the heights of happiness and the depths of despair and I would move with equal ease with duchesses or dustmen. Everything she said seems to have come true, except, of course, about my death which still lies in the future.

Once again, this is anecdotal and cannot be held in any sense to *prove* precognition. It could be said that, since the old lady's visit took place over half a century ago, my friend's memory was at fault, or that coincidences do happen, or that the prophecies were self-fulfilling. Against that, I have to say that I have complete trust in the integrity of my friend, and that in helping her with her autobiography I came to realise that she has a very clear and detailed memory of the past; and it is hard to believe that the actual occurrence of all these events was mere coincidence or that all of the old lady's prophecies were self-fulfilling.

Here was psi in ordinary life. I would investigate it all as best I could. It was worth looking into. And I found a good many other instances of what is called 'psychometry', that is, telling the past or the future of some person simply by holding in one's hand something belonging to the person concerned. I found many striking accounts.

Some of the other cases are better attested. G N M Tyrrell tells how Dr J Hettlinger, between 1935 and 1937, carried out a series of experiments in psychometry. Sixty-three different persons were used, and the sensitives made 1,266 statements about them, 605 of which were found to be correct (Tyrrell, p.128). Tyrrell suggested that no information is 'locked up' in the object, but it serves to canalise the sensitive's faculty and to concentrate it in the right direction, although he admitted that he had no idea how this happened. Tyrrell also reported on research carried out over many years by Dr Eugene Osty, a doctor who became interested in the paranormal, and who gathered round him what seems a remarkable collection of sensitives. He was Director of the Institut Métapsychique International in Paris, who gave this example of psychometry that he had witnessed:

Osty received a letter enclosed by a certain Captain C, and was told only that the writer of the letter was now dead. On the 18 May 1922, he gave this letter to Madame Viviana, who crushed it in her hands and said that the writer was dead; a soldier; in the war; sunburnt; had a very direct gaze; was strong willed and combative, unsentimental, intelligent, good, energetic, amiable, Catholic, had a tendency to mysticism, would pray when sad or troubled, not bigoted, high-minded; came of a religious family and from a country where they give boats the names of saints, as in Brittany; had an elder brother in whom he placed confidence; his only anxiety was for a dearly loved woman; there is a child; a feeling of swaying, rolling, or humidity and water... as if he were on the water; 'my lips are salt as if I were on the sea'; an officer; young; died at the end of the war; not from a wound; suffocation; a sudden pain in the head; did not die in bed; small houses, soldiers, engineers, pickaxes, tents round him.

Tyrrell notes that the points in the information are condensed. The letter could not have given all this information even if it had been read by the sensitive. Twenty-five points were found to be correct, and four were unverifiable. There was no false statement. The writer was the brother of Captain C, and the letter had been written on board in a rough sea. The captain had died of influenza. Dr Osty, four days later, put the captain's sister-in-law in touch with another sensitive (without the letter), and she also made no false statement (Tyrrell, p.179ff.). Thus psychometry cannot be claimed to be the only way of producing information about someone. But mistakes can always be made, because there is bound to be an element of subjectivity even if the bulk of a statement may be accurate.

Psychometry is the rather strange name given to this faculty of obtaining knowledge of persons or events by contact with a physical object linked to them. Usually, handling the object is believed to enable a sensitive to produce information concerning what has happened in the past, or what will happen in the future. Psychometry is therefore a form of telepathy or clairvoyance, produced under particular circumstances. Whereas telepathy, if it occurs, can be explained by positing that our minds exist in a field, and are not simply part of our brains, making it possible for one mind to be in touch with another, it would be more difficult to give that kind of explanation of psychometry. One would have to imagine either that a person somehow imprints on an object a memory of his or her own past and/or a knowledge of future destiny, or (less improbably) that by handling a physical object a person is brought into the field of another person's mind to whom the object belongs; but even that would not explain the ability to foretell the future, unless the 'field' of the mind is believed to extend beyond the spatio-temporal order.

Psychometry is only one of many paranormal phenomena. All manner of strange happenings have been recorded down the centuries. It was not until the Society for Psychical Research (SPR) was founded in 1882 that there was a serious attempt to investigate these phenomena. The object of the Society, set out in its publications, 'is to examine without prejudice or prepossession and in a scientific spirit those faculties of man, real or imagined, which appear to be inexplicable on any generally recognised hypothesis'. Its first president was Professor Henry Sidgwick, Professor of Moral Philosophy at Cambridge, aided by his wife, who became the first principal of Newnham College, Cambridge. It included at its foundation very distinguished figures from the academic world. Among its members have been professors of subjects ranging from Greek to Zoology, and even a winner of a Nobel Prize. Such a distinguished body should reassure people that 'it is not a playground for superstitious cranks', as Arthur Koestler put it. The archives of the society (the majority of which are unpublished) contain thousands of cases of alleged psi phenomena.

The first major work to be laid before the general public was *Phantasms of the Living* (Gurney, Myers and Podmore, 1886), some 1,400 pages long and containing 701 cases selected from more than seventeen thousand submitted to the Society. More than half of these were 'narratives or appearances or other impressions coincident either with the death of the person seen or with some critical moment in his life's history'. Since then, in addition to the SPR's Proceedings, there has arisen quite a large body of literature. Among this is *Apparitions* (Green and McCreery, 1975), which included material taken from the SPR and fifty cases selected from some 1,300 which were received as a result of a broadcast on apparitions and haunted houses.

In continuing my investigations into the paranormal, I now go on to relate some paranormal phenomena that have happened to ordinary people in ordinary life. I start with those who have had veridical glimpses into the future.

Precognition

Telepathy (if it happens) takes place when the events or thoughts of another person are perceived at the same time as they occur. This is a different matter from the ability to see or hear or intuit an event before it takes place in situations when it could not have been inferred from information obtained beforehand. There are many people who would say that this is impossible. But others have been convinced from experience that it can actually happen. Foretelling the future conjures up images of old ladies examining tea leaves in a cup, or gazing into a crystal ball, or simply shutting their eyes and telling a person about his future. It brings to mind a gypsy's tent at a fair. Nonetheless, remarkable predictions have occurred. Keith Hearne has made a study of them and he has published over one hundred such cases. Here is an example, anecdotal but paralleled by others involving similar dreams.

> I was planning to travel with my two children to visit my husband in West Africa. The night before the flight, I had a very bad dream in which my husband, a deep-sea diver, was drowning. Two months later, my husband did die in a drowning incident, just as I had dreamed in every detail. It shook me to have seen the future.
>
> Hearne, p.27

A charming story is told by a notoriously truthful Prime Minister, Clement Attlee.

> One night years ago I had a very vivid dream, so vivid that not only did I wake up but I remembered every detail the next morning.
>
> I was at a dog meeting, and suddenly I knew that I held in my hand the winner and second of the Grand National. The ticket had a diagonal stripe on it, with a number in each segment. Perhaps I should mention that I don't bet on horses, except very

rarely, and I don't go to the dogs! This dream took place about a week before the National, and I told everyone in the office that I had dreamt of backing both the winner and the second horse.

On Grand National day itself, I was very busy, and it was only by chance that I heard someone call out and ask if anyone wanted to place a bet on the race. I said I did and was asked which horse I wished to back. In reply I gave the two numbers I had dreamt... Someone fetched a paper and looked up the names of the horses running under the numbers I'd given. I placed a modest bet on them.

They came in first and second. That was the year in which the form was upset, because several of the fancied horses fell soon after the start.

How did I dream the winners? If I had dreamt the names of the horses, it could have been put down to my subconsciously having heard or read about them. But I didn't. I dreamt the numbers under which they would be running – well before those numbers had been allocated.

Enright, p.286ff.

Coincidence or precognition?

Precognition was believed to exist in many ancient cultures, often embodied in dreams, omens and auguries. Even Cicero told how a certain Simonides had a dream warning him not to go on a certain ship for a sea voyage, and the ship sank with all hands on board. In the seventeenth century, the diarist, John Aubrey, a Fellow of the Royal Society, made a collection of strange sayings.

Three or four days before my father died, as I was in my bed about nine o'clock in the morning, perfectly awake, I heard three distinct knocks at the bedhead, as it had been with a rule or ferula.

Aubrey, p.166

Interesting, but hardly proof of precognition! Other cases are much more persuasive. One of the most extraordinary cases is a premonitory hallucination that occurred to the niece of a good friend of Hearne. She foresaw the massive explosion at the Flixborough chemical works in the UK on 1 June 1974. Leslie Brennan was a married woman with two children. At the time, she was in the process of divorcing her husband. At noon she sat in a Cleethorpes house alone, watching television.

> The word 'newsflash' occurred on the screen, and a male voice gave news of an explosion at Flixborough, some forty kilometres away. Several people had been killed or injured, the voice said. Leslie felt shocked, and shortly afterwards she told a couple who were staying in the same house when they came in for lunch. That evening they saw television reports, but could not understand why the time of the explosion was given as late afternoon. The next day, in reading that the explosion had indeed happened, Leslie and her friends realised that she had had a premonition.
>
> At 4.53 p.m. on Saturday, 1 June 1974, at the Nypro (UK) Ltd chemical plant at Flixborough, South Humberside, a massive explosion occurred which virtually destroyed the sixty-acre complex. The disaster happened suddenly and unexpectedly, resulting in twenty-six deaths and hundreds of injured…
>
> The two witnesses were questioned closely. One was a male welder in an engineering firm, and the female worked in the same bank as Leslie. Both witnesses signed statements confirming that Leslie had reported the explosion to them at lunchtime on 1 June 1974.
>
> Hearne, p.74ff.

Both BBC and ITV confirmed that no newsflash on any topic was broadcast that lunchtime. They were witnesses, not of the phenomenon itself, but of being told about something before it occurred. It is not easy to find an alternative explanation for Leslie Brennan's experience, other than precognition. Coincidence seems improbable.

Another well-known case of precognition concerns the Aberfan disaster when, on 21 October 1966, a huge slag heap shifted and descended on a school at Aberfan in Wales, killing 144 people, including 128 schoolchildren. John Barker, a consultant psychiatrist, was so moved next day at the site that he wondered whether there had been any premonitions of the disaster. An appeal was put out, with no less than seventy-six responses. After checking for witnesses, this was reduced to twenty-four. The local minister, the Revd Glannant Jones, wrote a letter, confirmed by the parents of a ten-year-old child, Eryl Mai Jones:

Eryl was an attractive dependable child, not given to imagination. A fortnight before the disaster she said to her mother, who at the time was setting aside some money for her, 'Mummy, I'm not afraid to die.'

Her mother replied, 'Why do you talk of dying, and you so young? Do you want a lollipop?'

'No,' she said, 'but I will be with Peter and June (school-mates).'

The day before the disaster, she said to her mother, 'Mummy, let me tell you my dream last night.'

Her mother answered gently, 'Darling, I've no time now. Tell me again later.'

The child replied, 'No, Mummy, you must listen. I dreamt I went to school and there was no school there. Something black had come down all over it.'

Her mother replied, 'You mustn't have chips for dinner for a bit.'

The next day, off went her daughter to school as happy as ever. In the communal grave she was buried with Peter on one side and June on the other.

Enright, p.339

It might be said that, with the heap overhanging the valley, many local people could have dreamt about just such an accident. Doubtless Professor Dawkins would dismiss this as pure coincidence (Dawkins, 1998, p.160). But the number of people in different parts of the country who appear to have had premonitions of the disaster is impressive.

In addition to alleged cases of precognition that occur spontaneously, there have been several attempts to produce precognition under 'laboratory' conditions. In the 1930s, experiments in Cambridge to produce telepathy led to the remarkable conclusion that some people got the correct result one or two nights before or after the night on which they were attempting to produce telepathy. Later, J B Rhine used card guessing to produce evidence of precognition at Duke University in the USA. Further experiments in the USA were conducted by Helmut Schmidt, Rhine's former Director of Research, using a random number generator. Soal, who had been unable to get good results from card guessing, published some excellent results, but before he died in 1978 it was established that he had tampered with the figures (Markwick, pp.250–277). W J Levy, who succeeded Schmidt as Rhine's Director of Research, was also found to be cheating (Rhine, 1974, pp.215–250). I mention this to show how important it is to examine the possibility of fraud when dealing with alleged paranormal phenomena. Rhine's reputation, however, was unblemished and he confirmed his position, and indeed he set the future course for paranormal studies, by his 'laboratory' approach to the testing of phenomena.

Research on precognition was also conducted on dreams using a 'dream machine' that woke a person when her breathing rate increased, indicating that she had entered into REM (Rapid Eye Movement) sleep during which the phenomenon of 'lucid dreaming' may take place (that is, conscious and controllable dreaming). Some seemingly significant results were obtained. There appeared to be precognition of scenes that were afterwards seen by the dreamer (Hearne, p.82ff.). But there could be no guarantee that the person had not previously seen a picture of the sight she foresaw in her dream. Experiments have also been carried out on animals, which are said to show that mice can experience precognition and thereby avoid electric shocks (Duval and Montredon, pp.153–168), but the results are not clear-cut.

J B Rhine's wife, Louisa, compared evidence of telepathic experiences with those concerning precognition, with interesting results. Most alleged cases of precognition appear to come from dreams, 60 per cent compared with 19 per cent of telepathic experiences (L E Rhine, 1954, pp.93–123). Louisa also looked into cases where premonitory experiences resulted in intervention. She found no less than 131 cases out of 433 where intervention was successfully undertaken. For example, a couple were staying in a small hotel when the husband was awoken in the middle of the night by his wife telling him that they must leave at once as she had just dreamt that the hotel had been demolished by an explosion. The husband protestingly complied, and they left, only to find next day that a lorry loaded with dynamite had crashed into the hotel, exploded and demolished the building (L E Rhine, 1955, p.17).

Many attempts have been made to explain alleged cases of

precognition. The most common objection is that too great an emphasis has been given to the improbability of a coincidence. It is difficult to maintain this view in the face of the 'laboratory' conditions under which some experiments have been carried out, beginning with J B Rhine. Some people try to explain alleged cases of precognition as self-fulfilling prophecies, in the sense that the prophecies give rise to later events; but it is difficult to explain all prophecies in this way; and, in any case, there is often no connection between the two that could possibly be shown to be causal. Dunne's views, encapsulated in *An Experiment With Time* (Dunne, 1962), according to which, when we are asleep, we move forward along a fourth dimension, have not been well received. Other purported explanations are equally speculative, based on such concepts as subatomic particles conveying psi information by moving backwards in time and interacting with neurons in the brain (Feynman, 1949, pp.749–59), or acausal theories advocated by Jung and Pauli, in which two separate events, deriving from a common archetype, provide a meaningful coincidence, with the one causing the other (Koestler, pp.91–101).

A great majority of those who claim precognitive experiences are women. The reason for this might be that such experiences are connected with the right hemisphere of the cortex, which is more developed in women. Hearne noted that most experiences are premonitory of death or disaster, which may indicate that they are functional alarms rather than ordinary occurrences (Hearne, p.109). However, when we come to examine apparitions, we shall find that they, too, are often connected with death, and it is difficult to substantiate a theory of functional alarms for all of them. I do not think that, if these experiences are genuine, they invalidate the concept of free will. When we decide what we shall do or what we shall not do, we actually decide one way or the other; and outside time all past history and all future events appear as one. What is paranormal is the experience of what is 'outside' time by those who live within the spatio-temporal universe. If precognition does indeed take place, we have no idea how or why it happens.

Precognition is important because (granted that it takes place) it shows that the mind can receive information other than through the normal working of the brain. It is the death knell of materialism; and so materialists have a vested interest in trying to disprove that it can take place.

Telepathy

There is a natural affinity between precognition and telepathy. If precognition means receiving a message about the future, telepathy refers to receiving a message from another person without any form of bodily communication. Before considering whether this happens between human beings, it seems sensible to start with animals, to find out whether telepathy, if it exists, has been inherited from our evolutionary forebears. It could be that telepathy developed before animals could communicate with each other through bodily means.

There are certainly aspects of animal life that have not yet been explained by the laws of physics, chemistry or biology. There is no satisfactory explanation of the way in which shoals of fish and flocks of birds can twist and turn at considerable speed without running into each other. There is no satisfactory explanation for the extraordinarily complex evolution of colonies of bees, or the even more complex achievements of ant colonies. E O Wilson, after describing a marauding and leaderless column of several million African driver ants, wrote:

> To speak of a colony of driver ants or other social insects as more than just a tight aggregation of individuals is to speak of a super-organism.
>
> Holldobler and Wilson, p.110

Even stranger are termites. In one experiment, a steel plate was driven into a termitary so as to divide it in two, but nonetheless termites built up sides of an arch on either side of the plate that perfectly matched each other when the plate was removed, even though the termites were blind and could not know what was happening on the other side of the plate. Yet, the moment the queen was killed, the termites immediately ceased work. The experimenter put this down to a 'group soul': Sheldrake prefers to think in terms of a 'morphic field' (Sheldrake, p.82).

Again, no one really understands how homing pigeons find their way back to base. It has been suggested that they are dependent on the arc of the sun, on polarised light, on smell or on magnetism, but none of these can fully account for their return. Is there an unknown sense of direction, or something akin to quantum non-locality (cited in the introduction to this book)? The explanation appears to be beyond the reach of the natural sciences.

Higher up the scale in nature come mammals. Domesticated horses and dogs, it is claimed, have been found to be telepathic to their masters. Horses have been directed by telepathy to their food, and an owner has been directed by telepathy to a horse in need and can be alerted to its death. It is said that horses in the wild can direct their companions by telepathy to food and water, or one horse can be directed to another over long distances (Blake, 1975, pp.112–122). Domesticated dogs have been found to know not simply when their master is coming home, but when he decides to come home (Sheldrake, 1994, p.14; 2000, p.126). No doubt the faculty of telepathy in the animal world would have furthered 'the survival of the fittest'. Now that human beings have instant means of communication by radio, television, telephone and electronic means, their faculty of telepathy, if it exists, may be expected to decay.

From telepathy in animals, we pass naturally to telepathy among human beings. Most of us have had the experience of thinking about somebody and at that very moment the telephone rings, and we find that that same person has rung us up. We say to ourselves, 'Telepathy!' But we forget the number of times when we think of people and they do not ring us up. Stronger evidence than this is required before it can be established that one person can communicate with another at a distance without using known means of communication.

Such evidence does not seem to be lacking. One of the objects of the SPR's first book, *Phantasms of the Living*, was to show that 'experimental telepathy exists'. It records interesting experiments in which tastes and words were communicated, seemingly telepathically. Experiments have also taken place in France, and a good deal of work has been undertaken in Russia. As an example of this, in April 1966 Karl Nikolaiev was reported to have recognised in Novosiberk twelve out of twenty ESP cards transmitted to him from Moscow 1,800 miles away, far higher than the five out of twenty-five predicted by statistical theory (Ostrander and Shroeder, p.31ff.). It has been reported that, since then, there have been successful transmissions of emotions, images, kinetic impulses, sensations, sounds and tastes. Dr Nikolai Semyonov, winner of a Nobel Prize and vice-chairman of the USSR Academy of Sciences, said in the Russian journal, *Science and Religion*, in September 1966, 'It is very important to scientifically study the psychic phenomena of sensitives like Wolf Messing.' (p.60) Messing is reported to have proved to Stalin his ability to project his thought telepathically into the minds of others, thereby controlling or clouding their minds (*Science and Religion*, 1965, 7, 8) Impressive as these reports are, we do not know what controls were exercised in these Russian phenomena, and therefore they can hardly be accepted as solid evidence of telepathy.

Many cases of spontaneous telepathy have been reported. In 1889, the SPR asked members of the general public 'whether they had ever had the impression of hearing anything, or being touched when they were awake, which impression, as far as they could see, was not due to any external cause'. Seventeen thousand people replied! Ten per cent answered 'Yes'. Many of these impressions turned out to be veridical. Here is an example.

18 June 1883

My husband was dressing a few months ago one morning, about a quarter to nine o'clock, when he came into my room and said… 'I feel sure X (an old friend of his) is dead.' He said that all at once he felt there was someone in the room with him, and X's face came vividly before his mind's eye; and then he had this extraordinary conviction of X's death. He could not get the idea out of his mind all day. Strange to say, next morning he had a letter saying X had died the day before, at a quarter to nine, just the very time that my husband came into my room. About two months before, we had heard that X had an incurable complaint, but we had heard nothing more, and his name had not been mentioned by anyone for weeks. I ought to tell you that my husband is the last person in the world to imagine anything, and he had always been particularly unbelieving as to anything supernatural.

Gurney, Myers and Podmore, p.152

This kind of incident was carefully checked. Not so carefully checked, but even better known in the Roman Catholic Church, is Sister Briege Mackenna, a Poor Clare nun from Ireland, who acts worldwide as a counsellor to priests, and who understands telepathically their needs. After putting her hand on a priest, and saying some prayers, she is said to be able to gain an intimate knowledge of his problems. She has been called a kind of successor to Padre Pio (see p.264) with remarkable healing powers, a strange gift of prophecy and even, it is alleged, of bilocation (Cornwell, pp.113–19).

Telepathy was also investigated under laboratory conditions by J B Rhine (see p.28). Later, in 1974, Honorton, a former member of Rhine's team, introduced the *ganzfeld*.

The ganzfeld technique is so called because it exploits the effects of exposing the subject to a uniform visual field or ganzfeld. The simplest way of producing the effect is to make the subject wear translucent goggles (half ping pong balls make a convenient device) through which a light can be shone. To complete the total absence of perceptual patterning, earphones should be worn into which a white noise (something like the shushing sound of waves breaking) can be fed, while, to obviate tactile and somatic sensations the body should be relaxed and cocooned with ample cushioning... In a typical ganzfeld experiment, the target is selected at random from four different pictures. After ten minutes or so in the ganzfeld, the subject's imagery should start to become enhanced, and, hopefully, to reflect the objects on the target picture. When after a lapse of, say, half an hour, the subject is aroused from this condition, he or she is presented with all four potential targets by the experimenter (who is of course ignorant of the actual target) and has to rank them according to the degree to which they correspond with the images experienced in the ganzfeld.

Beloff, p.167

Lately, using the ganzfeld technique, Professor Morris of the Koestler Parapsychology Unit in the Department of Psychology at Edinburgh University has been putting in hand a wide range of parapsychological research and has recently produced positive results in telepathic communication (Dalton *et al.*, 1995).

The conditions in the ganzfeld are not dissimilar to those experienced when dreaming. Dr Krippner of New York carried out research on alleged telepathic communication during sleep. A 'sender' made contact with someone who was known to dream a lot, and established rapport. The dreamer was isolated and had electrodes attached to his head. Every ninety minutes or so during sleep, Rapid Eye Movements (REM) take place and electroencephalograms (EEG) are significantly different at those times, recording alpha waves, which are characteristic of wakefulness, not sleep. The sender, with a sealed envelope, was locked into a different room and, when the envelope was opened, concentrated on transmitting its contents to the person dreaming. Every ninety minutes, the person who had been asleep was awakened, and spoke into a tape any impressions that may have been received. Dr Krippner, who was appointed research director of this project at the Maimonides Hospital in 1964, claimed some very striking results, but as these have never been replicated, critics have raised doubts about their validity (Beloff, p.164).

Dreams have from time immemorial been believed to contain messages from another world, or to foretell future events, or to bring someone in touch with some other person. However, in more recent times, such views have been ridiculed in favour of more 'scientific' explanations. Dreams are said to be a way of flushing out past debris from the human brain, or they are explained in Freudian or Jungian terms as symbolic expressions of the tensions and feelings locked in the unconscious mind. Some dreams seem to be absolute nonsense, while others do appear to give expression to unconscious feelings. (As a working bishop, I used regularly to have my anxiety dream.) There may be some truth in any or all of these alleged explanations. But it may well not be the whole truth. When dreaming we seem to enter an altered state of consciousness in which the unconscious mind may be open to suggestions from outside. We have no idea how this could happen, but there are some indications that it may happen.

There is a great amount of testimony to the existence of telepathy, and due weight must be given to this. There is no cause of telepathy known to science. Professor H H Price was convinced that telepathy exists, and indicated the importance he attached to it.

> We must conclude, I think that there is no room for telepathy in a materialistic universe. Telepathy is something which ought not to happen at all if a materialistic theory were true. But it does happen. So there must be something wrong with the materialistic theory, however numerous and imposing the normal facts which support it may be.
>
> Price, p.109

The Sense of Being Stared At

The sense of being stared at behind one's back is very common. Many readers of this book will have experienced it. It may in some ways be related to telepathy, if there is an unconscious telepathic message passed from the person staring to the person being stared at. I was interested to find out that there has been some investigation of this experience.

> In informal surveys in Europe and America, I have found that about 80% of the people I asked claimed to have experienced it. It is also taken for granted in countless works of fiction, as in the phrase, 'she felt his eyes boring into her neck'. It is explicitly described by novelists such as Tolstoy, Dostoevsky, Anatole France, Victor Hugo, Aldous Huxley, D H Lawrence, J Cowper Powys, Thomas Mann, and J B Priestley.
>
> Sheldrake, 1994, p.101

Knowledge that one is being stared at would have had evolutionary value in the animal kingdom, giving warning of a predator's silent approach. In humans, the experience may well be connected with that of the 'evil eye', prevalent in traditional societies. It survives in such phrases as 'he looked daggers at her'. The 'evil eye' is an accepted concept in many countries. It is often connected with envy, a word derived from the Latin *invidia*, meaning originally 'seeing intensively'. Recent experiments have been carried out in schools on people who can sense that they are being stared at, with statistically significant results (Sheldrake, 1998, pp.311–23). No physical explanation can be given. More research is needed, but it seems as if the phenomenon may well be an instance of extra-sensory perception.

Dowsing

There is not much similarity between the knowledge that one is being stared at behind one's back, and the ability to know where underground water lies. I include dowsing here because, like the sense of being stared at, it is a gift with which a good many ordinary people are endowed (although most of them have never used it), and no natural explanation has been found for it any more than it has been found for the sense of being stared at. Water divining has been practised for many centuries. I once had a holiday home in remote Wales that was always seriously short of water in the summer: we called in a water diviner, and he found water nearby.

A forked twig of hazel is held in both hands. When a person crosses underground water, the twig twitches violently, seemingly of its own accord. Sir William Barrett, FRS, Professor of Physics at the Royal College of Science in Dublin (and a founder member of SPR) made a comprehensive investigation into dowsing way back in the late nineteenth century. He found that the best results were obtained when a person made his mind a blank, not wholly dissimilar to a trance condition. He noted some symptoms of the same kind found in hysteria; a trembling, for example, when underground water was crossed. Someone without the gift of dowsing began to twitch if a dowser put his hands on him; and in turn a dowser ceased to twitch if a non-dowser put his hands on him.

Dowsing has also been investigated in Russia. They used materials other than wood. In the 1960s, Professor Bogomolov worked in connection with two hydrology engineers. He claimed to be able to determine the depth of underground streams and cables. In later tests, dowsing was found to be successful in determining a stratum of lead, zinc or gold to a depth of 240 feet (Ostrander and Shroeder, pp.195–207). Abbé Mermet alleged that through dowsing he had made archaeological finds at the request of the Pope himself (Ostrander and Shroeder, p.206). It was indeed useful for locating underground cables, etc. In fact, the Russians found it so useful that they demystified its name, calling the practice 'BEM' – the Biophysics Effects Method. During the Brezhnev era, a manual was actually written by three professional dowsers and commended by academics under the pseudoscientific title *The Use of the Bio-locational Method in the Search for Ore Deposits and in Geological Mapping* (Inglis, p.239ff.). It is perhaps strange that under a regime of dialectical materialism such official recognition was given to paranormal phenomena. At the same time, the West has made use of dowsing too. The need to find water in dry lands has made Western companies employ water diviners; and Uri Geller is said thereby to have become a multi-millionaire (Inglis, 1989, p.241).

Various explanations have been attempted, including sensitivity to micro electro-magnetism generated by water or deposits; but this is mere speculation. How could this produce a physical force strong enough to make a diviner's rod react with such violence that it can scrape the skin of a person's hand because of the presence of water or ores far below the surface of the earth? In the absence of any physical explanation of dowsing, a paranormal one must be considered.

Electronic Voice Phenomena

Having looked at these well-known psi phenomena, I now pass to one that is less well known, but which is engaging the interest of ordinary people interested in the paranormal, namely Electronic Voice Phenomena (ERP). At first sight, this seems so incredible that it is not even worth considering. But one must not dismiss alleged phenomena for that reason without examining them.

Sir Oliver Lodge, who interested himself in radio as well as in the paranormal, predicted many years ago that there might be communication with the spirit world through electrical equipment. In 1959, Friedrich Jurgenson claimed that he had found strange and unaccountable voices on his tape recorder. Jurgenson had friends among leading figures at the Vatican, and was even decorated by the Pope. Five years later, his friend and pupil, Konstantin Raudive, a Latvian psychologist, published a book in German about the electronic voice phenomenon under the title *The Inaudible becomes Audible*. This was later published in England under the title *Breakthrough* (Raudive, 1971). Peter Bander, a trained psychologist turned publisher, and a former senior lecturer in religious and moral education, who was in charge of the English publication under the title *Breakthrough*, began by being deeply sceptical of the possibility of hearing the voices of the dead on a tape machine, but he changed his mind after hearing what he believed to be his mother's voice (Bander, 1972). Something similar is alleged to have taken place in the Scole group (see p.40ff.).

Breakthrough is a book with an involved and complex argument, matched by the complexity of style in which it is written. Of the thousands of voices which Raudive claims to have heard, some can be shown to have a natural explanation. (It is sometimes possible for a tape machine to pick up voices from radio broadcasts.) Some of the 'Raudive voices' spoke in Latvian, with which comparatively few people are conversant. Nonetheless, Raudive made remarkable claims, and before the English translation was published, he came over to England in March 1971 to confront the media. The *Sunday Mirror* set up an elaborate experiment, under the supervision of the chief engineers of Pye, using a diode and microphone as well as a recording machine; and over two hundred messages are said to have come through. The Pye engineers were baffled. Dr Raudive also went to Belling and Lee's laboratory which was specifically designed to screen out radio signals. There he met Peter Hale, who was then the leading British expert in electronic screen suppression. Hale, who before this had believed that the voices came from normal radio signals, could no longer explain the voices in this way, and reported:

From the results we obtained last Friday, something is happening which I cannot explain in normal physical terms.

Bander, p.66

These voices cannot be heard during the running of a tape machine, but only when the tape is being played back. It has been suggested that, while tests with the voice printer show that the voices are only just within the frequency range audible to the human ear, it is different for some animals (Bander's dog, Rufus, showed strange behaviour at the very times when the voices could just be heard). The voices themselves are very weak to our ears and are often mixed up with other voices, so that it is difficult to determine with accuracy just what is being said. Advice given to those who wish to receive the voice phenomenon emphasises that it takes some three months to hear anything at all, and much patience is required to persist (Sheargold, p.2ff.).

How are these voices to be explained? While some of them may well have emanated from radio stations, the experiment at Belling's laboratories shows this to be an insufficient explanation. The most obvious view is that the voices are imaginary. The noise made by the tape passing the playback head, plus that generated within the recorder amplifier itself, is that of a loud rushing sound, akin to that known to electronic engineers as 'white noise'. Prolonged listening to this is well known to result in voices being heard that do not exist. But in the case of voices alleged to come from the dead, this cannot be the case, since the voices have been captured on a visible speech printer and seen on oscillographs.

The idea that the voices are transmitted by an unknown method from another planet or from some other intelligent source in the universe may also be discarded, for the messages are relevant to the persons present at the tape recorder, and therefore purport to come from people known to them. A further suggestion has been that the electronic impulses sent out by the subconscious mind may be registered as human speech on a tape. This extraordinary hypothesis hardly accords with the fact that the messages have been received in a language unknown to any of the persons present at the experiment. There seems to be only one remaining explanation – that the voices originate, as they claim, from the dead getting in touch with those they have known on earth. It could be, however, that these voices emanate from fragmenting entities of those formerly living (see p.314) rather than the souls of the departed, and this could account for their often fragmentary nature. A further suggestion has been made that the voices are 'leftovers', rather similar to a haunting that has been imprinted on a locality.

Protagonists of electronic voice phenomena have formed themselves into the International Network for Instrumental Transcommunication, and a periodical called *Contact!* is published three times a year. Claims have been made not only for messages from tape recorders, but also for sideband radios, telephones, computers and the television screen. David Ellis, who held the Perrott-Warwick Studentship in Psychical Research at Trinity College, Cambridge, when Raudive came to England nearly thirty years ago, was involved in the investigations into 'Raudive's voices'. He claims that most serious parapsychologists agree with his sceptical conclusions. Raudive had claimed the paranormal nature of the voices because of what they said. But the voices are admittedly very weak, and Ellis found that, when he was investigating Raudive's claims, even the best voices were not quite clear enough for what they said to be unequivocally determined. If one cannot quite hear something being said, one is reduced to guessing, and in so doing one perhaps tends to read more meaning into the sounds than is warranted (Ellis, 1978). On the other hand, protagonists of the voices claim that when the electronic voices of Dr Raudive (and of others) after their death are compared with their voices when they were still alive, computer analyses of the vocal patterns conclusively show that the voices of the living and the dead are identical. (Highly sophisticated voice machines can now accurately measure voice variables, for example, pace, rhythm, accents, origins, etc.) If this vocal identity can be sustained, it seems to negate Ellis's suggestion that the voices are not authentic. At the same time, it is completely unknown how voices on tape could be produced by entities that have no physical means of producing them.

The Scole Report

I am ending this chapter with a brief mention of the Scole Report because it includes a report of an alleged paranormal experiment which has some similarities to electronic voice phenomena.

A recent project took place when three members of SPR cooperated with a group experimenting in psychic matters in Scole, a village near Diss in Norfolk, between 1995 and 1997. A lengthy report has been produced (M Keen, A Ellison, D Fontana, 1999). There was, however, a difference of approach between the Scole group and the SPR members. The latter were concerned only with the authenticity of phenomena and wanted more safeguards against fraud than were allowed by the 'spirit team' under whose orders the Scole group allegedly was operating. Infrared equipment and image enhancers were forbidden, and proceedings took place in the dark, with only luminous bands on arms and equipment by which fraud could be detected. The Scole group was ordered to experiment with new means of spirit communication, since more traditional means had failed to convince scientists of their authenticity.

The phenomena were various. Single-point light performed various functions. Although there were no materialisations, the silhouette of a graceful full-sized hand could be seen. Recorded on tape were the conversations between the investigators and the 'spirit team' on a broad range of subjects, from gravity waves to Wordsworth's poetry. There was talk about early members of SPR (most of which could have come from a book by Sir Oliver Lodge). Images (some of which have been identified in a rare printed book) were said to be imprinted on unexposed film placed in sealed containers during a sitting, although some doubts have been raised about the security of the film. Various apports appeared, including a genuine copy of the *Daily Mail* which gave an account of Helen Duncan's trial (see p.49). The 'spirit team' seemed to wish to tease the investigators into finding solutions to puzzles. A box containing an amplifier and a tape recorder attached to a 'germanium box' but without a microphone were set up to provide 'direct voices' of spirits, following technical details discussed between one of the investigators (a professor of electrical engineering) and a spokesperson for the 'spirit team' speaking through a medium. The 'spirit team' found it difficult to express in earthly terms the source of these phenomena. It was a novel type of pure energy. It was used much like carrier waves, and these forces, it was alleged, could penetrate material in our world. There is some affinity here to electronic voice phenomena.

There are those in the SPR who have cast doubt upon the authenticity of these phenomena. The investigators in their report leave the matter for readers to decide. The SPR report, which includes not only an account of what happened, but also queries that have been made, ought to be read before any conclusion can be reached about the authenticity of what is alleged to have happened. It should be remembered that the trained SPR investigators were without doubt impressed, and the initiative to have joint meetings between the Scole group and the SPR investigators did not come from Scole: they did not ask to be investigated.

Chapter II
MEDIUMS, GHOSTS AND APPARITIONS

Mediums

So far we have considered phenomena that, to a certain extent, can be tested out in 'laboratory' conditions. I turn now to a range of alleged paranormal phenomena that in no way can be subjected to such tests. Mediums obviously need to be investigated (or sensitives as they are often called, that is, people sensitive to psychic influences). Today they are often associated with spiritualists. There are not so many of them as there were in the Victorian age, and there has been so much fraud that they have fallen into disrepute. Whereas then, psychic research was concerned primarily with mediums, today parapsychology (to use the name preferred by contemporary investigators) prefers research under laboratory conditions. As a result, research with mediums nowadays falls mostly under the aegis of the College of Psychic Studies rather than the SPR.

So far as communication with the dead is concerned, mediums usually go into a state of altered consciousness, a trance in which they cease to be conscious of themselves; their voices change and they are taken over (possessed) by a control, who can call up spirits of the dead to communicate with people or who can speak on their behalf. They claim to function only in a darkened room (which particularly lays them open to fraud, or charges of fraud). And fraud has frequently been observed. Tyrrell has explained the situation:

> One can see how fraud can creep into physical mediumship. Mediums may start by being honest: but genuine phenomena are

rare, and sitters, especially if they have paid a fee, expect a continuous supply. Even then the medium may not consciously wish to be fraudulent, but, when she is in a semi-conscious state, the desire to satisfy the sitters overcomes conscious scruples, and simple trickery begins.

Tyrrell, p.223

Because some mediums have been found to be fraudulent, it does not follow that all mediums practise fraud. It is the task of research to investigate them, and to discriminate between what is false and what is true. The sheer triviality of what purports to come from the world of discarnate spirits may tend to make people reject them out of hand. But it has to be recognised that most conversation in ordinary everyday life is very trivial, and there is no reason to believe that people's characters should immediately change when they die and enter the next stage of their existence.

There is, however, one grave difficulty in trying to sift out the true from the false, and that lies in the inevitably subjective factor in what the mediums say. Even though they may appear to be 'taken over', whatever is said passed through their brains, and so it is likely to bear traces of their vocabulary. The messages which mediums purport to bring may be influenced by multiple factors. There may be telepathy involved. There may be contributions, additions, and embellishments (unknown, of course, to the person concerned) from the subconscious mind of the sensitive herself. And even if there is a genuine contribution from a discarnate spirit, it is possible that there could also be discarnate spirits who mislead the sitters and who pretend to be other than they are. And it is not inconceivable, although it may well appear very improbable, that mediumistic séances result in mass hallucinations.

Eileen Garrett is a good example of ambiguity. She had a reputation as a reliable medium in the 1920s. She offered her services to Duke University when she heard of the serious parapsychological research being undertaken there. Her record at Duke characterised her as a serious, sensible and responsible person. She had controls, but they acted sensibly, not like some controls at spiritualist séances. They participated in tests and from time to time they would introduce communicators to reassure loved ones of their continued existence. But when Eileen Garrett was asked for her own assessment of her mediumship, she said that it must not be forgotten that she had acting qualities, and also that she was telepathic, so that when asked about someone who had died she could pick up from her interrogator telepathic messages about the dead person concerned. She simply did not know, she said, whether her messages were genuinely from a discarnate spirit or whether they resulted from telepathic communication with the living, as a kind of dissociated part of her own personality. However, shortly before she died, she said she then believed that she had been indeed receiving genuine messages from the dead (Inglis, p.234ff.).

Interest in mediums began with table turning in America. In 1848, two young girls, aged twelve and thirteen, were living in a haunted house in rural New York State. The girls discovered that they could communicate with the spirits which seemed to be the source of these disturbances by their giving a specific number of raps in answer to the girls' questions (one for yes, two for no). There soon developed a code by which the spirits could speak by spelling out words made by yes or no answers to their pointing to letters in the alphabet. From this, spiritualism developed. It spread like wildfire in the USA and became popular (and even fashionable). It came to Britain, not only to London, but also to the North.

People would gather round a table in a darkened room, with their hands on the table, and soon (if all went well) it would begin to tilt, and the séance would begin. There is considerable testimony that even heavy mahogany tables could perceptibly move. The medium would usually go into a trance, and find herself 'possessed' by a control, or supposedly by a control. There is, however, an interesting case when a group, instead of waiting for a spirit to manifest itself as a control, invented one for themselves and provided him with a historical identity and called him Philip (Inglis, p.236). Soon they found that they could summon him and conjure him up so that he seemed to be independent of the group, capable of communicating with them through raps and table movements. This shows what a large part the subjective element can play in such matters.

Tyrrell produced instances where, in his judgement, there is no doubt that the messages were genuine communications from the dead. He instanced the case of Mrs Talbot, who arranged a sitting with a well-known and well-respected medium, Mrs Osborne Leonard. Through her control, Mrs Leonard told Mrs Talbot a lot of details about her dead husband which she could not possibly have picked up by telepathy. Suddenly, she began a description of something like a book, which was leather-bound and dark, with writing in it. Mrs Talbot could not think what was meant, but at last recalled that her husband had had a red leather notebook. This was thought probably to be what was being referred to, and Mrs Talbot was told to look at page twelve or thirteen for something written that would be relevant to this conversation. Mrs Talbot had not thought much of the notebook, and she was not sure whether she had thrown it away. Reluctantly, she searched for it and eventually she found it tucked away at the back of a top bookshelf. Inside she was astonished to read: 'Table of Semitic or Syro-Phoenician Languages'. On page 13 she found:

> I discovered by certain whispers which it was supposed I was unable to hear and from certain glances of curiosity or commiseration which it was supposed that I was unable to see that I was near to death... Presently my mind began to dwell not only on happiness which was to come, but on happiness which I was actually enjoying. I saw long-forgotten forms, playmates, schoolfellows, companions of my youth and of my old age, who one and all smiled upon me. They did not smile with any compassion, so that I felt that I was no longer needed, but by the sort of kindness which is exchanged by people who are equally happy. I saw my mother, father and sisters, all of whom I had survived...
>
> Tyrrell, p.199ff.

Without passing any judgement on the experiences that lie behind these remarks in the notebook, without doubt this was the 'something written' which would be of interest to Mrs Talbot in her situation as a widow. It is hard to see how the medium could have come across this information by telepathy, but easy to understand if she had received a genuine communication from a discarnate spirit.

Nowadays there are few mediums compared with the number a century ago when it became fashionable to consult them. I think that Dr Martin Israel's viewpoint should be taken seriously.

> I have alluded to spiritualist communication. Few outside that field are very sympathetic, because, as in the case of hypnotherapy conjuring up last lives [see p.183ff.], one does not know the veracity of the medium's 'guide' or 'control' – a spirit who allegedly puts the medium in touch with the dead entity. Spiritualism, little more than a century old, has some startling cases in which reliable mediums of unquestionable veracity have brought forth apparently accurate evidence of the spirit of the entity still in communication with those who knew the person when he or she was still alive in the flesh. But the number of such mediums is very small indeed – and so we all wait for the new genius to appear. The sporadic nature of psychic communication and its variable accuracy, to say nothing of the honesty of the medium (for the area of professional mediumship is a minefield of fraud) makes the practice of spiritualism of limited importance in releasing the unquiet dead.
>
> Israel, p.40

Mediums are not concerned only with communication with the dead. From a few there is even alleged materialisation of the dead. Mediums are believed to function better when they are set apart from other people at the séance, separated from them by a cabinet or curtained recess. It is also believed that the face of a materialised spirit can be seen only if the medium's face is hidden. All this easily gives rise to fraud. A well-known medium in the last century, Catherine Wood, was said to be possessed by a control called Pocha, but on one occasion Pocha was seized during a séance, and turned out to be Catherine Wood 'on her knees, partially undressed, and attempting to hide a quantity of muslin' (Owen, p.71).

Another well-known medium, Mary Rosina Flowers, said to have a control called Florence Maple, was also caught out. At a private séance at the house of a private investigator called Cox, his married daughter approached the cabinet in which Miss Flowers was sequestrated, and looked behind the curtains. According to the investigator, 'Florence Maple' fought desperately with the intruder and in the struggle with the inspecting lady the spirit's headdress fell off (Owen, p.71). However, the existence of such fraud is no proof that all mediums have been fraudulent.

Some mediums (such as the Frenchwoman, Marthe Béraud) were said to be able to produce 'ectoplasm', a substance apparently like cheesecloth (and, in the case of bogus mediums, actual cheesecloth) out of which human figures would materialise. Photographs have actually been produced of such apparently materialised bodies. These have been met with accusations of fraud, and it is this kind of phenomenon that has tended to make those interested in parapsychology concentrate on laboratory-type research. However, whether it was possible in those early days of photography to produce faked photographs and whether these alleged materialisations were always fraudulent remain open questions. Some reports suggest that either there was mass hallucination or that materialisations did actually take place.

Florence Cook (known as B or Miss Blank) was a medium who claimed to have experienced the paranormal even as a young girl. She is said to have achieved the full materialisation of 'Katie King', the daughter of 'John King', the spirit name of Sir Henry Owen Morgan. Professor Crookes, FRS, was said to be too fond of touching her! The *Daily Telegraph* of the day reported the séance.

In a short time Katie – as the familiar Miss B was termed – thought she would be able to materialise herself so far as to present the whole form, if we arranged the corner cupboard so as to permit her doing so. Accordingly we opened the door, and from it suspended a rug or two opening at the centre, after the fashion of a Bedouin Arab's tent, formed a semi-circle and sang Longfellow's 'Footsteps of Angels'. Therein occurs the passage: 'Then the forms of the departed enter at the open door'. And, lo and behold, although we had left Miss B tied and sealed to her chair, and clad in an ordinary black dress somewhat voluminous as to the skirts, a tall female figure draped classically in white, with bare arms and feet, did enter at the open door, or rather down the centre between the two rugs, and stood statue-like before us, spoke a few words, and retired, after which we entered the Bedouin tent and found Miss B, with her dress as before, knots and seals secure, and her boots on! This was Form No. 1, the first I had seen. It looked as material as myself.

Owen, p.48

Perhaps the most bizarre case of alleged ectoplasm concerns a Scottish lady, Mrs Helen Duncan. In 1944, she was convicted at the Old Bailey of pretending to conjure up the spirits of the dead under the Witchcraft Act of 1736, and sentenced to nine months' imprisonment. (The Act was later repealed in 1951.) Mrs Duncan, who had from childhood claimed psychic gifts, and who as a married woman had six children and a frail husband to support, earned a living giving séances in various parts of the country, using 'Albert', her spirit guide, to introduce spirits who were allegedly materialised by ectoplasm.

Was she genuine? Once in her early career, she had been caught cheating, but that was not unknown among genuine mediums. A disgruntled former maid alleged that she had bought cheesecloth for her for a séance, and Price (who photographed the alleged ectoplasm) believed that she had swallowed it before the séance, regurgitated it during the séance, and then swallowed it again before being searched (Price, 1931). This would have been almost as difficult as producing ectoplasm: it would have meant swallowing several metres of the stuff, complete with drawing pins, and re-swallowing it all before being searched (Rivaldini, 1998). (Her orifices were searched before and after a séance.)

As for her alleged production of ectoplasm, I witnessed and spoke with materialisations produced by Helen Duncan at very close quarters, and in a light that was strong enough to permit the exchange of facial expressions with other sitters at the séances.

Ivedell, p.151

During the last war, a spirit is said to have told of the sinking of HMS *Hood*, at a séance in 1941, at which Brigadier Firebrace, Director of Military Intelligence for Scotland, happened to be present, who thus learnt about the disaster before the Admiralty knew it had taken place!

As D-Day approached, Mrs Duncan seems to have been regarded by the authorities as a security risk. A police raid took place at a séance during which a spirit claimed to have been drowned on HMS *Barham*. In fact, the sinking of this ship had been concealed from the public for reasons of national security! Naturally, her disclosure that it had been sunk did not go down well with the authorities. She was charged with pretending to conjure up spirits under the Witchcraft Act which had custodial provisions, instead of under the Vagrancy Act under which bogus mediums were usually fined. No actual evidence of a conspiracy against her has been found. When she was in Portsmouth there had been gossip in the town that she would soon be in prison. She was! Her trial was sensationalised in the press, to the great annoyance of Winston Churchill. No physical evidence of ectoplasmic fraud during the séance was produced. Some of those present can still remember what happened. Many witnesses paid tribute to her extraordinary psychic powers, including ectoplasmic materialisation (although the prosecution alleged that they saw what they wanted to see). A nurse testified that, before the séance, Mrs Duncan had been stripped naked and subjected to a body search, before being clad in her séance gown. But the large number of witnesses for the defence alienated both the judge and the jury. Her lawyer asked for permission for her to demonstrate her psychic powers in court: the judge left this decision to the jury, which refused to allow it. After her release from prison, Mrs Duncan continued to give séances, and she died in 1956, shortly after another police raid. People differed strongly on whether the jury was right to find her guilty (Gaskill, 2001). She had earlier been fined at Edinburgh for fraud, but if she was bogus, why did she, on release from prison, have a premonition at Edinburgh Station of a rail crash, leaving her daughter behind, and hurling herself into a train lavatory just before the train did crash?

Mediums also engaged in spiritual healing. Some used a sort of hypnotherapy or what we could call today 'alternative medicine'. Some healing was by clairvoyance: the mediums 'saw' into the body of the patient and made a diagnosis to help the spiritual healer. Many healers were women: they might be married or single, slim or heavyweight: all that mattered was whether they could heal.

Mrs Olive, a long-lasting and popular healer, believed she was controlled by a Dr Forbes. He had been a well-known doctor and physician to the Prince Regent and the Queen's household. He died in the 1860s. Despite his own orthodox practice, he had scandalised his colleagues by his open attitude to complementary medicine.

> When Florence Marryatt consulted the medium on a delicate matter, 'Dr Forbes' whispered the name of her condition and what she must do about it. 'He' then wrote out a prescription in Latin and in the medical man's usual shorthand, so that there would be no mistake with her medication. When Miss Marryatt showed this slip of paper to her orthodox practitioner he was highly offended that she had sought a second opinion, but acknowledged the value of the remedy.
>
> Owen, p.118

Here is a testimony to Mrs Olive.

> I was a great sufferer for some months, and under the care of an experienced surgeon, but finding myself no better, and the remedies worse than the disease, I was advised by a friend to consult 'Dr Forbes', Mrs Olive's medical control, which I did, and feeling very greatly relieved after my first visit, I continued daily to attend for some weeks, during which time the tumour was entirely absorbed, my nervous system regained its vitality, and I am now completely cured.
>
> Owen, p.119

These are striking cases of healing, but there is a great variability in human disease and illness, and regressions can take place, so that (unless a 'miracle' occurs) it is very difficult to show with complete certainty that healing was due to some paranormal agency.

Automatic Writing

Mediums are said to be a verbal means of communication with spirits. But there is another kind of alleged communication, by means of automatic writing. A sensitive holds a pencil in the writing hand, relaxes, withdraws conscious control and finds himself or herself writing automatically. This differs from a trance in as much as the sensitive is conscious when writing, but not conscious of what is being written. Because it is the easiest form of mediumistic activity, it needs particularly rigorous scrutiny. Liebault, a French hypnotherapist, wrote way back in 1868 of one of his patients at Nancy:

> I have seen her rapidly writing page after page after page of what she called 'messages' – all in well chosen language and with no erasures – while at the same time she maintained conversation with people near her.
>
> Inglis, p.102

Automatic writing (or directed writing, as it has also been called) is certainly the result of an intelligence of which the writer is not aware; but whether it is a form of extrasensory perception or comes from a person's subliminal consciousness is hard to assess. It could be an effect of dissociated personality.

There is the case of an American woman, Mrs Curran of St Louis, Missouri. She was a lady of limited education who left school at fourteen; at the age of thirty-one she had never even seen the sea. As a result of using an Ouija board, she found herself allegedly in communication with a person called Patience Worth, a seventeenth-century Dorset woman who said that she had gone to America where she had been murdered by Indians. From this lady there came an enormous literary output, said to be three million words. Her case was carefully investigated by Walter Prince who found that these works of historical fiction covered very different subjects, and he was puzzled to understand how one person could have all the knowledge that was contained in them as well as the literary skill with which they were composed. This made it hard to credit that Patience Worth was part of Mrs Curran's dissociated personality. Mrs Curran either had remarkable telepathic gifts, or she was the channel for a discarnate spirit. The scope and powers of the unconscious may be far greater than is generally recognised, but on the other hand automatic writing may be the vehicle of discarnate intelligences (Inglis, 1989, p.139ff.).

Tyrrell described remarkable conversations recorded in automatic writing made by a lady referred to under a pseudonym as Mrs Willett. She belonged to a Cambridge group of ladies around the turn of the century who all practised automatic writing. Mrs Willett's powers developed, and Tyrrell reproduces conversations (among others) between Myers and Gurney (founders of SPR and by then dead) and Sir Oliver Lodge, together with Mrs Willett's own running commentary; and the script even records that Gurney explained how, before communication could take place, he had to use words that Mrs Willett could understand so that he could channel them through her subliminal mind. Mrs Sidgwick, the wife of the founder of SPR, gradually become convinced of the genuineness of the communicators, and Tyrrell himself commented:

> If this is all a piece of play-acting on the part of some fragment of Mrs Willett's personality, it discloses a quintessence of dramatic skill which strikes one dumb with amazement.
>
> Tyrrell, p.151ff.

Perhaps the more convincing instances of automatic writing are those that have cross references. A group of highly educated ladies (not mediums), referred to above, discovered around the turn of the century that they were able to produce automatic writing. Correspondences were found in their automatic writing, as well as in the productions of an American medium. All were asked to send their writing to the SPR without knowing what the others had written. It was found that their writings were complementary to one another, and moreover the scripts were signed and purported to come from the now deceased founders of the SPR, Henry Sidgwick, Edmund Gurney and F W H Myers. It is not inconceivable that telepathy in some way was involved, but it is strange that each one should have produced material from the founders of SPR without knowing that the others had done the same. Their communicators said they were doing this because a single theme, distributed among the various automatists, would show that a single mind or group of minds was the cause of the automatic writing (Tyrrell, p.144ff.).

The instances given all took place some time ago; but more contemporary is the case of Matthew Manning. It was carefully monitored and investigated by both Peter Bender, then editor of *The Psychic Researcher* and Professor A R G Owen, geneticist, biologist and mathematician, and at that period a Fellow of Trinity College, Cambridge. In 1971, while he was still a school-boy living near Cambridge and away at a residential school, Matthew Manning became the focus of poltergeistic disruption (see p.90ff.). He discovered he could divert this poltergeistic activity through automatic writing, as though the surplus psychic energy behind the former was used up by the latter. Most striking is the variety of handwritings, scripts and languages in which he took down these writings, including three different Arabic scripts which of course he could not himself understand, and also messages signed in their handwriting alleged to have come from Sir Stafford Cripps, (the Labour Chancellor of the Exchequer after the last war) and Bertrand Russell (who in his lifetime strongly disbelieved in survival after death).

Even more remarkable were the drawings that Manning produced by automatic writing, in the styles of and signed by Dürer, Rowlandson, Klee, Beardsley and Picasso among others; and all this despite the fact that Manning himself had no talents in this direction. Some of these are illustrated in the book that he wrote about his experiences, together with the messages he received signed by eminent people and reproduced in his book (Manning, 1974). Manning was psychically gifted to a remarkable extent, and attracted the attention of both Bishop Mervyn Stockwood and Archbishop Bruno Heim, the RC Apostolic Delegate in Britain, who sent reports to Pope Paul VI! He even attracted the attention of royalty. It is hard to evaluate these phenomena. It is difficult to believe that, if these writings and drawings did come from discarnate personalities, they would have retained after death the ability to communicate using the handwriting and styles of drawing that they had had when they were incarnate. On the other hand, it is difficult to explain how else it could have come about that Manning involuntarily produced these phenomena.

Psychokinesis

It is one thing allegedly to communicate with spirits verbally or by means of automatic writing: it is quite another allegedly to move objects at a distance by paranormal means and without the use of physical force. I mention this here because people who have this gift have been called 'physical mediums' to distinguish them from 'spiritual mediums' who are said to communicate with the dead.

The most famous of these physical mediums is usually acknowledged to have been D D Home (1833–86), about whom much has been written. Here is a succinct account.

> His most active period was roughly from 1855 to 1875 and he is unique in that he preferred to hold his séances in daylight or good artificial light. In his presence heavy tables and chairs rushed about the room, or rose from the ground; accordions were seen to play suspended in mid-air with no one touching them; on many occasions Home was levitated and floated round the séance room, visible to all present; phantom hands and arms appeared and were touched by the sitters and more than once a fully materialised form was seen; he handled burning coals and put his head into a fire without harmful effects; his body was elongated a matter of a few inches [this is a phenomenon attested among mystics as well as mediums], and what is perhaps most evidential for the psychical researcher, he was investigated by one of the most eminent scientists of the nineteenth century. Crookes' experiments with Home are so simple that it is difficult to see how the effects could have been produced by deception on Home's part. In my opinion the value of Home as evidence of the objective reality of ostensibly paranormal physical phenomena lies in the cumulative accounts of reliable witnesses combined with Crookes' painstaking experiments.
>
> Spedding, p.40ff.

Another striking person to have had the power of telekinesis is a Neapolitan girl, Eusapia Palladino. An Italian professor of forensic medicine and psychiatry, near the end of the last century, who was sceptical of all psi activities, was challenged to investigate this lady, thirty years old and illiterate. As a result, he became convinced that she could indeed move objects at a distance, cause musical instruments to play and levitate tables. Her demonstrations finally convinced him that he was not the victim of trickery. The lady was later investigated by several teams of scientists. For these tests, her hands and feet were securely controlled. Richet, President of the SPR and later a winner of a Nobel Prize, witnessed her powers in a number of trials and was convinced by them. Later, in his Presidential Address, he said that 'after we have witnessed such facts, everything conspires to make us doubt them. May it not all have been an illusion? May I not have been monstrously deceived...? We end up by letting ourselves be persuaded that we have been the victims of a trick'. Further trials took place in 1898, when one of the sceptical scientists was taken aback to feel himself being slapped and tickled, although at some distance from the lady (Inglis, p.99ff.).

It would be hard to find better evidence than tests of paranormal phenomena before sceptical scientists who were forced to change their convictions. But there are those who find such results so fantastic that they are convinced that they – and others – have been deceived. Certainly, psychokinesis on this scale is most rare, and if it be accepted as true, one can suppose only that the person concerned has such a surplus of psychic energy that it can be transmuted into physical energy and directed towards objects in ways that are completely unknown to us.

Apparitions of the Living

I pass next to another kind of paranormal phenomenon which may occur to ordinary people. Psychokinesis means deliberately willing objects to move without any known means of their so moving: but there are also people who have claimed deliberately to will apparitions of themselves to other people.

When the SPR early in its life published its 'Report on the Census of Hallucinations', it reported more visual apparitions than any other kind of ESP. Apparitions of the living fall into two categories: those that are deliberate (termed experimental) and those that are spontaneous. It may seem strange that one person can will that another should have an apparition of himself; but that is precisely what is claimed. One case that I shall cite appears in *Phantasms of the Living*, from which I quote a summary (Mackenzie, pp.77–88). It was sent to Frank Podmore by a clergyman friend, Frank Godfrey.

> After retiring to bed at 10.45 p.m. on 15 September 1886, Godfrey had determined if possible to appear to a friend, and accordingly he set himself to work with all the 'volitional and determinative' energy that he possessed to stand at the foot of her bed. His effort was sustained for perhaps eight minutes, after which he felt tired, and was soon asleep. He awoke at 3.40 a.m. feeling that he had succeeded in his experiment and made a note of that impression at the time. The next day he received from his friend an account of her experience. That morning, at about 3.30 a.m. she woke up with a start and a feeling that someone had come into her room. She rose, lit a candle and went downstairs to get some soda water. 'On returning to my room I saw Mr Godfrey standing under the large window of the staircase. He was dressed in his usual style, and an expression on his face which I have observed when he is looking very earnestly at anything. He stood there, and I held up the candle and gazed at him for three or four seconds in utter amazement, and then, as I passed up the staircase, he disappeared.'
>
> Both witnesses were questioned by Mr Podmore. Mrs – told him that the figure appeared quite distinct and lifelike at first. As she looked, it grew more and more shadowy, and finally faded away. Godfrey, at the Society's request, made two other trials, without, of course, letting his friend know of his intention. The first of these attempts was without result, but a trial made on 7 December 1896 succeeded completely. Mrs – writing on 8 December, stated she was awakened by hearing the cry 'Wake' and by feeling a hand rest on the left side of her head. She then saw stooping over her a figure which she recognised as Godfrey's.

Commenting on this last experience, Podmore said that the dress of the figure did not seem to have been seen distinctly, but in the apparitional experience on 16 November the suit was that ordinarily worn by Godfrey during the daytime, not the suit he was actually wearing at the time. The conclusion he drew from this was that 'the dress and the surroundings of the phantasm represent, not the dress and the surroundings at the time, but those with which the percipient was familiar'.

This is, of course, only anecdotal evidence, and coincidence cannot be entirely ruled out. It is strange that although Mr Godfrey on 15 September made the effort to appear before the lady around 11 p.m., she did not actually claim to have seen him until she woke up next morning around 3.30 a.m. There seems no reason why there should have been this lapse of time, unless (if the apparition was indeed the result of Mr Godfrey's efforts the night before), his friend was not in a position to receive the hallucination until she had been asleep and her brain had been at rest.

A different kind of hallucination appears not through some-one's effort, but spontaneously (Gurney *et al*, p.427).

24 February 1885

About September 1873, when my father was living at 57 Inver-ness Terrace, I was sitting one evening at about 8.30 p.m. in the large dining room. At the table, facing me, with their backs to the door, were seated my mother, sister and a friend, Mrs W. Sud-denly I seemed to see my wife bustling in through the door of the back dining room, which was in view from my position. She was in a mauve dress. I got up to meet her, though much astonished, as I believed her to be at Tenby. As I rose, my mother said, 'Who is that?' Not, I think, seeing anyone herself, but seeing that I did. I exclaimed, 'Why, it's Carry,' and advanced to meet her. As I ad-vanced the figure disappeared. On inquiry, I found my wife was spending the evening at a friend's house, in a mauve dress, which I certainly had never seen before. My wife recollected that at that time she was speaking to some friends about me, much regretting my absence, as there was going to be dancing, and I had promised to play for them. I had been unexpectedly detained in London.

Alex B Beaumont

This story was corroborated by Captain Beaumont's mother, and the friend who was present, and Mrs Beaumont was confident that he could never have seen the mauve dress before.

The most striking and the most frequent phantasms are those

associated with the moment of death. Indeed, there must be some kind of (unknown) connection between death and these apparitions. Many striking cases are given in *Phantasms of the Living*, such as this one.

9 January 1884

If anything I can say to you will be of any use, I will willingly give my testimony to what my husband has said. I remember perfectly ten years ago my visit to my mother's, and my husband's unaccountable restlessness on the particular day mentioned, also Mr Bee asking me, after I have come downstairs, if I had met a lady on the stairs. I said, 'No, I do not think there is anyone in the house but us.' Mr Bee then said, 'Well, a lady has passed me just now on the landing; she came out of the small bedroom and came downstairs; she was dressed in black bonnet and shawl.' I said, 'Nonsense, you must be mistaken.' He said, 'I am certain I am not, and I assure you I feel very queer.' I went to ask Mamma if there was anyone in the house, and she said no, only ourselves; still Mr Bee insisted that someone had passed him on the landing, although we tried to reason him out of it.

In the morning, while we were in bed, we received a telegram stating that Mrs Bee had died suddenly the night before. I said at once, 'Robert, that was your mother that you saw last night.' He said that it was. When we got to Gainsborough we asked what time she had died, and we were told about ten minutes to eight, which was the exact time; also that she was taken suddenly ill in the street (wearing at the time a black bonnet and shawl!) and died in ten minutes.

Gurney, 1918

Of course, the apparition may not have been connected with his mother: the fact that she died wearing a black bonnet and a shawl at that time could have been a coincidence. On the assumption it was not a coincidence, we must ask what was the point of the apparition. Although Mr Bee was certain that he saw a person on the landing, dressed in a black bonnet and shawl, he did not recognise this person as his mother. If the reason behind the apparition was to inform him about her death, it failed lamentably. It seems rather that there might be some strong bond between a son and his parent which is activated by death and which results in an apparition at that moment.

Here is another striking case reported to SPR. On 7 December 1918, Lieutenant McConnel, a trainee pilot, was unexpectedly asked by his commanding officer at Scampton, Lincolnshire, to fly a Camel aircraft to Tadcaster, sixty miles away. At 11.30 a.m., McConnel took leave of his room-mate, Lieutenant Larkin, saying he expected to be back for tea. McConnel nosedived and crashed his plane when landing in thick fog. His watch stopped at 3.25 p.m. Lieutenant Larkin was smoking in his room when he heard someone walking up the passage. He half turned and saw McConnel standing in the doorway, the doorknob in his hand. He was dressed in his usual flying clothes, but wearing his naval cap. The two men exchanged a few words. McConnel said, 'Well, cheerio.' The time was roughly a quarter past three. Someone remembers coming into the room at 3.45 to ask if McConnel was back. Lieutenant Larkin had recognised both his face and his voice. He had seen him at the time of his death (Mackenzie, p.22ff.).

Occasionally an apparition can avert death.

November 1884

When I was a child I had many remarkable experiences of a psychical nature, which I remember to have looked upon as ordinary and natural at that time. On one occasion (I am unable to fix the date but I must have been about ten years old) I was walking in a country lane at A, the place where my parents resided. I was reading geometry as I walked along, a subject little likely to produce fantasies or morbid phenomena of any kind, when, in a moment, I saw a bedroom known as the White Room in my home, and upon the floor lay my mother, to all appearances dead. The vision must have remained some minutes, during which my real surroundings appeared to pale and die out; but as the vision faded, actual surroundings came back, at first dimly and then clearly.

I could not doubt that what I had seen was real, so instead of going home, I went to the house of our medical man and found him at home. He at once set out with me to my home, on the way putting questions I could not answer, as my mother was to all appearances well when I left home. I led the doctor straight to the White Room, where we found my mother actually lying as in my vision. This was true even to minute details. She had been seized suddenly by an attack of the heart, and would soon have breathed her last but for the doctor's timely advent. I shall get my father and mother to read this and to sign it.

Gurney et al., p.137ff.

It is hard to explain away such an apparition as a coincidence. Although the story was told some time after the event, the lady affirmed that she had a very clear memory of the phenomenon (which is hardly surprising), and her story was attested by her parents, who would hardly have done so had they doubted the details of the story.

Hauntings and Apparitions of the Dead

It is strange that an apparition of a person may appear to another at the moment of death: but an even stranger paranormal phenomenon is claimed when an apparition of a dead person is said to appear in order to assure someone of their continued existence. Myers gives a remarkable instance of this.

13 January 1888

In 1867 my only sister, a young lady of eighteen years, died suddenly of cholera in St Louis, Mo. My attachment to her was very strong and the blow a severe one to me. A year or so after her death, the writer became a commercial traveller, and it was in 1876, on one of my Western trips, that the event occurred.

I had 'drummed' the city of St Joseph, Mo, and had gone to my room at Pacific House to send in my orders… My thoughts of course were about these orders, knowing how pleased my house would be at my success… I had not been thinking of my late sister, or in any manner reflecting on the past. The hour was high noon, and the sun shining cheerfully into my room. When busily smoking a cigar and writing out the order, I became aware that there was someone sitting on my left, with one arm resting on the table. Quick as a flash I turned and saw the form of my dead sister; and so sure was I that it was she that I sprang forward with delight, calling her name. As I did so, the apparition vanished. Naturally I was startled and dumbfounded, almost doubting my senses; but with the cigar in my mouth and pen in hand, with the ink still moist on the page, I satisfied myself that I had not been dreaming and was wide awake. I was near enough to touch her, had it been a physical possibility, and noted her features, expression, details of dress, etc. She appeared as if alive. Her eyes looked kindly and perfectly natural into mine. Her skin was so lifelike that I could see the glow or moisture on its surface, and on the whole there was no change in her appearance, otherwise than when alive.

Now comes the remarkable *confirmation* of my statements which cannot be doubted by those who know what I state actually occurred. This visitation, or whatever you may call it, so impressed me that I took the next train home, and in the presence of my parents and others I related what had occurred. My father, a man of rare good sense and practical, was inclined to ridicule me, as he saw how earnestly I believed what I stated; but he too was amazed when I told them later on of a bright red line or scratch on the right hand side of my sister's face, which I had distinctly seen. When I mentioned this, my mother rose trembling to her feet and nearly fainted away, and as soon as she had sufficiently recovered her self-possession, with tears streaming down her face, she exclaimed that I had indeed seen my sister, that no living mortal but herself had been aware of that scratch, which she had accidentally made while doing some little act of kindness after my sister's death. She said she well remembered how pained she was that she should have, unintentionally, marred the features of her dead daughter, and that, unknown to all, she had carefully obliterated all traces of the scratch with the aid of powder, etc., and that she had never mentioned it to a human being from that day to this. In proof, neither my father nor any of my family had detected it, and positively were unaware of the incident, yet I saw the scratch as bright as if just made...

Myers, p.205ff.

This certainly seems an authentic case. It seems very unlikely that her son would have unconsciously found out about the scar from his mother by telepathic communication. Nonetheless, there will be some who will decide whether or not apparitions of the dead are genuine by reference not to the facts of the face but to the tenets of their faith.

According to Catholic tradition, departed souls fall into three categories; those who are damned, in hell; the blessed, in heaven;

and the rest, who are consigned to purgatory in preparation for heaven. But Catholic tradition has never denied that those in purgatory may appear on earth, sent by God for some specific purpose, and dressed, we may imagine, in such a way that is consonant with propriety. At the Reformation, Protestants, in the belief that a person's eternal destiny was settled at death, denied the existence of purgatory, so according to their tenets, ghosts could not be genuine apparitions of the dead: they were evil spirits sent by the Devil.

Dr Dover Wilson pointed out how Shakespeare's *Hamlet* represents this diversity of belief. 'All the contemporary conceptions of the spirit world are represented among the characters to whom Shakespeare introduced his ghost' (Dover Wilson, 1959, p.75). Protestants of the day had a strong belief in the Devil, and anything paranormal could be attributed to him. Thomas summarises Wilson's description of their way of thinking.

> Much of the drama of the play's first act hinges on the uncertainty of the ghost's status. Horatio begins as an out and out sceptic. Even Hamlet himself is uncertain. Despite the truth of the tale the ghost had to tell, every firm Protestant in the audience would have felt justified in regarding the apparition as a devil in human form, and in view of the ultimately catastrophic results of his appearances, we may add that this may well have been Shakespeare's own view. The Devil's aim is always to capture men's souls and he was ever ready to exploit every situation to do so. By revealing the truth of his father's death to Hamlet the ghost sets off a train of consequences which involves Ophelia in the ultimate sin of suicide, and Hamlet in a series of murders. If the ghost had never appeared, and if Hamlet had refused to listen to its promptings, these events, and the terrible consequences to soul and body, would never have occurred.
>
> Thomas, p.704

Today, there are also differences of belief in ghosts, but nowadays few would explain them by reference to the Devil. Many would prefer to explain them by 'melancholie', or rather, in the light of increased medical knowledge, by schizophrenia and some other mental illness. I have pointed out the difficulties involved in such an explanation in some cases. There remains the third type of explanation, that ghosts are either earthbound departed spirits, or those who communicate with the living from another sphere of existence. If ghosts are explained by this third type of explanation, different theories have been advanced about how this happens.

Mackenzie has summarised five alternative theories of apparitions:

1. Gurney's hypothesis, which interpreted apparitions as mental hallucinations created by individual percipients in response to telepathic impulses directly or indirectly received from the appearers.
2. Tyrrell's hypothesis, which regarded apparitions as idea patterns produced currently or very recently by subconscious levels of the percipient with or without the assistance of the appearer.
3. Myers-Price hypothesis, further developed by Raynor C Johnson, which suggested that apparitions consist of the astral or etheric bodies of the appearers, with clothing and accessories created ad hoc.
4. Occult theory, which held that apparitions are of etheric images created currently or in the past by some mental act.
5. Spiritualist theory, which assumed that apparitions of the dead were spirits of the departed.

Mackenzie, p.28

Combination of Psi Phenomena Focused on a Single Individual

So far I have discussed various kinds of psi phenomena separately, but many kinds of such phenomena may be focussed on a single individual. I end this chapter by citing the case of Matthew Manning, whom I have already mentioned. He is still alive and he has given in his writings the names of those who witnessed (albeit in the 1970s) the paranormal events listed below, so his accounts are still open to investigation. Like Uri Geller, he seems to have many psychic gifts, but unlike Geller, he has submitted himself to investigation. For example, if he is connected to an electroen-cephalograph (and also to an electromyograph to exclude the use of physical force in psychokinesis), when he switches on his 'psychic energy' to bend metals, there is a large increase in theta and delta waves, which are characteristic of deep sleep. When electrodes are attached to his scalp, the ramp function of these waves is seen to emanate from the limbic region, the 'old animal brain' which lies beneath the neocortex (Manning, 1977, p.xiff.). Kirlian photography (high frequency electro-photography which registers radiation from all living and non-living objects) shows a large white area beyond Manning's fingertips, whereas normally only white squiggles appear.

I take the following from Manning's own writings. I make no attempt to assess them, although sometimes I give his own self-assessment.

CONTACT WITH A GHOST

Manning has made contact through automatic writing with Robert Webbe, a previous owner of the family house in Milton, near Cambridge. On occasions, Webbe materialised before him. Manning said he wanted to shake hands with him.

> As soon as I spoke, it was as though a warmth kindled suddenly inside the worn figure... I saw that my hand was shaking the air. Robert Webbe had not vanished – he was still standing in front of me, but my hand passed straight through his.
>
> Manning, 1978, p.96

Manning felt that it was his taking notice of Webbe that energised and vitalised him.

COMMUNICATION WITH THE DEAD

Manning received a cry for help in automatic writing from 'Graham', who had recently died and who had been the friend of a Roman Catholic Monsignor unknown to Manning, but known to Peter Bander, who was then acting as Manning's manager (Manning, 1977, p.52ff.). Graham's mother attested to his handwriting in the automatic script, which shows Graham's dyslexia. If this automatic writing was due to telepathy and was not a communication from the dead, it is strange that it was from someone who was unknown to Manning, but known to his friend.

ELECTRONIC VOICE PHENOMENON

On playing back a tape of an experiment being carried out by Professor Bender in Freiburg, Manning was heard to say 'Once more' and then 'All right'. Manning agreed that he had thought to himself, *Once more*, but those present were certain he had not spoken the words. After the tape had been played a dozen times or so, the words vanished (Manning, 1977, p.28).

PRECOGNITION

Manning had a vivid dream of a large jet landing by marshy ground too close to trees, and as the jet tried to climb, its right wing hit a pylon and he saw people carrying stretchers. Bander sent a postcard to the UK about this, which arrived in the country just before a Boeing 747 crashed at Kennedy Airport, New York, in just this way, killing 122 people (Manning, 1977, p.102).

TELEPORTATION

While carrying out tests with Manning in Sweden, Jan Fjellander locked his lab door and, arriving home for lunch with Manning, left the keys on his table at home. They disappeared. On borrowing a spare set of keys from a colleague in order to get into his laboratory, Fjellander found his own keys in the top drawer of the lab (Manning 1977, p.123).

APPORTS

While in England making a television programme, which was shown live in Japan, extraordinary poltergeist activity broke out in many Japanese homes when the programme was being watched. The TV company had 1,200 calls. Among other phenomena, cigarettes, coins, dolls and even a boiled egg suddenly appeared in Japanese homes (Manning, 1977 p.153).

METAL BENDING

Manning has bent many spoons, and conceived a distaste for so doing (see Appendix II). He also 'tested' some special Clejuso handcuffs, of which there were less than two dozen in the country. They bent and were only with difficulty removed from his wrists. Machinery with sufficient force to do this was too large to be hidden in the house. Tests at police forensic laboratories showed that no physical force had been applied, and that the molecular structure was intact (Manning, 1977, p.43ff.).

PUTTING MACHINES OUT OF ACTION

On many occasions, Manning unintentionally disabled machines, but with no discernible damage, except for the blowing of fuses. For example, a special machine for Kirlian photography which carries energy up to 35,000 volts was disabled in ten seconds. On a David Frost show, with an audience of 550, all four units to be used in the telecast were brought to a halt. At a signing session for a book at a Madrid seven-storey shop, all the electricity failed; but when Manning left, all was well again. When a TV director asked, 'What can Manning do?' his fridge exploded! During a test in Amsterdam, a large computer went haywire, 'caught in a loop'. During a programme, made in England but going out live in Japan, a camera went out of action in Japan! Manning believes that psychic energy is built up by worry about the telecasts in TV studios, and by the expectations of large numbers of people, and that he is the catalyst that lets loose the energy (Manning, 1977, pp.73, 77, 93, 144ff.).

MAKING SEEDS GROW

At a test in Stockholm, Manning concentrated positively on one tube containing seeds, and negatively on another. Three weeks later he was told that the tray of grass that he had treated positively was 'growing like hell' (Manning, 1977, p.134).

MEDICAL DIAGNOSIS

Manning would give someone's date of birth, and receive by automatic writing from 'Thomas Penn' a medical diagnosis with treatment which he says was correct 85 per cent of the time. He could not find out anything about Penn: when he tried, chaos ensued. For a long time he thought he came from inside his own head, but he came to think of him as a force, an entity. When the Pope, aged seventy-seven, became ill, the Apostolic Delegate gave him his birthday, among three others, for diagnosis! Archbishop Bruno Heim has even suggested, from certain little signs, that 'Thomas Penn' is in fact the spirit of Thomas Hodgkin whose centenary took place recently and who gave his name to Hodgkin's Disease. This particularly interested me, because Dr Hodgkin became the friend of Sir Moses Montefiore and acted as his medical attendant on his journeys abroad on behalf of Jews, and died near Tel Aviv.

TELEPATHY

Circling in a plane 430 metres above Stockholm, Manning sent telepathic messages to all who could pick them up; first three numbers, then a colour, then an image of a fish. Manning writes that he does not think that telepathy is a psi faculty, but rather something left over from our animal past. (Why not both?) He did not feel a loss of energy after sending out a telepathic message, and he did not have to empty his mind so deeply. Manning found he could send telepathic messages, but not receive them. In fact, in a test he sent a message to the other person, thus influencing the message sent to him, which he would then be able to give correctly! He could read what other people were thinking (Manning, 1977, p.23). Since Manning was residing at the time near Chequers, he was evidently regarded as something of a security risk, and was under scrutiny by the security forces (Manning, 1977, p.38ff.)

AUTOMATIC WRITINGS

Manning produced automatic writing from famous people (see p.54), even including one from John XXIII which included one of his favourite proverbs. Was Manning really in touch with these people or did his unconscious mind pick up their words and style from some other source? As for their signatures, the Official Examiner of Handwriting and Documents at the Central Criminal Court in London has said that it is not possible for a person to fake five such distinctively different handwritings. However, a passage from 'The Shipwreck', a poem written in 1796, of which Manning had never heard, showed in automatic writing some small divergences from the true text, which suggests some subjective input.

As for the pictures that Manning drew, allegedly signed by famous artists, Manning believed that 80 per cent came from his subconscious, but he could not account for the remaining 20 per cent. When Dr Bender in Freiburg gave him simply the pseudonym of a living artist, he drew a remarkably accurate 'harlequin', which was just as Dr Bender's own artist daughter had described herself and had even dressed up in the character, without of course his knowledge (p.63). As for the drawings allegedly by famous artists, Professor Easton of Hull University said that no one could have copied the style of so many artists. The Belgian art expert, Dr Jageman, declared of one drawing: 'It is Matisse' (p.68).

One of his drawings, that of a hanging man, was later identified as Leonardo da Vinci's drawing of the hanging of Guliano de Medici on 28 December 1478, with writing on it in mediaeval Latin. This was new to Manning (p.71). Were these drawings telepathic in origin, or what other explanations can be given of them?

Can one person really produce such a multiplicity of psychic phenomena? Even if a naturalistic explanation of some of them can be given, what are we to think of them taken all together? Naturally the reader does not have in front of him cast-iron evidence that they all took place. Most of them are inexplicable in our present state of knowledge. *Exit in mysterium*: it is almost beyond belief.

I call the paranormal phenomena which I have discussed in the first part of this book 'secular' because they have no immediate concern with religion. Before I pass to the second part, I must deal with a subject that is not generally regarded as paranormal at all; and then, in the second part I shall consider a whole range of phenomena that are, in one way or another, intimately connected with religion.

Chapter III
ASTROLOGY

This chapter sticks out like a sore thumb. Those concerned with parapsychology would not regard astrology as within their remit; yet I include it here, because if it is true that we are influenced by planets and stars, we have no reasonable explanation about how it happens. It never occurred to me that I would ever investigate astrology. Like most people who regard themselves as reasonably intelligent, I didn't believe a word of it. I grew interested by chance, happening to finger a book on the subject in a university library; and what I read both amazed and fascinated me. It is, of course, mostly rubbish.

Astrology has been described as 'the art of judging reputed occult influences of stars, planets, etc. on human affairs' (*Concise Oxford English Dictionary*). Belief in astrology is very ancient, and in primitive times there was probably little or no distinction between astrology and astronomy. In the ancient world, there was great interest in, and knowledge about, the movement of heavenly bodies, and ancient monuments were often built with a particular orientation of astronomical significance, as at Stonehenge, the Great Pyramid and elsewhere in the ancient world.

The claims made for astrology are very bold. It is alleged that a person's character is influenced by the position of the heavenly bodies at the time of birth, and also that a horoscope may be used to foretell future events in a person's life. It is even claimed that there are particular moments, dependent on the movement of heavenly bodies, when it is particularly appropriate to stage an event or to initiate a movement.

The casting of a horoscope is a somewhat complex business. It involves noting the sign of the zodiac through which the sun is passing at the time of birth. (The heavens are divided into twelve equal parts of a 360° zodiac, and the sun passes through each sign in the course of a year.) There are also twelve 'houses', and all the constellations will appear to pass through them all in the course of twenty-four hours, taking two hours to pass through each house. It is important to know the ascending sign, that is to say, that part of the zodiac on the eastern horizon; and for this it is necessary to know the exact time of birth. This is included in details of a birth registration in most Western European countries, including Scotland, but not in England. Popular astrology, as found in the tabloid press, is based solely on the 'sun sign', and so it is easy to see why it is regarded with contempt by professional astrologers. Another measurement important for astrology is the 'aspect', or the angle between planets or other significant points. (In astrology, the sun and the moon are regarded as planets.) Special significance is attached to a 'conjunction' (when one planet is superimposed on another). If they are in opposition (180° apart), or 'square' (at right angles to each other), then they are thought to be difficult or hard, contrasting with the easy or soft angles of 60° or 150°. This is only a very rough outline of an astrological chart, and there are very many other complex and complicating features.

The interpretation of a horoscope is even more complex than casting it. Each planet, sign and house is said to have its own characteristics, as do particular combinations of various heavenly bodies, including their 'aspects': these help to form the basis of the interpretation of an individual horoscope. The interpretation may vary greatly according to the interpreter. The complexity of the subject, together with the great variety of studies which seek to correlate astrological prediction with actual events is so great that I am dealing with the subject here only in very brief outline indeed.

Astrology seems to have begun in ancient Babylonia, from which it passed to the Greek and Roman worlds (and also to India). By the Middle Ages, it had spread throughout the known world. It lost credibility at the time of the Enlightenment and with the invention of the telescope. It has had a remarkable resurgence in modern times. It is said that the number of people making a serious study of astrology in the Western world is roughly the same as the number of psychologists!

Is this merely because of the prevalence of superstition? At first sight, this would seem to be the case. But it is unscientific to approach a subject with a closed mind, however fantastic its claims may seem to be. There is a clear way of testing the claims of astrologers, and that is by casting horoscopes of known individuals and by comparing their characters and the events of their lives with the interpretation of their horoscopes. Many people have over the years attempted to do this, and the celebrated psychologist H J Eysenk, in collaboration with D K H Nias, has made an informed and critical study of their findings. In what follows, I have borrowed heavily from their book *Astrology: Science or Superstition?* (1982).

Astrology, Personality and Destiny

In order to provide convincing evidence of some correlation between the position of the heavenly bodies at birth and people's characters or future events, it is necessary to take a large number of cases and examine the results through the cold eye of a statistician. A properly matched control group is needed, besides the group being investigated, and any project must be replicated, for the initial result could be a coincidence. Empirical projects which set out to prove the truth of astrology often fail because these principles have not been followed. Sometimes other factors are taken into consideration. For example, eighteen astrologers were asked to comment on a fictitious forthcoming marriage (Eysenk and Nias, p.40). In addition to birth details, they were sent other information that was either favourable, negative or neutral in respect of the forthcoming marriage. Only in one case did the reply seem to be based purely on astrology!

Alternative explanations must always be investigated. For example, the only study where there was apparently some correlation between character and time of birth concerned army officers. The birth dates of 16,000 army officers in Britain and 12,000 US Army officers showed peaks in summer and autumn, as against the general prevalence of birth dates in the spring. Is this astrologically significant, or is there some other explanation? It has been suggested (Eysenk and Nias, p.64ff.) that traditions of army service tend to run in families, and officers are usually away on duty during the year, but often return over Christmas, around the time when the peak of conceptions take place. For many this is a more probable explanation than one based on astrology.

When examining the correlation of astrological predictions with actual personal destinies, it would be hard to find a more extreme case than that of suicide. The records of suicides in New York City between 1969 and 1973 have been examined (Eysenk and Nias, 1982, p.80ff.) and 311 suitable candidates for research were found, all of whom had been born in the city and whose birth certificates showed the time of birth. These were divided into three groups according to the time of the suicide and carefully matched with three control groups of others who had not committed suicide. Computers were used to examine some 100,000 different factors in the 622 charts. Not a single one of these correlated in a statistically significant way with suicide. Eysenk and Nias conclude:

> We have looked at the major claims of astrology to predict personality and destiny, and we are forced to conclude that these claims are at best unproved. Wherever a properly scientific test has been carried out on a large enough sample and reported in enough detail for its validity to be judged, and has then been replicated, it fails to support the beliefs of traditional astrology.

p.94

Sunspots

Nobody quite knows what sunspots are, or why they are caused. The largest of them can sometimes be seen by the naked eye. Sunspots are comparatively colder than surrounding areas on the sun's surface, and they are associated with a high magnetic intensity. Although they radiate less light than other areas of the sun, they emit large amounts of other radiation and charged particles (giving rise to the phenomenon of the Northern Lights), and they also give added strength to the solar wind with its ionised gases. There is a cycle of about eleven years when they reach a maximum, and also periods when sunspots are minimal.

I mention sunspots because of the theory that planets

influence their occurrence, depending on the angle that the planets make with each other, their aspects, to use the language of conventional astrology. Most astronomers hold that sunspots are caused by internal processes in the sun, but a second theory which concerns the planets builds on the fact that various planetary combinations have periods closely matching those of the sun. Any such planetary influence would be due to gravitational effects, but critics point out that this would be far too weak to produce any effects on the sun, but others hold that in complex and unstable conditions a small force could trigger a large event such as a sunspot. Its proponents emphasise the 'resonant frequency' of the solar system, and point out that since at least 2000 B.C., whenever the planets Pluto and Neptune have been in opposition and in the solar equatorial plane, there have been prolonged periods of sunspot activity.

The radiation and charged particles from sunspots were known to affect high frequency radio, and in 1946, John Nelson, a radio engineer employed by the Radio Corporation of America, was asked to investigate their relationship. He found that the worst period of interference had taken place when there was a number of critical aspects among the planets. As he continued his research, he found that nearly all radio disturbances coincided with hard aspects of the planets, and the degree of disturbance was proportional to the number of planets involved. This enabled Nelson to make predictions about bad days for future HF radio reception, for which he claimed 90 per cent accuracy. However, those who checked his work found that Nelson, following a method used by the US Bureau of Standards, employed a statistically useless method of calculating the percentage of successes! They could not find any statistically significant correlation, although Nelson certainly did occasionally predict occasions of very bad interference correctly, and it could be that his theory worked only for those.

Further suggestions have been made. Marine organisms can respond to the earth's magnetic field, which itself is affected by the moon. The sun and the planets also have magnetic fields. It has even been suggested that all organisms have magnetic fields that are 'tuned' or resonate with the specific fluctuations of the earth's magnetic field. It is held that bees use the magnetic field, and that birds may use it too for navigation. Shielding from the earth's magnetic field has been found to influence responses of the human nervous system. Just as electrical circuits can be influenced by fluctuating magnetic fields, so also may the neurons of the central nervous system (Seymour, p.158). There could be resonant interactions between a human being and magnetic radiation from the sun; and this in turn could be affected by aspects of the planets triggering sunspots. Such a theory is highly controversial, but if planets could influence human beings, it might possibly provide an explanation of how it happens. There is not, however, much evidence that it does happen.

The Moon

The moon causes the tides on earth through its gravitational attraction, which is twice the strength of that of the sun. The height of the tides depends on the relative positions of the sun and the moon. Studies have shown that the moon can be used to predict the probability of rain around new moon or full moon, but the effect is slight. It has long been held that, to gain the best results, the phases of the moon should be taken into account in agriculture. Studies have been made, but they have not been replicated, and they therefore cannot be accepted as hard evidence. In any case, positive results may be due to other circumstances, such as weather or the fertility of the earth. Some species of marine life appears to be influenced by the moon, but probably their time clock has been set by the tides.

Whatever may or may not happen in the natural world, what is the effect of the moon on human beings? Research has found little correlation between the full moon and the time of birth. The moon has long been believed to influence those who are mentally ill. The very word 'lunatic' is derived from the Latin word for moon. There is some slight evidence that murderers tend to choose a time near full moon for their crimes, but another study, relating the phase of the moon to 34,318 criminal convictions, found an increased rate at full moon for crimes other than murder (Eysenk and Nias, p.174)! Studies have found the tendency for suicides to be more frequent at full moon, but the effect is very slight. As for admissions to mental hospitals at the time of full moon, there is a slight tendency for these to peak around this time, but the statistics are unreliable because of the delay in patients being admitted to hospital.

The moon is a well-known and ancient symbol of female fertility. A Nobel Prize winner in chemistry once studied the moon in connection with the onset of menstruation: he found that this peaked on the eve of a new moon, but other studies have given different results. It is striking that the length of the female cycle, which averages 29.5 days, is the same as the lunar cycle; but it is hard to see a connection here, since oestral cycles for other mammals differ in length.

It has been said that the moon influences blood flow, but there is no clear evidence of this. Eysenk and Nias quote with approval Abell who wrote:

> There may well be undiscovered lunar influences, and some of the alleged influences may turn out to be real. But many of the incredible 'facts' concerning the effects of the moon turn out not to be facts at all.

p.181

Cosmo-biology

A brief examination of traditional astrology has produced an almost entirely negative result. If there is solid evidence to show that astrology can predict a person's character or destiny, and that the planets or sunspots can influence human beings, that evidence so far has not been forthcoming. Even if the planets or the sun or the moon do have any influence over human beings, we have found nothing to connect this with the time of birth.

I have been amazed, however, to find out that there has been some remarkable research carried out last century with professional thoroughness and care which suggests not that conventional astrology is true, but that there is an inexplicable correlation between particular planets and people of outstanding character. (In what follows, I am particularly reliant here, as elsewhere in this chapter, on the work of Eysenk and Nias.)

Michael Gauquelin, a Frenchman from Paris, had been obsessed by astrology from early youth. After studying psychology and statistics at the Sorbonne, he came to realise the need for proof if the claims of astrology were to deserve acceptance. After finding negative results from researching the sun signs under which people were born, he next considered planetary positions at the time of birth and death. He was able to show that those who claimed the importance of their positions at the time of death were relying on faulty methods and controls.

However, when Gauquelin turned to planetary positions at the time of birth, he began to produce results that were statistically significant. He noticed that certain planets were likely to be in particular positions at the time that famous people were born (in cases where he was able to obtain not only their date of birth, but also the precise time when they were born). Not only did Gauquelin possess considerable knowledge about astrology, but he also used the strict discipline of scientific method in his researches, for none of which did he receive any grant or payment whatsoever, nor did his wife, herself a statistician. As a result of their work, he became very critical of professional astrologers on account of their lack of rigorous methodology, and he came to believe that much of what they claimed was simply untrue.

His first positive result came from his research into members of the French Academy of Medicine. He chose 576 doctors who had achieved distinction as a result of their research. He found that these outstanding doctors, contrary to what one would expect, tended to have been born when Mars or Saturn had just risen, or had just passed the zenith. He divided the path of a planet into twelve segments (rather like the twelve houses of traditional astronomy) so that, if there was an even spread of birth times, 8.33 per cent of these would fall in any one sector, or 16.7 per cent in any two sectors. Gauquelin found that, in fact, a higher percentage of eminent doctors' births occurred when Mars or Saturn had just risen or had just passed the zenith. He also assembled a control group drawn at random from birth registers covering the same period of birth times, and with these the spread was what would normally be expected. Was the result of his work on eminent doctors just coincidental? Gauquelin replicated his research with a further group of 508 eminent doctors, with results similar to those he had obtained from the original 576. It could hardly be a random coincidence.

Gauquelin decided to widen his research to include other professions and other countries, assembling some 25,000 birth dates. Positive results again emerged. Eysenk and Nias give two examples. He contrasted 5,100 successful artists with 3,647 successful scientists. The distinguished scientists, in contrast to the eminent artists, tended to be born under Saturn. When similar groups of distinguished soldiers and musicians were studied, the soldiers, in contrast to the musicians, tended to be born under Mars, traditionally regarded as the god of war. With the soldiers, he found that the planet Mars was rising or at the zenith in 660 cases out of 3,438 cases, when only 572 would be expected if there was an even spread.

Gauquelin further discovered that these results obtained only for those who were pre-eminent in their professions. When he looked at the birth times of those who had not achieved eminence, he found that the percentage dropped to what would be expected if there was an even spread.

Furthermore, Gauquelin examined soldiers of distinction whose lives had been cut short in war. He found the same results as among soldiers of distinction who had died a natural death later. This was an important finding, because it suggests that, if the planets do indeed influence certain eminent people, it influences only their character and not their achievements.

Further research was undertaken with 2,089 eminent sportsmen, 1,409 actors and 3,647 scientists. The results showed that, regardless of occupation, personality was associated with particular planets being in one of the critical zones. Sportsmen, who needed aggression for success, tended to be born under Mars. Gauquelin published a list of particular traits associated with particular planets: Mars, Jupiter, Saturn and the Moon; and later research has associated tenderness with Venus.

Gauquelin made another astonishing discovery. It used to be thought, as Kepler put it, that 'there is one perfectly clear argument beyond all exception in favour of astrology. This is the common horoscopic connection between parents and children'.

This Gauquelin found to be untrue as far as sun signs are concerned; indeed, it is common knowledge that children's birthdays are often at different times of the year to those of their parents. But when a comparison was made with the birth times and dates of 15,000 eminent couples and their children, Kepler's observation was found to be true! When Gauquelin later replicated this research with a further 15,000 eminent couples and their children, he obtained the same result. Moreover, he found that the gender of a parent had no impact on the effect, but that the effect was heightened if both parents had the same planetary heredity. It is interesting that the effect is more marked in the case of those planets that are nearer to the earth, Venus and Mars, and then Jupiter and Saturn.

Gauquelin further tested his hypothesis by dividing his group into those whose children were born naturally, and those whose births were induced (whether by drugs, or by forceps, or by Caesarean section). He found that the planetary effect applied only to natural births. It follows, then, that there seems to be a connection with the planets and the natural time of birth, with an increased likelihood that a person with a certain character will naturally be born at a certain time.

Criticisms of Gauquelin's Findings

Gauquelin's findings are so extraordinary, and so contrary to what one would expect, that inevitably he has had to face strong criticism, despite the fact that he has verified his findings by further replication and he has always been entirely open in his facts and findings. In particular, he has been opposed by the US Committee for the Scientific Investigation for Alleged Paranormal Phenomena (CSIAPP) which has often functioned like a committee for disproving paranormal phenomena.

After fifteen years' study of Gauquelin's results, in which they could find no fault, the members of the Committee decided to undertake their own replication, choosing famous sportsmen for their project and selecting 535 sports champions from Belgium and France. If the spread had been equal, 16.7 per cent of them would have been found to have Mars either just rising above the

Eastern horizon or just past the zenith. In fact, CSIAPP found 22.2 per cent, more even than Gauquelin's 21.4 per cent. Even so, the Committee issued a statement to the effect that the result might be due to artefact, and added, 'The Committee Para cannot accept the conclusion of the research of M Gauquelin based on hypotheses on which the Committee has found inexactitudes.' (Their objection was founded on the fact that Gauquelin had assumed that the birth frequency of 16.7 per cent was stable over the course of every twenty-four hours during the period in question, ignoring the fact the Gauquelin's results from his various control groups showed that this was actually the case.)

An American journal called *The Humanist* had been very critical of Gauquelin's claims, and called in a professional statistician as a referee in the debate. Eysenk and Nias tell the story of what then happened (p.198):

> He (the referee) pointed out that ideally a control group should be assembled which matched the sportsmen as to the approximate time and place of birth. If Gauquelin's result was due to some demographic artefact, then such a control group should also display the Mars effect. In response to *The Humanist*'s offer to publish the results of such a test, no matter what the outcome (previously they had only published criticisms of astrology), the Gauquelins went back to their birth data and constructed charts for 16,756 people born around the same date and in the same areas as 303 of the champions (matching control data were not readily available for the others). Upon analysing the newly assembled data it was found that the Mars effect was apparent for the subgroup of 303 champions with 66 of them born in the critical zones. It was not apparent for the control group. Even for 474 controls who had been matched with the 66 champions born under Mars, only 82 had also been born under Mars (again close to the chance expectation of 16.7%). This result effectively answers the Committee's objection about theoretical expectancies.

Even then the CSIAPP and *The Humanist* were not satisfied and decided on another study, this time with American sports champions; but they could obtain the birth times only of 128, which was too small a sample, so more were added to bring the study up to 605 US champions, with the result that the number with the Mars effect was well below the chance figure.

But the additions were not all champion sportsmen, nor did they select only natural births, despite the fact that the Gauquelins had claimed in earlier studies that the Mars effect was apparent only in champions who had had natural rather than induced births. When Gauquelin divided the total into highly successful and less successful sportsmen, he again found the Mars effect among the former. He later studied 432 new international outstanding sportsmen in Europe, with a control group of 423 new sportsmen below international level. He found the Mars effect in 24.5 per cent of the former group. Eysenk is not the only academic who has checked on Gauquelin's work. Dr Ertel, Professor of Psychiatry at Göttingen, has analysed his figures in detail, highlighting the dubious methods of Gauquelin's critics and showing that in fact much of the evidence is even stronger than previously claimed (Ertel and Irving, 1996)!

Further criticisms concern not Gauquelin's work so much as the findings themselves. Why is it only the eminent in the professions that are affected? Are the findings the result of a deficient probability theory? Did those who had the Mars effect have any previous knowledge of astrology, so that eminent athletes took up sport, for example, because they knew that they had been born under Mars, the god of war? In view of the heredity effect, this seems improbable. It seems hardly likely that a parent who had been an eminent sportsman, if he found his offspring also had been born under Mars, decided to persuade him to take up sport, because on this account he was likely to follow in his father's footsteps.

Yet it must be admitted that the percentage is never greater than seven per cent more than would be expected if there were merely a random spread. Nonetheless, the number found is statistically significant. There is no indication why the time of birth should be important: one might have thought that future potentialities were decided at the moment of conception rather than birth. It seems improbable that there is here a psi effect similar to those discussed earlier in this book, because the circumstances are so utterly different. Again, it seems unlikely that the effect is due to gravitational or radio magnetic impact, since there is no significant aspect between planets such as those that have been found to be significant with sunspots. So it is not surprising that many intelligent people are sceptical of Gauquelin's claims, although we must remember that these have little to do with conventional astrology, and in fact the two relevant positions, the period just after the rising of a planet and its position just past the zenith, are regarded by astrologers as 'weak houses', unlikely to have any influence.

Unable to make up my own mind on these matters in view of my ignorance of astrology and of statistics, I prefer to end with Eysenk's and Nias' conclusion (p.208).

> For ourselves, faced by Gauquelin's research at its present stage of development, we feel obliged to admit that there is something here that requires explanation. However much it may go against the grain, other scientists who take the trouble to examine the evidence may eventually be forced to a similar conclusion. The findings are inexplicable, but they are also factual, and as such can no longer be ignored: they cannot just be wished away because they are unpalatable or not in accord with the laws of present-day science.

Theological Considerations

If it be accepted that Gauquelin has proved his point, what are the theological consequences? I do not think that there are any. There is no predestinarianism here: Gauquelin's research does not imply that a person is bound to take up a particular profession just because he will have characteristics that ensure he will be good at it. Eminent sportsmen or doctors are not predestined to their professions: if they are born at a certain time and place, there may be influences, unknown to us, which may enable them to be pre-eminent in particular professions, if they decide to concentrate on these later in life. But this is hardly a new situation: people born with certain inherited characteristics may have similar potentialities for later development in particular professions.

If we accept Gauquelin's findings, we would have to admit that it is entirely unknown to us, in our present state of knowledge, how a planet which at the time of a person's birth is just about to rising or just past the zenith can possibly affect the character of a small number of eminent people, but not others. But then there are many others things that are mysterious to us in our present state of knowledge.

PART TWO

Religion and the Paranormal

Chapter IV
CLEANSING UNPLEASANTNESSES

Poltergeist Activities

In the second part of this book, which is concerned with religion and the paranormal, I deal first with poltergeists, because – contrary to many people's belief – they have nothing to do with religion! So I want to get them out of the way.

Poltergeists are unpleasant. The word in German means 'noisy spirit'. Thumps and bumps occur, electricity may go on and off, glass and crockery may be thrown across the room and get broken; and all this apparently without a cause. People find this difficult to believe – certainly Professor Richard Dawkins does (see p.xii) – unless they have actually seen it happen. And it does happen, and has happened since antiquity; and it has been well documented (Price, 1945).

Not long ago, two competent researchers published an account of some 500 cases of poltergeist activity (Gauld and Cornell, 1979). Sometimes the disturbance is very considerable. For example, there is a record of 225 objects being displaced in a gift warehouse in Miami where a nineteen-year-old Cuban clerk was employed (Roll and Pratt, *Journal of the American Society for Psychical Research*, 1971). In Long Island, USA, a dwelling was so badly affected that the house was nearly pulled to bits by builders, electricians, etc. to find the cause, but nothing was discovered (Pearce-Higgins, p.163ff.). It is, fortunately, a feature of poltergeist activity that usually no one gets hurt. For example, glasses may be thrown across the room, but they narrowly miss hitting people. A witness reported in one case that babies were removed from their cots when no one else was present and were found lying on the floor beside them, though there was no possible way by which they could have achieved this on their own; yet, after each occurrence, the baby was quite unhurt, and no bruises or any other damage could be detected on them (Petitpierre, p.109).

Phenomena connected with poltergeists differ in certain respects from hauntings (Pearce-Higgins, p.167). Whereas hauntings only disturb people, poltergeist activity is by its very nature antisocial. Unlike a haunting which lasts for years, poltergeist activity soon settles down, seemingly of its own accord. While haunting is associated with buildings, poltergeists are connected with people, and can even accompany a person if he or she moves house. Furthermore, certain phenomena that are common in hauntings, for example, footsteps, seldom appear with poltergeists.

Sometimes the disruption is almost laughable. There is a charming reminiscence in Petitpierre.

> People who have had no experience of poltergeists tend to find some of the things that happen quite incredible. I know that when I mention bowls of flowers disappearing into thin air, some of my friends often look askance at me. Yet I investigated one case at Hemel Hempstead where two women were having tea one day when a whole spray of tulips vanished from a flower bowl. There had been poltergeist phenomena in the house, and one lady had just said laughingly to the other, 'Well, at least the tulips are still there,' when they found that the flowers that had been there a moment before had vanished.
>
> Petitpierre, p.103

The disruption can be very distressing and upsetting. People who suffer such nuisances usually imagine that the building where they happen to be is haunted, but attempts to solve the problem by releasing or expelling spirits is useless: indeed, sometimes it actually aggravates the problem. Exorcism should not be carried out, nor any ecclesiastical or other rite. Here is an example which illustrates the point.

> A family of 'born again' Christians was experiencing poltergeist activity. They had curtains billowing at a window where there was no detectable draught. Electric lights began to flicker, an electric clock started to go backwards and then religious objects

would be found thrown on the floor. On one occasion the Bible was thrown across the room while they were having a family prayer session. Thinking they had a demonic attack, they prayed for deliverance and then began a fast, but at the end of the fast things were worse rather than better, so they decided to call in the elders of their particular church who confirmed that it was indeed a case of demon possession. The elders anointed the doorposts and windows of the house and commanded the demons to leave. Again, the activity increased, and the family were banned from attending their church on the grounds that they had invited the demons into their house and were hiding something from God and needed to repent. The family in desperation called in the local vicar.

At the centre of the activity was their eleven-year-old son. When away from his parents he told the vicar that he didn't like his parents' church and was play-acting and pretending to share his parents' faith but he hated going to church twice on Sundays and to join in the family prayer sessions. The vicar recognised that the boy was receiving mixed signals from his parents. They told him how precious he was and how much they loved him, but they added that they loved him so much that they only wanted him to be saved and to know the Lord. The boy did not recognise this as unconditional love and felt that he had to pretend to share his parents' faith to gain their love. The vicar counselled the family together and assured them that they were not under demonic attack, and within days the activity died down.

Walker, p.18ff.

Poltergeists are not the work of evil spirits, but are due to the psychic disturbance of individuals. Many other examples could be given of the cause of poltergeist activity being due to this kind of disturbance on the part of a member of a household. Poltergeist activity seems to be either the unconscious projection of this disturbance onto the environment, or to be caused by the psychic nature of a member of the household which releases some pocket of psychic energy. Two-thirds of all cases of poltergeist activity have been traced to disturbed adolescents and young people, and the rest to adults who are frustrated or otherwise emotionally disturbed. For example, the trouble at the gift warehouse in Miami ceased abruptly when the disturbed nineteen-year-old Cuban clerk left. The trouble in the Long Island house which had been ripped apart to find the cause of the disturbance was eventually traced to the parents' twelve-year-old son.

Very few people who are emotionally disturbed cause this kind of unconscious chaos: and the mechanism involved is entirely unknown. It seems to show the power of the unconscious. Of course, some apparent poltergeist activity is fraudulent. But there are so many cases where it has been attested that it is hard to deny that some unknown force is at work. It is typical of scientists that they assume that a physical force is involved.

> The discoverer of the new energy field which links mind to mind, or of the new fundamental force which moves objects without trickery around a table top, deserves a Nobel Prize, and would probably get it.
>
> Dawkins, p.128

It seems more likely that a psychic force is at work, the mechanism of which is quite unknown, although its effects are well known. It is certainly not a fit subject for exorcism. Often it settles down of its own accord. All that is needed is proper counselling all round. Often the emotional disturbance will be eased simply by verbalising the problem and sharing it with another person.

But not always. One of the stranger cases of poltergeist activity was focussed on Matthew Manning. An account of the outbreak when he was aged eleven, living at home in his parents' house at Queens House, Linton, near Cambridge, and of the further outbreak when he was a boarder at Oakham School, has been in print for many years (Manning, 1974). There is no room for fraud here. The happenings are very well attested.

The headmaster of Oakham School, a level-headed man who had courageously kept Manning at the school despite the disturbances he was causing and the worries voiced by other boys' parents, issued a statement after Manning had completed his studies there.

> The things that happened when Matthew was at Oakham are simply mind-boggling. He must be the most unique boy I have ever met in twenty-eight years as Master and Headmaster. Of course, I am a sceptic about psychic matters, but I know that

something quite extraordinary was happening. I bent over back-wards not to get involved, but I am sure there were paranormal powers at work to produce such mysterious happenings. I person-ally witnessed none of the happenings but plenty of people in his school house did. I had him under my personal care for about three years and I became very worried about all these happenings. There was never any explanation as to how all these disarrange-ments of dormitories, etc. occurred. Knives, bricks, glass, pebbles and suchlike appeared without any clue as to their origin. And yet nothing ever appeared to be missing from other parts of the school. The boys who shared Matthew's dormitory and whose bunks moved about were absolutely adamant that it had hap-pened: they were honest and nice boys and I know they did not tell lies.

Manning, 1974, p.iv

Professor Dawkins does not believe such things can happen.

If you put a brick on a table, it stays there until something moves it, even if you have forgotten it is there. Poltergeists and sprites don't intervene and hurl it about for reasons of mischief or ca-price.

Dawkins, p.28

In view of the headmaster's testimony, this remark of Dawkins' seems a somewhat ignorant generalisation.

Soon after the school outbreak began, the headmaster received a letter from Dr A R G Owen, who had been a Fellow of Trinity College, Cambridge, when the first outbreak took place took place at Manning's home near Cambridge. He wrote:

I investigated a minor outbreak of poltergeist activity at Mr Manning's home a few years back. I believed that they were not due to trickery, but real phenomena. The evidence did not allow them being ascribed to Matthew in particular as the invol-untary source. The probabilities were that they would not recur. This latter guess has been proved wrong.

It was naturally awkward for a boy to discover that he was the unwilling focus of chaos and disruption. How could he stop it happening? It happened by chance. One day, when writing an essay in his study, with his pen in his hand, his attention wandered, and he found that he had written words in a handwriting other than his own. He was apparently in contact with the Webbe family who had owned and lived in the house two centuries earlier. Manning cultivated this automatic writing and found that it was the best way of controlling or preventing poltergeist activity.

> If it looked as though disturbances were imminent, I would sit down and write. Later it became clear to me that writing was the controlling factor. It appeared that the energy I used for writing had previously been used for causing poltergeist disturbances.
>
> Manning, 1974, p.65

For those who accept the genuineness of psychic phenomena, this illustrates their interconnection.

Psychic Imprint on a Local Environment

Poltergeists are attributable to the present members of a household. But disturbances also seem to be caused by the past actions of dead people. When some terrible action has taken place, involving strong emotions, it seems that there can be a psychic imprint in the local environment which can manifest itself to those who have psychic sensitivity. Such an imprint can, it seems, gain strength by repetition, or by a similar episode nearby.

> There are various places which are reputed to have ghosts. Usually it is claimed that they not only appear, but also walk around and sometimes carry out various actions. In some ways it appears like a video replay, in which the same action is repeated each time the apparition is seen. It could, the sceptics say, be a matter of folklore and psychological suggestibility, so that the story is planted in someone's mind causing them to expect to see the apparition; then, after a few drinks, or in a poor light, they see the ghost just as they imagined it would be. Such an explanation may well account for some cases. There are, however, cases where people have not been forewarned and where different people at different times and without collusion have witnessed the same ghostly happening.
>
> Walker, 1997, p.28

Dr Martin Israel calls these ghosts 'non-material deposits of an obsessional nature which have arisen from past experiences of people who have lived in a particular place'. He has recounted one particular incident of this kind in which he was involved.

> One case with which I was involved concerned the recurrent appearance of a nun running down a flight of stairs. It seemed that centuries ago a nun who had stolen a small amount of money was eventually found out. In order to escape she had run precipitately down the staircase, but during the course of her flight she had fallen and sustained fatal injuries. Apparently the horror of the incident had implanted itself on her mind and perhaps the community's mind also. It had persisted as a permanent psychic landmark which seemed to reveal itself in the presence of psychically sensitive people. Some of these saw the form of the young woman on the stairs, others a nun fully dressed in a habit, and others still were aware of someone falling on the stairs, accompanied by screaming. I am aware that, for a time after death, each of us becomes a discarnate entity, before we move on to higher things according to the worthiness of our life on earth. But I do not believe such an entity was present in this case. The form was a psychic imprint of a horrifying episode, similar in its own way to the tape recording of a speech or a concert. It can live on for ever, even though the incident ended in a couple of minutes, or at the very most hours.

> Israel, p.66ff.

Of course, materialists and scientists who believe in material causes will not accept such testimony, but it comes from someone much experienced in this field. If indeed there is a psychic imprint, no explanation can be given of it, except perhaps to compare it with what seem to be cell memories of a worm (see p.172) or of a transplanted heart (see p.171). The location where such apparitions take place is often oppressive. My wife and I once looked over the Abbey House in Cambridge, adjacent to the former Barnwell Priory, a twelfth-century Augustinian foundation. The house happened to be for sale at a time when we were bursting out of our house in that city. The Abbey House had a very oppressive atmosphere and we both decided that we did not want to live there. It was only later that we discovered that it was indeed haunted; a nun was accustomed to appear in a bedroom at the foot of the bed, and a strange animal ran up the stairs. When I told Professor Stratton, a Fellow of the College where I was Dean, that I had thought of living there, he was bitterly disappointed that we went elsewhere and I subsequently discovered that he had made a special study of the place, and that 'The Haunting of Abbey House, Cambridge' has been featured in a publication of the Society for Psychical Research (Mackenzie, pp.186–195).

One of the characteristics of a psychic imprint is that often the repetition of the incident takes place at exactly the same time of day or night. For example, the Society for Psychical Research was sent a manuscript by a Canon Robinson of York after his death about the haunting of the first vicarage he had lived in after his ordination. All hell broke loose in the attics during their first night in the parsonage house.

> The great noise which greeted us on the first Sunday morning, as it was the most startling of all the phenomena, so it was the least frequent. Weeks sometimes passed without us hearing it at all. But whenever we did hear it – we always found it occurred at two o'clock on a Sunday morning... As the winter passed away, we had few visitors... One of the visitors was a young lady, a very near relative of my wife... At length Sunday morning arrived, and we met at the breakfast table. 'Whatever was the matter last night?' was our kinswoman's first greeting. 'What a clatter some-one made... As I stood in the darkness, looking out of the window, I heard the church clock strike two.'
>
> Mackenzie, pp.77–88

The story was later corroborated by Canon Robinson's daughter. Something terrible must have happened in the past at that hour that made a psychic imprint on the house. Unfortunately, the clergyman made no attempt to silence the trouble, probably being ignorant of what could have been done. Incidentally, one may well ask why accounts so often feature parsonages and convents. They tended to have been built long ago, and so, like the old stately homes of England, there has been more opportunity for strange happenings in them. I suspect, however, that the real reason is a mysterious connection between religion and the paranormal.

Sometimes there can be a happy outcome from a psychic imprint. In *The Oxford Dictionary of the Supernatural* the following record can be found:

> As Mrs Agnes Kelly of Fartown, Huddersfield, drove her car into a sharp bend, the glare of incoming headlights picked out the figure of a fair-haired boy. Horrified, she swung the steering wheel over as the boy's freckled face loomed up in front of the windscreen. That single act probably saved her life. She smashed into a parked car, but suffered only shock. As she waited for an ambulance, she asked a policeman, 'Have I killed the boy?' But there was no boy.
>
> A court heard, in January 1981, that what Mrs Kelly saw as she took the bend in Summerfield Road, Huddersfield, was a vision of an eight-year-old child who had been knocked down and killed by a car on the same spot many years before. After the case she said, 'But for that vision I am sure I would have driven straight into the car coming up the hill towards me.'
>
> Whitaker, 1983, quoted by Enright, 1995, p.16

Those who refuse to believe in ghosts will presumably dismiss all these accounts as either fraudulent or merely hallucinatory. Others, however, may think that they pass the criteria that I set out in the first chapter of the book concerning the integrity of percipients, the time elapsed between the event and the written record, and the coherence of the accounts.

Earthbound Spirits

Can those who have lived and are now dead affect us in any other ways? Those who do not believe that there is any further existence after death will likewise dismiss the possibility that there are discarnate spirits of dead people who are for some reason earthbound. How could there be, if there is no existence after death? It is a perfectly understandable position. Nonetheless, it is wise to consider what evidence there is for holding the view that some spirits, perhaps many, become earthbound. The reader is referred in particular to the dialogue that I had with a Christian visionary on this subject (see pp.238ff.).

Those who believe that they have psychic gifts which enable them to deliver earthbound spirits are clear that such spirits do not need exorcising. It is not the spirits of the dead, but evil spirits who need to be expelled from their infestation of localities and human beings. Earthbound spirits, they tell us, have lost their way, and need help.

Why have they become earthbound? They may have died a violent death, and their souls were not committed to God. They may have committed some violent crime, and although they may be consumed with guilt, they may not have repented of the crime. They may believe that they still have important work to do on earth, and so are obstinate about leaving this worldly existence, even though they have only a spirit existence here. They may have been so committed to the place where they lived that they have refused to leave it (and they may get very upset when they find others are inhabiting a house that they regard as their own). They may be so materialistic that they are unable to recognise that there is a spirit world, and remain wedded to the material world. Some of them, perhaps most of them, may not even realise that they are dead, and so are extremely confused by the differences of today's world from the world that they knew. Since they no longer belong to the spatio-temporal world, space means nothing to them (so that they seem to walk through material objects) and the passage of time is meaningless to them (so that they think that they still belong to the period when they were alive). Some of them realise that their position is unsatisfactory, but they cannot move on without help; and so they intervene in our lives to attract attention and make their presence known, thereby often causing fear and distress. Few of them have actually decided not to seek the Light, although to do this will require a change of heart. So they are usually glad to move on when it is explained to them that this will bring them under God's loving care and protection.

Those with special psychic gifts are able to explain this to them. For those of us who are not gifted in this way, prayer and a celebration of the Eucharist with a special intention on their behalf will usually suffice, unless an earthbound spirit is very obstinate and seems likely to take the fundamental option against the Light. Whatever be the cause of their being earthbound, and whatever be the state of their soul, they should be offered not deprecation and denunciation, but assistance and help. This is the message about them that those who seem psychically gifted to help them bring to the rest of us.

Dom Robert Petitpierre, who had long experience in these matters, has described the case of an earthbound spirit with which he was involved. His account is too long to be included here, so I cite it in a shortened form:

> A big house in London had ceased to be a convent more than twenty-five years earlier... Two young London businessmen shared a five room flat in the converted building. The old convent chapel still existed, and more than once, I believe, the young men saw the ghost of a nun there. It may have been an imprint or a ghost... (In the flat) matchboxes were continually being thrown across the rooms and on one occasion a metal matchbox holder was tossed right across a room and forcefully struck a sister of one of the young men. When I visited the flat the sister was there to show me the metal holder and to describe the incident in detail... One night while one of the young men was in bed and asleep, he was suddenly woken up to discover that somebody had tossed three votive candles onto his chest. There were no votive candles in the bedroom; the inference was that they had been thrown there by the shadowy nun...
>
> On the face of it, this was a typical poltergeist set of phenomena. Both the young men were fairly strongly psychic and could have been unconsciously responsible. They were both practising Christians, one being churchwarden of a neighbouring parish... The stories told me by the two men and the sister whom, as I have indicated, I also interviewed, convinced me that, to the best of their ability, they were telling me the truth. On the whole I was inclined to accept what they had to say at face value...
>
> On the Saturday morning, assisted by the churchwarden's vicar, I celebrated Mass in the flat. Late that night, the two young men went out to enjoy their Saturday night and when they returned they found that strange things had occurred in their flat while they were gone. In the kitchen they found a burnt out matchbox, with every match inside also burnt. In another room they found another matchbox with every match burnt out – but with the matchbox intact. Finally in one of the men's bedrooms they found that talcum powder had been scattered all over a chest

of drawers. And there, scrawled into the powder, in capital letters, was the word AMEN.

That was in fact the end of the trouble in that particular flat. There were, I know, other manifestations in some of the neighbouring flats so the Requiem Mass had obviously not cleared the whole house, but I was not called in to deal with these other problems. Although the phenomenon appears to indicate poltergeist activity – and I do not discount the possibility that some of the happenings were due to this – I am convinced that the nun was a ghost proper and that it was her spirit that scrawled the word AMEN into the talcum powder. It was her way of saying thank you for her release.

Petitpierre, p.78ff.

It is possible to hold that what the two young men really needed was a doctor or a psychiatrist and that they had hallucinated or made up some of the matters they reported. On the other hand, there are those who would agree with Dom Petitpierre who wrote:

> I find it difficult, with personal knowledge of the efficacy of prayer as expressed in exorcism, whether major or minor, to pay too much attention to theologians and others who like to suggest all these problems the working clergy have to deal with are better left to psychiatrists and doctors.

Petitpierre, p.70

Matthew Manning, whom I have mentioned elsewhere in this book (see pp.64ff.) has written an account of his dealings with a ghost in his parents' house near Cambridge in his youth. For the most part, he communicated with Robert Webbe, the ghost of a former owner of the house, by means of automatic writing. Manning seems to have been a young man with remarkable psychic sensitivity. Even discussing Webbe with his parents seemed to energise his interventions. Objects disappeared from the house, and objects appeared, including pages from an eighteenth-century book. At times, there was a strong smell of tobacco in the house, though the family were not smokers. Matthew Manning was researching the village of Milton for an O level project, and this seemed to interest the ghost of Robert Webbe, and no less than 503 names, many with dates, were found written on the wall of his bedroom in different handwriting. Sounds from the ghost were recorded on tape. Webbe seemed to have died of gout, and Matthew's father attested that on occasions he felt the presence of someone else in his bed and a tingling sensation in his lower limbs, as though Webbe were reliving the experiences of the end of his life, and communicating these to Matthew's father who happened to be lying where Webbe's bedchamber had been situated. If we accept Manning's own assessment, it seems that just as he had been the cause of polter-geist activity described earlier (p.90ff.), so also he somehow brought the ghost to life.

> The more I thought about it, the more convinced I became that Webbe's 'spirit' was some kind of incandescent light. A bulb will only light up when connected to a source of electricity, like a battery, and I came to the conclusion that I was the battery for Robert Webbe. I could not help thinking of how he had looked wax-like and lifeless until I spoke to him. He had almost come back to life then.
>
> Manning, 1978, p.99

It seems (if the evidence from automatic writing be accepted) that Robert Webbe was a self-made man who was proud of the house he had built and was deeply attached to it: he made it clear that he attended church without belief, and he was very materialist in his attitudes. All this points to his being an earthbound spirit (for those who believe that these exist). As Matthew Manning himself wrote:

> By now it was quite clear that Webbe was trapped in the house, reliving his past life.
>
> Manning, 1978, p.71

It is a pity that the offer of the local vicar to say prayers for him in the house was not accepted, on the grounds that Webbe would not have wished it.

One of the reasons why souls might become earthbound, it

was suggested earlier, could be that when they died, they had not been properly committed to God. Dr Kenneth McAll was an eminent British surgeon/psychiatrist, who became an international figure liaising between the medical profession, the international fraternity of psychiatrists and the Church. He believed that many supposedly 'incurable' patients are the victims of ancestral control, and he sought to liberate them. By drawing up a family tree, he believed he could identify the ancestor who was causing harm to his patient. The bond between the ancestor and the patient was then cut by celebrating, with a clergyman, a service of Holy Communion to deliver the earthbound ancestor to God.

> Molly, a well-educated, healthy, intelligent thirty-year-old woman, developed what she described as a 'a new and ridiculous phobia'; a paralysing fear of travelling anywhere near water, even for a short distance. Her two children had suffered a ducking the previous summer when they had been tipped into the water in a little boat in a very safe pond. Psychiatric treatment had not alleviated this phobia and she had been referred to me. We did not have to go very far back in her Family Tree to discover that an uncle of hers had been drowned in the *Titanic* disaster. As far as the family knew, no one had committed him to the Lord, so we decided to hold a Eucharist for him. The celebration of the Eucharist when our Lord is always present is the central act of deliverance and healing. Molly took part and afterwards felt completely freed from her phobia. Although the drowned uncle only seemed to need a committal service, Molly did accept a greater degree of spiritual discipline in her life from that time forward.
>
> McAll, p.12

Of course, it can be held that the dead uncle had nothing to do with her cure, and that the spiritual impact of the Eucharist had an effect on her psychiatric condition which doctors could not achieve by their techniques. The same explanation could be applied to Dr McAll's views about numbering unborn babies among the unquiet dead. On the other hand, babies are sensitive to love very early on in a pregnancy even before the brain has been properly formed. Those who have early on been deprived of love and life, Dr McAll claims, may also cause illness in others.

Dr McAll wrote:

> I have over six hundred recorded cases of direct healing which have taken place after a Eucharist has been held for babies – who were either aborted, miscarried, or discarded at birth or who had never been loved or committed to Jesus Christ in a burial service. When a Eucharist has been held for such infants, the results have been startling. Many have felt the healing power that was generated, including patients who were actually taking part, patients who were miles away in hospital and mental institutions and knew nothing about the services, and even disturbed relatives in foreign countries.
>
> McAll, p.49

Sceptics will doubtless explain such healings by assuming that the guilt which many women feel after having an abortion has caused the illnesses, and that the service of the Eucharist, with its message of forgiveness, has released the feelings of guilt. However, it is difficult to apply this explanation to those who knew nothing of such Eucharistic services having taken place, and Dr McAll gives an impressive list of healings. In our materialist culture, it seems incredible that Dr McAll's explanations should be correct; but, on the other hand, it is possible that an earthbound spirit awaiting release may have been trying to draw attention to itself by causing trouble to members of the family.

The Cleansing of a Polluted Environment

Not only people may be influenced; houses too are affected by their occupants, past and present. Why and how we do not know; but they are. When one enters a house, one can feel 'This is a happy place'. Or one can feel 'This place is oppressive: I don't like it'. Of course, this may be due to the layout of the place, or it may be overshadowed by trees. It is always best to seek a rational explanation for such feelings before considering the possibility of a psychic cause. But sometimes rational explanations do not suffice. The cause may be something psychic. A presence seems to brood over the place, not altogether happy, and sometimes positively evil. It may be an earthbound unquiet spirit; or it may be something worse.

We have already looked at some ways in which a locality can been disturbed when considering the phenomena of poltergeists, ghosts and psychic imprints. There are other ways in which a locality can be psychically polluted. It may be a place where, in the past, some dreadful deed has been done, or where some gross sexual behaviour has taken place. It may be that black magic has been practised there, or it may be the result of the use of Ouija boards or the planchette or some other occult practice, or it may be a desecrated place of Christian worship, or a spot where evil pre-Christian worship once took place. If the ghost is that of an evil person, he or she may become the channel of evil spirits. Then the situation can become serious.

But happily, this is not always the case. I remember, when I was Bishop of Birmingham, there was a parish in a post-war housing estate where a previous incumbent had by no means been all that he should have been. The present incumbent told me that the family dog would not enter his son's room in the vicarage, that the boy did not like the room, and that it was always cold, despite the central heating. (For reasons unknown, cold spots are a characteristic of psychic pollution, and this is sometimes accompanied by a pungent and offensive smell.) The vicar called in one of the priests whom I had designated 'diocesan exorcists', who simply said a few prayers in the room, and the trouble ceased, though things are not always as easy as that.

At other times, the situation is far worse.

> Sometimes properties may be haunted by such terrible atmospheres that produce such depression that nobody who is psychically sensitive could bear to be within reach of them.
>
> Israel, p.57

I have already discussed ghosts; but a malicious person who has died presents a different problem. Evil shows itself in a desire for the personal destruction of others, and a malicious ghost may become the channel for evil spirits which use the locality for their evil ends. (The question why there are evil spirits is as intractable as why there is any evil at all, but evil can serve as a challenge to people to overcome it.) This can have a devastating effect on those who later inhabit a house. A friend told me an experience of her youth.

> I rented a large bedsitter to share with a friend on the ground floor of a house in the corner of Onslow Square in London. On the left-hand side of the hall there was a passage, and down the passage on the right was the entry to my room, and opposite it was a small bathroom. On the right of the hall there was a spiral iron staircase leading to the basement. It was a beautiful house, completely refurbished. I was the first tenant, and my room was bright and airy. On the first night there, I went to have a bath, and got into it. I was sitting in the bath and suddenly I had a perfectly terrible feeling and awareness of something evil outside the bath and behind my right shoulder. I was terrified and I was afraid to look at what it was. If I'd thought it was a ghost, I would have looked at it.
>
> I'm not afraid of anything. I've been in the jungle, I've had snakes over me, I've waded across rivers with crocodiles. I even fight other people's battles. If I hear anything in the night I go and look. But not there. What I did was to get out of the bath, drape myself with a towel and bolt to my room without daring to look behind me. Once inside my room everything was normal, and the room was bright and cheerful. In bed I wondered whether I'd been imagining it, and thought I had.
>
> The next night I didn't think twice about having a bath. I got into it, and the experience was even worse. I was aware of something terrible coming out of the well of the staircase. I couldn't bear to look back to see it. I went to my room and locked the door: everything was perfectly normal in the room. Next morning, forfeiting my deposit of a week's rent, I moved out with my suitcase, leaving the key in my room, determined never to go back there again.

It would seem that some terrible deed had been done in the house, which had permitted the infiltration of evil spirits. Unfortunately, my friend, who had been brought up as a Presbyterian, did not realise that the Church had a ministry to deal with such things.

Although the following story shows what effect the ministry of exorcism can have, it happened too late to avert two tragedies.

A few years ago I was asked to cleanse a cottage on an estate near London. The cottage, quite unknown to its owner, had been used for black magic rituals and the nastiness within it struck me almost like a blow in the face. After the black magic tenant left, the cottage had been occupied by a married couple but the presence of evil was such that what had once been a happy marriage broke up. The next tenant was found dead with his head in the sink; he had fainted while washing up and fallen into the water. I said some prayers and attempted to cleanse the place. At the end of the ceremony we found ourselves very, very tired (an exorcist suffers great strains as he confronts evil), and thereafter the conditions within the cottage were very much improved.

Petitpierre, p.47

If an unquiet spirit is causing trouble, the exorcist must meet evil not only with Christian authority, but also with Christian love if he is to succeed. The Holy Communion should be celebrated in a polluted place during which the person causing the disturbance is charitably commended into the loving arms of God, so that jealousy and hate may be transformed into love and peace. The rooms should be blessed and evil spirits commanded to depart from that place.

Sceptics would say, in the case of the cottage mentioned above, that the people concerned were simply in need of marital counselling or psychiatric help; but I should very surprised if they continued to say that after they had actually experienced the atmosphere of a place of this kind, although I suppose that a person with no psychic sensibility at all would not have noticed anything strange about the cottage. Sceptics would also hold that the ministry of the Church in such cases, carried out with impressive ritual and authority, calms the people affected down and has a cleansing effect not on the locality but on the outlook of the persons concerned; and that it is for this reason that responsible psychiatrists, when they find patients who are beyond their care, often welcome the ministry of the Church. Such an explanation hardly applies to the physical manifestations in the environment (e.g. cold spots measurable by a thermometer which register several degrees lower than the surrounding environment), and it is not easy to apply it satisfactorily to all cases, for instance, where past evil has taken place unknown to later inhabitants of a place.

Assault by Evil Spirits

If buildings can become polluted, is it possible that human beings also can be adversely affected by spirits? There are those who hold that (apart from possible forms of intelligent life on planets elsewhere in the universe) Homo sapiens is unique, and there are no other forms of spiritual beings. This is only a presumption: it cannot be proven whether or not this is the case. It is equally possible that we are only one kind of spiritual being. There could be other forms of spiritual beings, in particular angels, good and bad. (We often picture angels as winged beings, because human language has to use such imagery to describe non-human entities.) Evil spirits are often equated with fallen angels, but if there are such, they could exist in their own right. Many of those who are prepared to concede the possibility of other forms of spiritual beings would regard it as superstitious to believe that a human being could be possessed by these powers of evil. Psychiatry, they would say, has replaced such primitive ideas. People who in past ages would have been thought possessed by a devil are now considered mentally ill and dosed with appropriate drugs. Mostly this is the case; but not necessarily in every case.

Human beings certainly can and do influence one another. If there are evil spirits, it is not so extraordinary that we can be influenced by them, especially if they are invoked. Usually when a person seems to have been polluted by evil spirits, there is a feeling of oppression, which can be relieved by what is called the 'lesser exorcism'; prayer and the laying on of hands and (if the person concerned is a communicant) by the Eucharist. Prayer will include the Lord's Prayer: the words translated 'deliver us from evil' would be better translated 'deliver us from the evil one', and these in themselves constitute a lesser exorcism. Prayer is usually effective in such cases.

I know a person who, when she was a young girl, during a long and lonely dinner break at school, drew a pentagon in the dust and used Faust's invocation of Mephistopheles. Thereafter, she felt a sneering presence with her until she could bear it no more and told her mother, who told her to pray, 'Dulce Jesu, libera me' (sweet Jesus, deliver me) and when she had spoken these words aloud, the shadow left her and never returned.

A person can be not only influenced by another person, but even possessed by another person. It is possible for people to be so dominated by a strong personality that they can no longer exercise a will and mind of their own, but merely produce the concepts, dispositions and responses of the person who dominates them. It is well known that 'mother love' can degenerate into 'smother love'. It follows that, if there are evil spirits, a person may similarly be possessed by one or more of them.

There are certainly mental states that produce symptoms akin to those expected in possession. We have already noted hysterical dissociative states in connection with mediums (p.45) and will consider it with reference to reincarnation (see p.186). Suddenly a person may assume one or more personalities quite different from their normal one, without being aware of the change, and with no knowledge of a change in the state of consciousness, and with no knowledge whatsoever of the other states. It is easy to assume, quite wrongly, that such a person is possessed. There are states of schizophrenia that can give a similar impression. Here the personality is not dissociated, but disintegrated. A person suffering from paranoid schizophrenia may hear voices inserted as it were into his head from outside; he may lose control over his life, and have no desire to reassert it. He is alienated from his true self. There are some similar symptoms with left lobe epilepsy, when there is a disturbance in the left lobe of the cortex in the brain.

Dr Anton-Stephens, a consulting psychiatrist who was quoted in the first chapter of this book, has suggested that it is possible that a hysterical or schizophrenic personality gives access to an outside agent so as to produce symptoms that we associate with hysteria or schizophrenia (Anton-Stephens, 1994, p.154). The same might be said of a psychopath, whose behaviour can be outrageously sadistic, and since some people seem to be born psychopaths, this would imply that they have been possessed from birth. The invasive agent is not necessarily bad. The agent might be good, bad, or indifferent. If good, it could be equated with a good angel, and this might account for some of the quasi-hysterical symptoms we shall note when considering the physical phenomena of mysticism (see p.273). If bad, it would account for the horrible phenomena that occur in rare cases of alleged possession. If indifferent, it would account for some strange phenomena, an example of which Dr Anton-Stephens provides.

> I have been present when a fully conscious clairaudient endeavoured to transmit words in a language of which she was ignorant. In that case the process had every possible appearance of the person involved listening to phonetic syllables which only became 'words' after one had worked out which phoneme belonged to a particular word and which to the one which followed it: the experience of the person involved was that of hearing unintelligible sounds which she did her best to vocalise accurately. That the result was Latin and intelligible must, I would think, exclude any cerebro-muscular malfunctioning, because the chances of a non-functioning brain producing that result must be on a par with monkeys tapping typewriter keys and producing a Shakespearean sonnet.
>
> Anton-Stephens, 1994, p.156

Dr Anton-Stephens has found, when interviewing patients with symptoms of alienation, especially schizophrenics, that in rare cases he seems to be interviewing the agent (if there be one) rather than the patient himself. None of this adds up to a proof of possession. Proof does not rest on impressions. There is always the alternative explanation of mental illness giving the impression of possession. Possession, if it does occur, is exceedingly rare. There is a 'syndrome' that goes with it: blasphemy, paranormal phenomena, abnormal strength, as well as behaviour markedly different from a person's norm (Perry, 1996, p.120).

Abbot Wiesinger, in a book on occultism, has quoted two horrific cases. The first, too long to quote here, concerned two foster children of a childless couple living in a little village on the Chiemsee in Upper Bavaria. The other account concerned two children, Theobald, aged ten, and Joseph, aged eight, from Illfurt near Mulhouse in Alsace.

The boys began, without any visible reason, to turn around rapidly, while lying on their backs, to 'thrash' the bedsteads and break them up: then they would remain for hours apparently lifeless; soon after this they developed an insatiable, wolfish, hunger, their bellies began to swell, their legs began to intertwine like flexible withies, so that no one could untwist them again. Then there appeared to them a hideous thing with a duck's beak and with claws and feathers. Theobald threw himself madly upon it and pulled out feathers which lay about and gave off a loathsome stink. This occurred twenty or thirty times in the presence of hundreds of people. The feathers, with their hideous smell, left no ash behind when burnt. Sometimes the boys were lifted up in their chairs and hurled into a corner; on another occasion they felt a pricking and tickling all over their bodies, and fetched incredible quantities of feathers and sea-weed out of their clothes, and this occurred however often their shirts and clothing were changed.

After the doctors had tried all they could without success, the parish priest was called, who took pity on the poor tortured creatures, and was anxious to bring some comfort to their parents who were almost in despair. The children, who had been well brought up with due regard to morality, found abusive names for all holy and consecrated objects, knew of things not taking place in their presence, and answered in French when they were asked questions in Basque. The devils did not want to go back to hell: their gave their names and answers to the priest's questions.

The children were taken to hospital where they were for a time more quiet. They were now deaf; also they avoided coming near any consecrated or religious object. At length an episcopal commission was appointed to examine the matter, which made a report in preparation for the exorcist. When Theobald was brought into the church so that the exorcism might be proceeded with, he trembled all over his body, developed a fever, and spoke blasphemously. When the priest recited the exorcism 'I command thee to depart from here', the devil spoke from the child, saying, 'My time has not yet come: I am not yet going.' When the priest further recited 'In the name of the Immaculate Conception' the boy called out in a deep bass voice, 'Now I must yield,' and fell down as though he were dead. After an hour he came to, and looked at all the people around him with astonishment. He knew none of them, although for four years they had constantly been about him. The only people he knew were his parents. His hearing returned, and he was the same well-behaved decent boy he had been before, simply four years older.

Wiesinger, E T, p.250ff.

Wiesinger adds that some weeks later the other boy was similarly cured and thereafter lived a normal life.

What are we to make of such a story? In the first place, there are no named witnesses and so we know nothing about the credibility of those who reported the phenomena. Secondly, the events are said to have taken place in 1874 but were not written down until forty years later. Wiesinger affirms that they were based on documents, but how can we be sure that details were not altered or exaggerated? Thirdly, Wiesinger wrote in German, and cited a German source for the account, *Satans Macht und Mirken in zwei besessenen Kindern* (Eckman, 1921) written by P Sutter, a book that he claimed had been translated into many languages. No such translations have been discovered, and a search in the database of the American Library of Congress has established that in all the main libraries in Europe and America only one copy of the German edition is known to exist! Fourthly, there are certain inconsistencies in the story. Why should the devil have stayed put when commanded to come out in the name of God, but agreed to depart when commanded in the name of the Immaculate Conception? Fifthly, there are certain vaguenesses in the account – 'hundreds of people' and 'twenty or thirty times'. In the light of this, the account certainly cannot be accepted as a validated instance of possession. This is not to deny that possession did happen to the two boys – we simply cannot be sure. If we had a copy of the contemporary account of the phenomena, which we were told was prepared for the exorcist, we would be in a better position to make a judgement. I cite the story as a good example of bad evidence of the paranormal.

An account of a very different case of possession is given by Dom Robert Petitpierre, the only case of genuine possession he could recall in all the years of his long ministry of deliverance.

In 1943, Gilbert Shaw, along with T S Eliot and Dorothy Sayers, had founded a discussion group at St Anne's, Dean Street, in Soho. The church itself had been bombed out, but the parish house remained. (The church has since been rebuilt.)

The case concerned a lady who was no more than five feet five inches tall. She had been involved with certain drug gangs at that time in London's East End. I do not believe that she actually took drugs herself. But she was unquestionably mixed up in an evil business and it seems clear that at times she came under demonic control. The symptoms were varied, usually involving continual blasphemy, often a display of telepathic knowledge beyond the ken of either the victim or those trying to cure her and frequently accompanied by a display of abnormally violent strength. One does not decide that a person has come under demonic control, of course, without a long period of observation and without a careful check of the medical and psychiatric condition of the victim. Gilbert Shaw, I and others concerned with the lady's case had satisfied ourselves that her case was beyond medical help.

At other times the woman would go into hour-long trances because of psychic attack by the drug groups. One day we managed to get her down into the basement room of the parish house – a large room about twenty by forty feet. For almost an hour Gilbert Shaw, myself and a deaconess prayed for her, calling her back to normality. At last she recovered, and then suddenly she stood up, and stuck one foot out in front of her. We grabbed her, but with her foot stuck out straight and hopping on one leg she dragged all three of us round that big room three times. There is no rational explanation, of course, for such extraordinary strength, strength far beyond the powers of even a mentally deranged person. Eventually we managed to sit her down, and Gilbert Shaw performed a major exorcism, exhorting the demon to depart and harm no one.

I warrant that even the most doubting of Thomases could not fail to have been convinced. As the prayers ended, an amazing transformation took place. The wild violent little figure suddenly became tranquil, serene, normal. It was as though she had sloughed off an enormous weight or come out of a deep sleep. She herself acknowledged the demon's control. 'Cor, that was a demon, wasn't it?'

Petitpierre, p.91

In trying to distinguish the various ways in which spirits, ghosts and poltergeists manifest themselves, I am conscious of attempting to make neat categories where these do not really exist. The reality is not so clear.

In my diary there are several cases where one finds a difficult mixture of sources for abnormal phenomena which demand a great deal of patience in unravelling. Ghosts proper, place imprints or memories, poltergeist effects – all get inextricably mixed up and it is not always clear which is causing which effect and why... There are cases where a departed spirit has been able to produce psychokinetic effects and instead of the usual manifestations – opening and shutting doors, footsteps, pale apparitions – quite fierce physical effects are produced.

Petitpierre, p.91

Profligate Use of Exorcism

Unfortunately, in some of the more extreme evangelical and charismatic circles, there is a profligate use of exorcism. In an American manual with the subtitle, 'Answers to Questions You Have Been Asking in This Age of Increased Demonic Activity', the numbers of evil spirits are explained as follows:

When you're engaged in spiritual warfare, it's as well to know your enemy. The following evil spirits, demons or devils are mentioned in the Scriptures. Each one is a personality and the word used expresses their nature.

Maxwell Whyte, p.55

The author then goes on to list twenty-one spirits lifted from texts in the Old and New Testaments. Some of these were not intended by the authors of the biblical books to refer to a discarnate spirit, but rather to an attitude which is the alternative meaning of the word 'spirit' in Hebrew, Greek and English (e.g. 'God has not given you craven spirit but a spirit to inspire strength' in II Timothy 1:7, or 'a spirit of wantonness that has led them many astray' in Hosea 4:12). In the world of the Old and the New Testaments, there was a greater belief in spirits than there is today, but the writers of the books in question were not intending to name particular spirits so much as to describe what the Book of Common Prayer calls 'the deceits of the world, the flesh and the devil'. There was no attempt to compile a definitive list of demons that can infest mankind!

A fundamentalist attitude to the Scriptures (and usually to the King James version) can have a disastrous impact on the practice of exorcism. Some fundamentalists believe that any kind of mental or emotional disturbance is due to an evil spirit and that a physical illness may well be caused by the infestation of a demon. Jesus distinguished between healing and exorcism, using the latter only when (in his day) he considered it appropriate. Fanatical sects now tend to use it wholesale for depression or any mental disturbance, and 'when a physical illness has persisted for a long time, and does not respond to fervent prayer, we should consider casting out the spirit' (Maxwell Whyte, p.115). To the question, 'How does a person come under the influence of a demon in the first place?' the following answer is given:

> Demonic influence occurs in many ways. In certain cases people have been born with demons. Years passed before I was persuaded by events and the Holy Spirit that an infant could be born with an evil spirit within him... Demons may also enter young children. Many adults have testified that a terribly frightening experience as a young child gave opportunity for the evil spirit to come in. Having entered in, the spirit will not leave readily, especially when a person waits fifty years before seeking deliverance. During this period the spirit digs in more and more tenaciously and may bring other symptoms such as fear, pains, arthritis, and stomach disorders...
>
> Maxwell Whyte, p.89

It is true that there have been cases when a child has apparently been possessed; but if this ever occurs, it is very rare indeed. The author of the book cited above claims many successes in commanding demons to depart from people whom he has believed to suffer from them. This success is possibly due to the psychosomatic nature of their complaint and to his authoritarian stance; or it may be due to the natural course of an illness. An authoritarian stance is itself evil, for people can become dependent on their pastor and unable properly to exercise their God-given free will.

It can be extremely dangerous to attempt to exorcise someone who is suffering from some mental instability or emotional disturbance. In 1974, Mrs Christine Taylor of Ossett near

Barnsley in Yorkshire was killed by her husband who tore out her eyes and tongue after spending a night being exorcised by seven people who believed that he had a demon. The exorcism had the effect of making the man mad. This is one case among others that led to an Open Letter to the bishops of the Church of England, written by several leading theologians of the day, that exorcism should not be practised or recognised within the Church, implying that the practice involves a gross misunderstanding of the doctrine of possession.

Although the signatories of the Open Letter were mostly my friends, and some were former colleagues, I personally regarded them as gravely mistaken in their views. *Abusus non tollit usum*: Abuse of anything does not invalidate its right use. It seemed to me that these academics were remote from the pastoral realities of life. I was then a bishop in South London, and there were quite a few cases of paranormal disturbance, especially among West Indian Christians. Mostly, these were of the poltergeist type. The diocese had appointed an experienced parish priest (who had served in the rural areas of South Africa) as its 'diocesan exorcist'. I believe that this practice is now fairly general. This priest's task was not to go round exorcising right, left and centre, but to deal sensitively with those who had been shaken by paranormal phenomena and who had been referred to him by their parish priests. Usually, all that was needed was some counselling and the ministry of reassurance, but occasionally more was required. When I went to the See of Birmingham, I appointed four experienced parish priests to carry out similar duties. I found that other parish priests called them in when they were faced with situations with which they could not easily deal. I wonder how the signatories of the Open Letter would have dealt with them in these circumstances. If people are terrified by paranormal phenomena, it only makes them worse to tell them that they are simply being superstitious.

Exorcism in the Church of England

By the middle of the third century, the early Church had established the office of exorcist as a minor order of the Church. Exorcisms continued in the mediaeval Church, and during the Counter-Reformation. But Puritans deeply disapproved. The power to exorcise was regarded as a special charisma bestowed on the early Church. The Devil could not be put to flight by holy water, the sign of the Cross and words from Scripture. Exorcism was rejected as papistical ritual. Jeremy Taylor wrote: 'If any man amongst us should use such things, he would be in danger of being tried at the next assize for a witch or conjuror.' The office of exorcist disappeared in the Church of England, together with minor orders, with the publication of the Ordinal of 1550.

Despite the official ban on exorcism, the apparent phenomenon of possession continued. What was to be done? Some Protestants took the words of Jesus in the received text of Mark 9:29: 'This kind can come forth by nothing, but by prayer and fasting', and they attempted to deal with cases of apparent possession by this means. But this, too, was forsworn after the exposure of a Protestant exorcist (Thomas, p.579). Under the new church canons of 1604, no minister, without the explicit permission of his bishop, could attempt 'under any pretence whatsoever whether of possession or obsession, by fasting and prayer, to cast out any devils, under pain of the imputation of imposture or cozenage and deposition from the ministry'. An interesting result was the great increase in the number of executions for witchcraft. The people of England, deprived of the traditional means of counteracting evil, took refuge in depositions against those whom they accused of being witches, who were believed to be in compact with the Devil. Doubtless, many of these cases of alleged possession were caused by psychological dysfunction; and as people became more aware of these, the number of cases brought to the courts dried up. As we have already pointed out, real cases of possession are exceedingly rare.

Yet they do occasionally occur. In 1972, a Commission set up by the then Bishop of Exeter issued a report that included rites of exorcism. In 1975, the bishops issued guidelines for the practice of exorcism, and most dioceses have appointed 'exorcists', whose main task is to deal with poltergeists and hauntings and to comfort those distressed by paranormal phenomena.

The ancient rite of exorcism in the Roman Catholic Church has been revised and recently published. That Church also authorises certain priests to carry out exorcisms, and in Italy the number of such priests is said to have increased from twenty to two hundred in the last few years. Very few, if any, will have carried out a 'major exorcism': their ministry of deliverance resembles that of Anglican priests.

The Church has ruled that major exorcisms should be undertaken only with the express permission of the bishop and that the officiant and his assistants (which must include a woman if the exorcism is to be performed on a woman) should be steeped in prayer and make a thorough preparation. The exorcist should be a person well versed in this aspect of his ministry and confident in the power of Christ to conquer all evil. People unknown to the priest should not be present, including unauthorised reporters, because of the spiritual danger in which they place themselves. If the exorcism takes place in a house, animals and children should be removed, and the latter given a prayer of protection before the rite of exorcism commences. During the exorcism, the evil spirit is commanded to depart to its appointed place and never to return, and prayer is offered for the person concerned.

Of course, there are those today who, like some Elizabethans of an earlier age, believe that there are no evil spirits that can infest or possess a person, and such people hold that the experiences of the person concerned should be attributed to schizophrenia or one of the other mental illnesses. It is, however, difficult on these grounds to account for all the symptoms of alleged possession, including telepathic knowledge and abnormal strength, and it is remarkable that exorcisms can achieve a return to normality in cases where psychiatrists admit that they can make no progress.

It would perhaps be helpful to listen to the words of someone who has had practical experience of these matters. An interview with such a person follows in the next chapter.

Chapter V

QUESTIONS TO THE CO-CHAIRMAN OF THE CHRISTIAN DELIVERANCE STUDY GROUP, THE RT REVD DOMINIC WALKER, OGS

ME: Tell me, have you been interested in psychic phenomena for some time?

BISHOP DOMINIC: Yes, I think it fascinates most people. I think for me the first time was when I saw poltergeist activity. I saw something moving in a house without anyone touching it, and that fascinated me.

ME: Was that in the course of your pastoral duties?

BISHOP DOMINIC: Yes, yes.

ME: So it was really after you were ordained that you were interested as a result of your pastoral work?

BISHOP DOMINIC: Yes, that's right.

ME: And then you became co-chairman of something—

BISHOP DOMINIC: The Christian Deliverance Study Group, it's called. It's the ongoing group from the Bishop of Exeter's Report [see p.114] which has been going on ever since. It comprises psychiatrists, psychologists and members of the clergy, and we lay on training courses for the Bishops' Advisers. We train about thirty a year, and we always have a waiting list for what are now called 'Deliverance Teams'.

ME: Do you find that you get people who are not Anglicans coming for help, because the Reformed Churches on the whole don't believe in psychic realities.

BISHOP DOMINIC: That's right. In the Christian Deliverance Study Group we have trained one or two Roman Catholic priests, but very few Free Church ministers, as they tend to think that psychic phenomena are all psychological in origin.

ME: Do think that the Church as a whole takes these psychic matters seriously?

BISHOP DOMINIC: I think it's rather embarrassed by them, and it doesn't know how to handle them. Bishops recognise the need to control deliverance ministries by having people who are approved to do it, and in a way to prevent other people from doing it.

ME: Isn't there something to be said for that, for some people indulge in wholesale exorcism if someone has a bad cold or something?

BISHOP DOMINIC: Yes, but it's rather like extended communion or the marriage of divorced people: it's something that happens so it has to be controlled!

ME: Isn't it really very sad, because it means that a whole aspect of spirituality is missing?

BISHOP DOMINIC: Yes, and I think very few people know how to give spiritual direction to someone who

117

is psychic. We are very used to dealing with spiritual gifts, but not with psychic gifts.

ME: It's very strange, isn't it, that psychic gifts often seem to run in families, almost as if there was heredity involved?

BISHOP DOMINIC: Yes, I think that's true; and certainly among some gypsy families there are very strong psychic gifts.

ME: Do you regard psychic disturbances that you have been called into or that you see in the course of your pastoral duties as relatively frequent, or very infrequent?

BISHOP DOMINIC: The most common problem that we deal with is poltergeist activity; for twenty or thirty years that's always been the main problem, and people are very frightened when they see things flying around.

ME: Have you actually seen things flying around?

BISHOP DOMINIC: Yes, I have. And also interference with electricity. I've seen clocks going backwards, or lights flashing on and off, controls or volume going up and down; but I have also seen objects move.

ME: Was this very scarifying?

BISHOP DOMINIC: Yes, it's very frightening when suddenly, as you're talking to someone, an object which was on the mantelpiece suddenly smashes in the middle of the room.

ME: And have you any idea about its causation?

BISHOP DOMINIC: On the whole it seems to be caused by the people in the house. Most of the cases involve youngsters, although amongst the adults it's almost always been with older people. In fact, I was called in a couple of years ago to an old people's home where it was quite fascinating because they'd recorded it on camera. It was sheltered accommodation, and people were being woken up in the middle of the night, and their doorknockers were going. They would open their doors and there was no one there. They thought someone was playing a trick. The council put in a camera, and it was captured on video. We weren't able to trace the source because there were too many people, about twenty in all.

ME: So what did you do about it?

BISHOP DOMINIC: I went and talked to them about it and tried to explain that this wasn't something from outside which had come to attack them, but a psychic phenomenon created by psychic energy, and I tried to reassure them. But the staff got hold of me and said, 'What will they do if you get rid of this, because this is the one thing that holds that community together?' People would invite each other in the morning into their flats and ask whether they had had a peaceful night.

ME: Yes. But, in other cases, have you been able to discover the cause?

BISHOP DOMINIC: Usually we can: it's a youngster going through puberty or someone in their late teens. They have no one to talk to, they're quite lonely people, and they're often cut off from their parents in some way. I had one case that involved a Pakistani girl, and the whole thing started after her father arranged a marriage. This poor girl was living in two worlds, really. At home, she had to speak Punjabi and wear Punjabi dress and was under the Islamic control of her father, and when she went to school she could talk about pop music and boyfriends and wear Western clothes. It was when the father arranged the marriage that the activity began.

ME: But there must be thousands of girls in that situation, but they don't produce poltergeist activity.

BISHOP DOMINIC: It may be just one method of letting off steam, and the others become ill or act it out in some other way.

ME: Do you find that people who were the source of poltergeist activity had psychic tendencies in any other way?

BISHOP DOMINIC: Sometimes we find that they had some psychic experiences before, so that they know that they have some psychic energy, or they bring it under control – that's fascinating, when they begin to control the poltergeist activity a bit.

ME: Can they ever shut it down?

BISHOP DOMINIC: I knew one woman who could move a piece of paper by looking at it—

ME: Consciously willing it? What's called psychokinesis?

BISHOP DOMINIC: That's right. I saw that happening. She had very violent poltergeist activity taking place, but she managed to bring it under control. She was having psychotherapy which seemed to cope with her problem, and as it progressed, so her psychic ability died away. Somehow it was linked with her frustration.

ME: I understand that poltergeist activity often dies down of its own accord?

BISHOP DOMINIC: Yes, it does usually. It seems to begin with things like raps and knocks and footsteps and then it affects electricity, and then objects begin disappearing and reappearing.

ME: Have you dealt with apports, I think they are called, objects that appear?

BISHOP DOMINIC: Yes, once. Sugar kept appearing in a house in Surbiton, and no one knew where it was coming from. About half a pound of sugar a day was appearing in the kitchen. While I was in the house, when I went back into the kitchen after an hour or so, there was more sugar than ever there had been at the beginning!

ME: Only sugar?

BISHOP DOMINIC: Yes, only sugar. But they also had spontaneous combustion and automatic writing, quite a lot was going on. I got called in because the Christmas decorations had gone up in flames.

ME: What did you do in that case?

BISHOP DOMINIC: I talked to the family to see what was going on. It was an extraordinary set-up. The father and son were just like Steptoe and son, an extraordinary couple. And the son had his mistress, whom he'd just moved in with her young daughter, a nine-year-old girl. The little girl was unhappy at school because her mother had taken her away from her father, moved her in with these two strange men and sent her to another school, and although this school had said that they would like to talk to the mother about her daughter, she never got round to it. First of all, they had poltergeist activity. They told the little girl to make friends with the ghost and to call it 'Polty', and so she used to talk to Polty, and to write letters to her, and she got replies, which had things like, 'I want to be your friend. Can't you see me? I am here all the time. I want to play with you.' These were all calls for attention. They would go to bed, and in the morning when they came down they said they found the replies on bits of paper which she had left there. They got out a big biscuit tin for me and it was full of these notes which appeared to be written by a child of the same age, although they told me it wasn't her handwriting.

ME: So helping people with poltergeists has been the major part of your deliverance ministry? But you have presumably come across other forms of psychic phenomena, such as a place memory, or whatever you like to call it?

BISHOP DOMINIC: Yes, I've been to quite a number of places where different people at different times see the same thing happen, and there's been no collusion between the people, so it appears there's some objectivity about it. Very occasionally they describe a slightly different minor detail, otherwise it seems to be exactly the same phenomenon. It's like a video shown over and over again.

ME: What sets it off?

BISHOP DOMINIC: Normally it's a disturbance to someone in the house. I remember one case near you in

Tooting where it had been triggered off by a cot death that they'd had.

ME: When the place memory took place, was it a memory of something awful that had happened there, or something nice, or just something neutral?

BISHOP DOMINIC: People appeared in period costume, walking through the house. They said they were carrying brown paper parcels which looked as though they might have been carrying their own dead children to be buried – they said it looked like a funeral procession.

ME: So it was probably an event of high emotional content?

BISHOP DOMINIC: Yes.

ME: Do you think that that had something to do with the memory imprint?

BISHOP DOMINIC: Yes, it seems to be. Or else it seems to be linked to something traumatic which happens to the building. I was involved in a television programme where there was a couple who bought a house in Yorkshire which needed a lot of repairs done to it, and each time they did any major work, they saw a little old lady wander through the house. She would always leave behind her a smell of either oranges or cigars, and neither of them smoked. And this little old lady would come out of a door where there wasn't a door and wander through, and she always looked in the same direction each time.

ME: So this wasn't a ghost? It does happen that earthbound spirits get tied to a building;

    they can't find their way to the Light because they are so wrapped up in the building.

BISHOP DOMINIC: The difference with an earthbound spirit is that it tries to make contact with the person to whom it appears. She never made contact, although they did find a picture of her in the local library: she was someone who had lived in the house two hundred years before them.

ME: What did you do about it? Did you let it go on, as it were?

BISHOP DOMINIC: Yes, it didn't worry them in the slightest!

ME: What would you have done if they weren't happy?

BISHOP DOMINIC: We would have prayed in the place. But normally we would try to find out what was under stress, the person to whom it happened or the building. If it was the building, it would only happen after major alterations and then it would die away.

ME: Yes. But there might be occasions when it was set off rather alarmingly for people, and I was wondering what kind of ministry you have for them.

BISHOP DOMINIC: I think we would celebrate a Requiem Mass, and that often calms things down. It wouldn't be with any particular intention for anyone, because that's normally reserved for some unrested soul.

ME: Why do you think that a Requiem Mass would have that sort of effect? Would it be because Christ is brought into the place in a special way?

BISHOP DOMINIC:	I think it's because Christ brings healing. Of course, he is universally present, but the Eucharist makes him present in a different way. I'm always intrigued by the word *anamnesis*, used of the Eucharist for making present what happened in the past.
ME:	Perhaps the anamnesis in the Eucharist of Christ's past victory on the cross over evil is made present and so banishes the anamnesis involved in a place memory. Tell me, have you ever come across people who have been worried, or perhaps very pleased, because they have seen an apparition of a loved one shortly after death?
BISHOP DOMINIC:	Yes, although that can be part of the bereavement process. I think that it's true to say that one in six people who lose a life partner see an apparition shortly after death. I think that this is due to the bereavement rather than to an unrested soul.
ME:	What do you think happens? Do you think it is the memory of a loved one which clothes itself in the form of an apparition?
BISHOP DOMINIC:	I remember dealing with a very interesting case in Battersea in one of the prefabs which were still surviving, and a family was living there who kept chickens. The mother had died, and the father saw her in the bedroom getting into bed with him and he said he actually cuddled her and went to sleep, and in the morning she wasn't there. He told his daughter who lived up the road, and his daughter then saw her mother coming down the stairs. They went to various mediums who convinced them that Mum didn't want to leave them. When I

125

went to see them, they told me an extraordinary thing: when they went to the funeral, the coffin wouldn't go down because the hole wasn't big enough, and when they got home, all the chickens had died. They hadn't been got at by a fox, or had their throats cut: they seemed to have died naturally. They saw all this as indicating to them that Mother didn't want to leave them. When I asked where the mother had been in hospital, and it was quite clear that she had died of cancer, they got very angry when I used the word cancer because the word wasn't used in the house. I think quite clearly this was all a bereavement experience. But what I couldn't explain was why the chickens had died, unless there was a psychic link between the mother and the chickens, and on the day of the funeral that link was broken.

ME: Has any other kind of psychic phenomenon come your way, for example, with unquiet spirits seeking help?

BISHOP DOMINIC: I've come across a few cases where people appear to have died and become earthbound in some way. When I was writing a booklet on psychic matters, I looked at the cases I had dealt with, and each time there seemed to be some unfinished business. It was as if it wasn't God who wasn't willing to take the person, but the person wasn't really ready to go. Either they didn't want to leave the place where they were, or else there was some inordinate attachment or relationship.

ME: Do you have psychic gifts yourself, if I may ask?

BISHOP DOMINIC: Occasionally, I can be in a place and feel that there is evil. Sometimes when I've been taken into a building where something's wrong, I say, 'Don't tell me where it is: I'll see if I can find it,' and I always seem to find it.

ME: I suppose, if you believe as I do, that there are not only evil people, but also evil spirits. They can – do you think – affect people?

BISHOP DOMINIC: Yes, I'm sure that there are evil spirits at work. Whilst many of them, I think, are internal spirits, I think there are forces from outside as well which affect people. There's a lovely saying that you don't catch demons like you catch a cold. In each case, you tend to find that the person is involved in something evil, and that seems to be something that attracts an evil spirit: an evil person becomes a channel for them.

ME: Have you come across people who have suffered as a result of planchette and Ouija boards and, if so, what kind of effect do these have on people?

BISHOP DOMINIC: They can become violent or depressed, and in one sad case, the person committed suicide.

ME: Do you regard these things as genuine means of getting in touch with the occult with evil effects, or is it an internal matter, as it were?

BISHOP DOMINIC: I think it's a mixture of both. It's often that they are in touch with their own dark side, their own shadow, bringing to the surface all sorts of things they can't handle, and sometimes that seems to attract something from outside as well. I always tell young people who have been using them that they are playing a dangerous game of psychodynamics.

ME: Have you come across places where black magic has been practised?

BISHOP DOMINIC: Yes, where there have been black arts as well as places where Satanic sacrifices have taken place.

ME: Have you cleansed them?

BISHOP DOMINIC: Yes, partly by blessing them, because I don't find any scriptural authority for exorcising a place.

ME: How do you distinguish a ghost from an apparition?

BISHOP DOMINIC: I think that most people who claim to see a ghost really project from their unconscious so that it's very real to them and not real to anyone else. It's usually a subjective phenomenon, whereas in other cases where you get different people at different times seeing the same thing, then you have to have another explanation, in which case it's either a place memory or else, as Henry Cooper said, some of the signs of the resurrected body of someone who has died.

ME: When you say someone has died, do you mean that someone is dead, but still hanging around, and hasn't gone off to the next sphere of existence?

BISHOP DOMINIC: Yes, something like that. I remember one ghost, which only the women in the house ever saw, and this was of a woman who had committed suicide, and it was an extraordinary phenomenon in the sense that she had only one leg. Then the people living in the house found that thirty years before there was a woman living there who had had her leg amputated; when she came back from hospital she found an eviction notice and she killed herself. We had a Requiem Mass and she wasn't seen after that.

ME: It always seems to me that the efficacy of the Church's ministry with people who are troubled with psychic disturbances is not sufficiently recognised.

BISHOP DOMINIC: Yes, I think that's right. But what is important is that the pastoral and the sacramental go together, because some people go in almost as magicians. There was a priest who phoned up the other day, and who had gone in and celebrated a Requiem Mass in a house where there seemed to be poltergeist activity. He used incense and holy water and everything, so that he exhausted his possibilities and so, when things were still going on, he didn't know what to do; and that was because he didn't begin in a pastoral way, but went straight to a sacramental ministry.

ME: Have you ever come across cold spots?

BISHOP DOMINIC: Yes, but it's strange because, if you use a thermometer, they don't appear to be any colder than the rest of the room, and yet when you go to the place you find yourself shivering.

ME: Is there anything else you would like to tell me?

BISHOP DOMINIC: Sometimes you get a case that you can't

explain; you may have people speaking in an unknown foreign language or people with unusual knowledge or people with unusual strength, who do not respond to psychotherapy or drugs and yet, after a rite of exorcism, they make an immediate recovery.

ME: Have you come across any of those?

BISHOP DOMINIC: Yes, very rarely, in two or three cases. And I came across an extraordinary case in the island of Fiji when I was taking a retreat for some nuns. Halfway through the retreat, they asked me to exorcise a girl from the village who was possessed by an evil spirit. And when I went into the chapel, there was a beautiful young Polynesian girl. As soon as we began the prayers of exorcism, she threw herself to the ground and became like a snake and she started moving round the walls of the chapel. Interestingly, the nuns didn't take any notice, they just carried on praying. Eventually, two of the nuns picked her up and I said the prayers of exorcism and Reverend Mother said, 'Her mother will take her home and she will come back tomorrow at the same time to thank you and to thank God for delivering her from the evil spirit.' To them it was a very natural phenomenon.

ME: You mean, it was not infrequent?

BISHOP DOMINIC: Yes.

ME: Why do you think that this is quite usual in Fiji, but very unusual in Britain?

BISHOP DOMINIC: It may be something to do with the culture, that we act out certain things in the way our culture expects us to do. If people had seen exorcisms, they might well begin to act out in that kind of way.

ME: Does that mean that the whole thing is subjective? If we act in accordance with our culture, that seems to suggest that there is nothing objective there?

BISHOP DOMINIC: I think that there is something objective there, but the way we act it out is in accordance with our cultural tradition.

ME: It is quite possible then that people who are possessed, as that Fiji young girl was, might act it out in quite a different way in our culture, and we wouldn't always be aware of it. That's a very sobering thought! Tell me, do you find at times that there are other strange phenomena or strange appearances that people are worried about?

BISHOP DOMINIC: Occasionally, you get strange smells that appear. I had one case when a smell appeared at five o'clock and disappeared at seven each night – it seemed an extraordinary thing to happen – and the smell was so bad that the couple would have to leave the house for two hours. They would go down to the local pub or library or go for a walk to get away from the smell. The interesting thing was that whenever a priest or a doctor went, or a helping agency, the smell didn't occur. I deliberately went along at six o'clock one evening to see if I could smell it; and they knew I was coming so the smell, they said, hadn't occurred. And then the wife eventually told me her tale. She said she had been a cleaner in a students' hostel, and, just as she was about to knock off one day, she remembered that she hadn't cleaned one particular loo because someone had been occupying it. She found it still locked. She banged on the door, and then she used a key to open it, and inside a student had hanged himself. She never went back to work after that experience. I asked her when she discovered the body, and she said, 'Just as I was finishing work, about five o'clock,' and I said, 'what time did you get home?' She said that the police kept her for two hours, until seven o'clock. Somehow, she had reactivated those events.

ME: But usually these reactivations take place in the locality where something happens, yet in this case it was in their own house! It's very unusual if it follows a person, isn't it?

BISHOP DOMINIC: Yes, that's right. It was much more in keeping with poltergeist activity rather than place memories.

ME: But I think it's very difficult, don't you, always to draw a hard and fast line in explaining psychic phenomena?

BISHOP DOMINIC: Yes, and sometimes you get two or three phenomena occurring at the same time.

ME: It has been really very good of you to speak so openly and to share with me your very remarkable experiences. Thank you so much.

Chapter VI
NEAR-DEATH EXPERIENCES

So far we have considered only paranormal phenomena concerning living people, the spirits of the dead or evil spirits. There is a further group of paranormal phenomena in which people claim to have had a glimpse of the life to come. I refer to Near-Death Experiences (NDEs). The capital letters show that this phrase refers, not to the normal process of dying, but to something very specific that can occur when people are near to death, or think themselves to be. It is not uncommon for people to have extraordinary out-of-body experiences (OBEs) and other out-of-the-ordinary experiences when they are, or believe themselves to be, in situations close to death.

Dr Moody, an American doctor, after being given, to his great surprise, accounts of NDEs that had a similar structure from two different patients, collected further descriptions and published them in a book that aroused great interest in the subject, largely because of the common pattern of experiences in the cases he described (Moody, 1975). Since then, a very considerable literature on the subject has developed, mostly in America; and an International Association of Near Death Studies (IANDS) has been formed. Most of those interested in the subject seem either to regard them as incontestable evidence of life after death, or they hold equally strong views that the experiences are hallucinations which can be adequately explained through modern knowledge of the functioning of the human brain, or that they have a psychological origin, for example, as an anxiety response to the imminent threat of death. People seem to be either for or against, and they often dismiss the arguments of their opponents as being well intentioned but utterly misconceived. I suspect that there is a hidden agenda on either side.

Each NDE is different, but there is a common pattern, although few people experience every item. One author has actually introduced a scale giving different weightings to particular items, thus enabling people experiencing an NDE to notch up their own score! His 'core experience' comprises feelings of peace, an OBE, entering the darkness and seeing the light (Ring, 1982). The first English collection of NDEs (12 per cent of which included hellish experiences) was published a few years later (Grey, 1985). Peter Fenwick, a consultant psychiatrist with an international reputation, once took part in a television programme on NDEs with the chairman of the British branch of IANDS, and as a result he received a large correspondence. He sent a questionnaire to five hundred people selected from his correspondents, three hundred of whom replied, and excerpts from some of their replies are given in this chapter.

The full 'syndrome' of NDE experiences may be summarised as follows:

1. feelings of peace, joy and bliss;
2. an experience of leaving the body and often looking down on the physical body from above;
3. entering a tunnel, usually dark, with a pinpoint of light at the end;
4. approaching a brilliant (but not dazzling) white or golden light;
5. meeting a 'being of light';
6. experiencing a barrier that marks a point of no return;
7. visiting another country, often a pastoral scene;
8. meeting relatives;
9. experiencing a life review, usually of the past, occasionally of the future;
10. reaching a point of decision, however reluctantly, to return to earthly life;
11. rapidly returning to the physical body, often with a thump;
12. aftermath, in which all fear of death is removed and the experience is regarded as the most vivid and profound of a lifetime.

Fenwick and Fenwick, p.9ff.

To those of us who have never had an NDE (although some people have experienced two or three), it comes as something of a shock to find that NDEs, which include some of these experiences, are not uncommon. An American NOP poll has suggested that nearly a million Americans have had NDEs. In 1982, a Gallup Poll, after conducting thousands of interviews, put the question: 'Have you yourself ever been on the verge of death, or had a "close call" which involved an unusual experience at the time?' to which 15 per cent answered affirmatively. A recent study, over a one-year period, of survivors from cardiac arrest in Southampton General Hospital reveals that over 11 per cent reported memories of an NDE (Parnia et al., p.149ff.). A review of available evidence suggests that gender, educational achievement, marital status, occupation and socio-economic grouping are irrelevant factors. It seems that personality is equally irrelevant, whether people are anxious, neurotic, intelligent or extrovert. Children can have an NDE. There seems to be a greater likelihood of an NDE through some sudden catastrophe, such as cardiac arrest or a car accident, rather than during gradual deterioration in a life-threatening illness.

NDEs, or rather certain elements of an NDE, can be found outside situations in which people face or think they are facing death. Out-of-body experiences themselves are not uncommon. Drugs can induce them. Sensory deprivation can induce hallucinatory phenomena. A survey in the medical journal, *The Lancet*, suggested that those who were actually near to death, compared with those who thought that they were near to death, were more likely to have a more enhanced perception of light and enhanced cognitive functions, although the size of the sample makes this kind of generalisation hard to establish (Owens, Cook and Stevenson, 1990, pp.1175–77).

Although the scientific study of NDEs is comparatively recent, there have been many who have been said to come back from the dead in earlier cultures and in different ages. Of course, these could be dismissed as the product of superstition, although it is dangerous to reject without evidence all ideas of earlier ages that run contrary to present received wisdom. Plato, at the end of *The Republic*, told of Er, a soldier killed in battle, who returned from the dead to describe the conditions of post-mortem existence. The eighth century Venerable Bede, in his *Ecclesiastical History*, recounts the near-death experience of a Northumbrian who lived at a place called Cunningham (Bede, Book 5, Chapter 12), with visions of purgatory as well as heaven. A phenomenon called *Delok* is known to Tibetans. *Delok* means 'returned from death', and it occurs when a person, seemingly dead, travels in the *Bardo* (transition), often accompanied by a deity as a guide who explains what is happening, and after a week the person returns to his body (Rinpoche, 1992, p.330). The *Bardo Thodol* (the 'Tibetan Book of the Dead') has descriptions in some ways similar to NDEs, except that the fifty-eight wrathful deities which face the soul after death are the personification of its own negative feelings and emotions (Evans-Wentz, p.130). Swedenborg (1688–1722), a man of great practical intelligence as well as seemingly gifted with strange psychic powers, retailed accounts of the next world. It is understandable that NDEs have only recently surfaced, since spectacular advances in medical technology have enabled people at the point of death to be resuscitated, whereas in the past they would have died.

In order to decide whether or not these NDEs reflect a brief but genuine experience of post-mortem existence, it is necessary to enquire with rigour into other possible explanations, especially in the light of our increasing knowledge of brain dysfunction. Are most of the symptoms of NDEs hallucinatory, caused by reduced oxygen supply to the brain (hypoxia) and excess of carbon dioxide (hypercarbia)? The stability of brain cells is maintained by inhibition, and without this the brain can run amok and dysfunction. The effect of hypoxia and hypercarbia, it has been claimed, is 'disinhibition' and consequent random excitation of brain cells.

> The very sudden anoxia and G-LOC (accelerated loss of consciousness among air pilots who are subject to intense gravitational forces) is associated with positive emotions, visions, sensations of floating and inability to communicate. The slightly slower anoxia with cardiac arrest and other associated conditions is also associated with the tunnel, bright lights and noises.
>
> Blackmore, p.62

On the other hand there are experts who disagree about the effects of anoxia being similar to NDEs. Dr Peter Fenwick wrote to me (in a private communication):

> From a scientific point of view, I have always thought that anoxia makes very little sense. I think it has been put forward by people who are not familiar with the effects of anoxia on the brain, nor intimately connected with brain injury and the dying process. Clear memories are not formed, mental content is disturbed, and even mild levels of anoxia can lead to unconsciousness. It is thus impossible to argue that anoxia should process the highly synthesised and coherent expression of the NDE. I also agree that there are a number of NDEs where the brain is not damaged in any way, so I do not think from a scientific point of view that anoxia in any way is a runner.

Before agreeing or disagreeing with Dr Fenwick, we need to look in greater detail at the various elements that can make up an NDE.

Feelings of Peace

Feelings of peace, joy and bliss are the most common and most memorable part of the experience. Any sensations of pain which the earthly body may have been feeling drop away. I give some testimonies from those who have had these experiences. (The references refer to the author of the book in which they can be found rather than the experiencers themselves.)

> Unconditional love. An astonishing love. A love beyond my wildest imagining.
>
> Wilson, 1987, p.62

> It was one of the most intense and happiest moments of my entire life which a quarter of a century has not erased or diminished.
>
> Blackmore, 1993, p.94

> I felt embraced by such feelings of bliss that there are no words to describe the feeling. The nearest that I can come to it in human terms is the experience of being 'in love', the emotion one feels

when one's first born is put into one's arms for the first time, the transcendence of spirit that can sometimes occur when one is at a concert of classical music, the peace and grandeur of mountains, forests, lakes and other beauties of nature that can move one to tears of joy. Unite all these together and magnify a thousand times and you get a glimpse of the 'state of being' that one is in.

Blackmore, 1993, p.94

All pain disappeared, comfort seized me. Time no longer mattered and space was filled with bliss. I was bathed in radiant light and immersed in the aura of the rainbow. All was fusion. Sounds were of a new order, harmonious, nameless (now I call it music).

Grey, 1985, p.33

Like all the components of an NDE, these feelings are intensely real to the experiencer. Nothing can shake their belief in their occurrence. They can occur to would-be suicides as well as to those who fall ill. Such intense feelings are to be distinguished from the sensations of tranquillity and acceptance experienced by someone falling when climbing a mountain, or by a person who has suffered a cardiac arrest without experiencing an NDE.

To what are such feelings due? Drugs such as morphine and heroin can induce a comparably blissful feeling, but those experiencing NDEs are not high on these drugs. The view that these feelings are a psychological means of escape from the terrors of approaching death is difficult to uphold, for in that case feelings would not need to be so intense. But are they the result of drugs released by the brain in an emergency?

Endorphins are now known to be synthesised in the brain and released into the cerebro-spinal fluid which bathes the cells of the brain and the spinal cord... Like the opiates they resemble, the endorphins have a variety of effects, including analgesia, or elimination of pain, and the induction of intense pleasure, peace and calm. The most powerful narcotic among them is beta endorphin.

Blackmore, 1993, p.107

These endorphins could be released to eliminate the suffering of death, just as they are released in animals to encourage mating.

They could account for the feelings of bliss in those who are, or who think they are, approaching death. At the same time as the endorphins are produced, the pituitary gland in the brain releases a hormone known as ACTH, which stimulates the adrenal cortex to produce a chemical that helps people to cope with stress. Its levels are known to rise at the approach of death. It also has the effect of lowering blood pressure, and presumably endorphins, released with ACTH, have the same effect.

Naloxone is a drug that acts as an antidote to morphine. When it was administered to a patient to bring him out of coma, he recorded later that his initially blissful feelings turned into horror. It has been suggested that this was because the original blissful feelings which had been brought about by the effect of endorphins were counteracted by the administration of Naloxone (Blackmore, 1993, p.109).

Those who do not favour a physiological or psychological explanation of these feelings of bliss claim that they are a foretaste of heaven (and presumably the occasionally bad feelings that are sometimes experienced are a foretaste of purgatory). They would say that the fact that these feelings may be brought about by drugs in no way invalidates their view, any more than religious feelings are invalidated by the fact that some of them may be artificially induced by pharmacological means. Such people base their conviction about the genuineness of NDEs on the total evidence rather than on one particular component. If these experiences really are a foretaste of heaven, there could be no way of proving this except by post-mortem experiences, which of course are not accessible to the living. Those who favour a physical basis for these feelings are looking for some testable evidence. However, no one knows the actual endorphin level of someone on the point of death, because doctors and nurses are rightly concerned at that point with helping a patient rather than with research into NDEs, so that the physical hypothesis is, if testable, likely to remain untested.

Out-of-body Experiences

Often, the experience begins with the person finding that he has left his body. He feels as though he is slowly rising out it, weightless and floating, and he can look down on himself from some objective vantage point, usually near the ceiling. We have already noted that out-of-body experiences are more common than is usually thought, with research suggesting that 15 per cent of the population have had them. For those who hold that the mind is the same as the brain, such experiences must be held to be hallucinations. For those who believe that the mind can exist without the brain, OBEs are possible, but still might be hallucinations. Some of them clearly are just that. They can be induced by psychedelic drugs. Susan Blackmore has recounted her own experiences with drug-induced OBEs (Blackmore, p.43), although it has been pointed out that these show some important differences from those experienced in NDEs (Wilson, 1987, p.96). Research also suggests that these experiences can also occur to people who do not engage in drug abuse or who have low levels of alcohol in their blood. They can happen when a person is wide awake, or meditating or drowsy. There is even a case of a clergyman having an OBE while delivering a sermon! It is said that people can even learn how to induce them. Their attraction is that they give people enhanced feelings and a greater clarity of mind.

Here are some accounts of OBE experiences during an NDE. The first is from someone who was ill during the flu epidemic of 1918.

I felt myself rise up, float into the highest part of the room and look down on myself lying there 'asleep' on my bed. I felt marvellous, no pains, free from ills, just floating there.

Fenwick and Fenwick, p.36

The next thing was that I was above myself near the ceiling, looking down. One of the nurses was saying in what sounded a frantic voice, 'Breathe, Dawn, breathe.' A doctor was pressing my chest, everyone was rushing round. I couldn't understand the panic. Then they rushed my body out of the room into the theatre. I followed my body out of the ICU...

Fenwick and Fenwick, p.25

It was as though I was standing on the wall of the ICU defying gravity and looking down at my body. I was shocked at what an ugly corpse I was. I was naked and a nurse was taking a drip out of my ankle. I vividly remember how purple my face was and how blank my forehead seemed. I appeared to have a black triangle from my hairline to my nose. My wife later confirmed that was how I looked when she was allowed in to see me.

Fenwick and Fenwick, p.33

Does the mind leave the body or are *all* these hallucinations? (Some of them certainly are, as in the case of the woman who watched her Caesarean operation and woke up to find she had given birth in the normal way.) Are they caused by a retreat from reality, an escape from psychological or physical pain? Are they symptoms of a psychiatric disorder? Or is the OBE what happens when the model of reality that puts 'me' in the centre of things breaks down, because of a lack of input, and because of insufficient information to make sense of and to give a plausible model of the world? Does the brain in such a case produce an alternative model which puts 'me' outside my body? This might account for the way in which people in OBEs sense their bodies as grey ghostlike figures that can move at will and even pass through solid matter. Does the brain in an OBE construct a whole new world in which a person sees everything not from where he is, but from the perspective of the ceiling? If so, why the ceiling? Is it really convincing to explain this by the suggestion that memories are modelled from a bird's eye view, as has been suggested (Blackmore, p.177)?

Or is an out-of-body experience in an NDE genuinely an experience of people who are out of their bodies?

It is true that levels of anaesthesia differ, so that people can sometimes hear things spoken in a hospital theatre when they can neither move nor speak and when they are thought to be unconscious. But people in OBEs allege that they have seen and heard things that are inexplicable if they were lying in a hospital bed.

Some stories which sound impressive could be explained in other ways. For example, half a century ago, George Ritchie had double pneumonia and fell unconscious while being X-rayed in Barkeley Station Hospital near Abilene in Texas, and he experienced an OBE which changed his life. He found himself taken at great speed on a long journey. He crossed a very broad river with a big bridge spanning it, and he noticed before 'touching down' the bright blue colour coming from a Pabst Blue Ribbon Beer neon sign in the front window of a café. He then found himself unable to communicate, even to be seen, by people in the street: indeed, he discovered he had no substance and could pass through solid objects. Eventually, he returned to his physical body and recovered. Some time later, he stayed the night in Vicksburg, Mississippi and noticed something very familiar. He saw it was the Pabst Blue Ribbon Beer sign by the river. The whole story sounds very impressive and, indeed, Moody dedicated his groundbreaking book to Ritchie (Moody, 1975). But the fact remains that there was no independent witness. Although it seemed so real, the whole experience could have been a hallucination, with a feeling of déjà vu later when he came to the neon sign.

There are other equally striking stories. A short-sighted woman from Connecticut who had an NDE on going into shock after post-operative complications found herself floating on the ceiling of the operating theatre. She reported:

> It was so vivid... They were hooking me up to a machine that was behind my bed. And my first thought was, *Jesus, I can see! I can't believe it, I can see!* I could read the numbers on the machine behind my head and I was so thrilled. And I thought, *They gave me back my glasses.*

Later, she went back into the recovery room and verified the numbers. Although the woman insisted that she had shared her findings with the anaesthetist, unfortunately he could not be traced (Wilson, 1987, p.100ff.). This case is rather similar to the woman in the Washington Hospital in Seattle who insisted that she had seen, in an OBE, a tennis shoe with a dent in its toe lying on a window ledge on the third floor of the hospital building. A social worker reluctantly went to look for it and eventually found it just as foretold. But no one has ever traced the social worker.

In another case, an army major, floating on the ceiling in an OBE, saw his wife coming to visit him in a red suit through the high windows of the hospital. It was quite impossible for him to have seen his wife from his hospital bed. But, of course, he had seen his wife in that suit before and he could have hallucinated the scene (Fenwick and Fenwick, p.34ff.).

In order to substantiate the near-death experience as a whole, it is necessary first to validate the out-of-body experience. Before it can be generally agreed that OBEs really are out of the body experiences, cast-iron proof (and witnesses) are needed that people did actually see in an OBE what they could not see from their hospital beds. I am glad that experiments are being set up in certain hospitals where objects are placed in positions where they cannot be seen from ward beds, in the hope that someone will have an OBE and see them. Then we shall know for certain. But people do not have OBEs to order, and they do not necessarily speak about them afterwards.

Into the Tunnel and Approaching the Light

In NDEs, there is often (but not always) a sensation of going down a black tunnel at great speed. People seem to pass down this very rapidly without making any physical effort. At the end of the tunnel, they see a pinpoint of light that, as they approach it, becomes larger and larger. For some people, it is a tunnel of light not of darkness. Three examples are given below:

> I was in a serious car accident in June 1986... I was in a black tunnel or funnel, shooting through it incredibly fast... There was a loud roaring, like the moment of birth. I had no time to feel afraid. I was very interested in what was happening, but I felt completely safe. While I was shooting through the tunnel, which was completely black to begin with, but seemed to be getting less dark and less clearly defined further on...
>
> Fenwick and Fenwick, p.4

> I started zooming down this really black tunnel at what seemed like 100 mph. Then I saw this enormous bright light at the end...
>
> Fenwick and Fenwick, p.50

> There was total blackness around me. I want to say that it felt like I was moving very fast in time and space. I was travelling through

a tunnel. It didn't look like a tunnel, but when you're in a tunnel, all you see is blackness around you. If you move very fast you can feel the sides moving in on you whether there are sides there or not because of the darkness.

Sabom, p.63

To those who believe that NDEs report a visit to another sphere of existence, the tunnel obviously marks the transition. Light is a common religious metaphor for divine realities, and holiness may actually be experienced in terms of light (see p.267). But why a tunnel? In a private communication, Dr Fenwick answered my query as follows:

In one or two of the NDEs, the person who had the NDE floated on the ceiling and expected to float out of the window, but no, they went down a tunnel... Most people imply a tunnel without seeing it and this is because they are floating towards a light. I think part of the impression of the tunnel is the movement to-wards the light, although some people do say that they see the light glinting on the sides of the tunnel. Whether the tunnel would be directly connected with the birth process or not, I do not know. I do know, however, that if you ask people whether or not they would connect it with the birth experience very few draw the conclusion.

If the experience of going down a tunnel and approaching the light is a hallucination, one must ask, 'Why a tunnel? Why approach the light?' Various attempts have been made to answer these questions. The tunnel may be an (unconscious) representa-tion of the process of birth (but why experienced at the point of death?). Perhaps there is a psychological explanation: at the approach of death, there may be a change of consciousness. In addition to attempts at psychological explanations, there may be a physiological explanation. This is based on the effects of anoxia on the human brain, causing disinhibition and excitation of brain cells, especially in the visual cortex. Stripes moving across the visual cortex, caused by disinhibition, are said to cause the illusion of a tunnel (but why stripes, and not lattices or cobwebs, which can also be caused by anoxia and hallucinatory drugs?).

There is a further refinement of this physiological theory. As a result of disinhibition, the cells in the visual cortex start firing in the centre, quickly spreading to the outside and, as anoxia proceeds, all the cells will start firing fast, giving the illusion of a speedy journey down a tunnel with a speck of white at the end which quickly changes into an all-white scene. Since this firing of cells takes place not in the retina but in the visual cortex, brilliant white light will not hurt the eyes. This is said to explain why the phenomenon takes place when a person is really ill, but not in less serious illnesses. Furthermore, since there is random excitation of the cortex, all colours would be represented; and so light appears white, as happens when colours are mixed together (Blackmore, 1993, pp.81–7). The difficulty about this theory is that, to the experient, there is nothing random about the journey down the tunnel: it seems ordered and orderly.

The Being of Light

Very often (but by no means always), those who experience an NDE report that they have met a person or presence described as the Being of Light, although the point in the experience at which such a meeting takes place may vary from person to person. If the experient is religious, this may be an obviously religious figure. Sometimes it is simply a presence which is felt to be God or godlike. It is nearly always an intensely religious experience, so much so that the experients cannot find words to describe their feelings. The experience is nearly always a positive one, and the description is that of a being who is warm and loving.

> I was moving through a tunnel of beautiful light towards something which I can only describe as a presence (either the light or something beyond the light).
>
> Fenwick and Fenwick, p.60

> I was surrounded by this light, and I realised that this light was a being.
>
> Wilson, 1987, p.143

In a Christian culture, the figure is often identified with Jesus.

> I was met by a figure of light and it was what can only be de-
> scribed as a 'Jesus' figure. But I knew that the purpose of the
> figure was to make me feel comfortable in a new place.
>
> Fenwick and Fenwick, p.108

But the figure was not always associated with Christ:

> At the time of my NDE I was a practising Roman Catholic. Had I
> died I would most certainly have expected that any visions that I
> had would be related to my faith, and if I was to see a Being of
> Light I would have related it to Jesus or Mary or an angel. As it
> was, when I suddenly found myself in the gently glowing light
> and standing a little below three people above me, they appeared
> to me as young Indian men.
>
> Fenwick and Fenwick, p.81

I cannot help noting a certain reserve on the part of those who
believe that the experience is a hallucination in their attempted
explanation of the Being of Light. How can they account for this?
Ring holds that it is oneself. 'The golden light is a reflection of
one's own and symbolises the higher self' (Ring, 1982, pp.240–
41). Although Blackmore does not agree generally with Ring's
theories, she concurs in this.

> Perhaps the Being of Light is oneself. In fact, in any materialist
> view of the NDE, it simply must be, because there is no other
> outside force or entity that it could be.
>
> Blackmore, p.201

It is noteworthy that those who have become blind can still see
the Being of Light, and those who prefer a physiological explanation observe that this is because the figure emanates from the
visual cortex rather than the retina. Those who have had an NDE
regard the Being as that of a real spiritual being; but the image
must surely be culturally conditioned to some extent. For
example, no one knows what Jesus looked like, but when he is
seen in an NDE, he conforms to the kind of mental picture that

people have of him from contemporary representations. The idea of a guide to meet one when one passes into the next world was not uncommon in earlier epochs. What is important about the Being of Light is that he has great authority, a figure of light who encourages and welcomes people who believe that they have entered a new dimension of reality.

The Barrier

People sense that there is some sort of barrier between them and the light, a barrier that in some sense marks a point of no return. Several see this as a physical barrier – a person or a gate or a fence – sometimes it is simply a feeling that this marks the limit beyond which they cannot go. The barrier is a point beyond which visitors may not pass rather like a demarcated area within a closed convent into which a visitor may not stray. About a quarter of those who filled in Dr Fenwick's questionnaire spoke of the barrier. Here are some of the answers that he cites.

> Between me and the place there was a little green trellis fence, which stopped, leaving a gap at the end. I could easily have gone through. But I knew without anyone telling me that I could not stay there. (p.110)

> As I was going down the slides, I could see a barrier at the bottom. It was like a black shiny leather bench. I knew that if I went over the barrier I would be dead. (p.111)

> I saw myself beside a door which began to open, shedding a white light… I consciously recall a great desire to pass through the door. I knew if I did there would be no recall. (p.111)

Why should there be no recall? Presumably, if the barrier were purely psychological, someone would have gone through it and returned to tell the tale. Dr Fenwick suggested that the explanation could be that we cannot picture our own death, and we always wake up in a nightmare just before that happens. But why experience a barrier? Why not simply return to the body without any barrier, just as people wake up from sleep after a nightmare when they are on the point of death? So far as the physical body is concerned, there may indeed be a point beyond which there is no return to life. Is this what the barrier is all about? Is an inability to cross a barrier an indication that life is returning? If so, why is there a representation of a barrier in an NDE? It is interesting that Susan Blackmore, while she mentions the barrier, does not venture any physiological explanation. Perhaps (for those who do believe that an NDE is a spiritual journey), the barrier is an indication that our life is regulated by providence, and providence has decreed that it is not yet our time to die.

Another Country

Those who have NDEs often say that they have visited another country – usually an idyllic pastoral scene, brilliantly coloured, filled with light and fragrances – or that they have glimpsed such a country beyond the barrier.

> I was just in a wonderful peace and wellness in a beautiful land-scape setting of grass, lanes and trees and brilliant life.
>
> Fenwick and Fenwick, p.75

> I went to this lovely land, green grass, blue sky, beautiful stream, so quiet and peaceful.
>
> Fenwick and Fenwick, p.104

> During this vision that I had, I couldn't see myself, but I was standing on something high because below me there was just the most beautiful, greenest pasture. There was just a small hill and then just flat meadow over to my right.
>
> Sabom, p.57

Here is a conversation between a mother and her two-year-old in Kashmir who was believed by her father, a doctor, to have been clinically dead for a quarter of an hour and who was later questioned about her experiences by her mother.

> 'And where did my little one go the other day?'
> 'Far, far away to the stars.'

148

'And what did my darling see there?'
'Gardens.'
'And what did she see in those gardens?'
'Apples and grapes and pomegranates.'
'And what else?'
'There were streams, a white stream, a brown stream, a blue stream and a green stream.'

Wilson, 1987, p.131

Why gardens and streams and pastoral scenes? Those looking for a psychological or physiological explanation have some difficulty in finding one. The endorphin theory could hardly account for the repeated vision of this kind, with a person consoling himself with a well-loved scene. I suppose it could be regarded as an escape mechanism when faced with death. The Greek word *paradeisos* is used in the New Testament in the words of Jesus to the penitent thief: 'To day shalt thou be with me in paradise' (Luke 23:43). The word originally meant a garden, and was used of the Garden of Eden and then, in inter-testamental literature around the time of Jesus, to designate a place of blessedness above the earth (Arndt and Gingrich, p.619). This seems to accord with the use of the word to describe an NDE experience. Obviously, there are no real gardens in another sphere of existence, but the word represents refreshment, beauty, peace and contentment, and so it is not surprising that that the mind should make an image of the next world in the form of a garden.

Relatives and Friends

Often there are relatives to meet the newcomer on 'the other side':

Then I saw a group of people between me and the light. I knew them: my brother, who had died a few years before, was gesticulating delightedly as I approached.

Fenwick and Fenwick, p.104

Suddenly I saw my mother, who had died nine years ago. And she was sitting – she always used to sit in her rocker, you know – and she was smiling and she just sat there looking at me and she said

> in Hungarian, 'Well, we've been waiting for you, we've been expecting you. Your father's here and we're going to help you.'
>
> Wilson, 1987, p.63ff.

> I came to some place, and there were all my relatives, my grandmother, my grandfather, my father, my uncle who had recently committed suicide. They all came towards me and greeted me... And all of a sudden they turned their backs on me and walked away and my grandmother looked over her shoulder and she said, 'We'll see you later but not this time.'
>
> Sabom, p.73

It is not unusual for those who die to believe that relatives have come to fetch them. But this is rather different: relatives and friends greet a 'visitor' who has come to the 'other side'. If people really did join the dead, it would be natural for their relatives to greet them and help them, and to be pleased to see them. On the other hand, the experience could be explained as a retreat from the fear of death to the comfort of known and loved ones. It would be difficult to produce a physiological explanation of the experience.

Life Review

A life review is a common component of NDEs. Sometimes these reviews take place in the presence of the Being of Light, sometimes in the presence of relatives, sometimes with neither present. Some have felt that they are being weighed up, experiencing a kind of Day of Judgement in which their past actions are being reviewed. Some have a life preview – events are unfolded to them which will take place in the future, and sometimes they are told that these are tasks ahead of them which they must go back to complete.

> Then I experienced a review of my life which extended from early childhood and included many occurrences which I had completely forgotten. My life passed before me in a momentary flash but it was entire, even my thoughts were included. Some of the contents caused me to be ashamed, but there were one or two

I had forgotten about of which I felt quite pleased.

What happened next was remarkable. All my past life and incidents passed through my mind in a flash, things I had forgotten,
right back to about two years of age, when I was given a rag doll.

Fenwick and Fenwick, p.114

During this stage my life just flashed in front of my face. My
whole life... Things that had happened to me in my lifetime, like
when we got married, just flashed in front of my eyes, flashed and
it was gone. When we... had our first child flashed in front of my
eyes. The biggest thing, I guess, and the longest thing that stayed
flashing in front of my eyes was when I accepted Jesus Christ.

Sabom, p.74

Life reviews may take place in other circumstances; among
mountaineers who fall (but survive), and among air pilots
approaching the speed of sound. It has long been known to be an
experience of those who have been saved from drowning. It has
been held to be the result of anoxia, when the temporal lobe of
the brain, as a result of lack of oxygen, undergoes random firing
and excitation. It is known that an electrode in the temporal lobe
can stimulate flashbacks to past memories and also out-of-body
experiences, floating sensations and religious experiences
(Blackmore, 1993, p.205ff.). If there is lack of oxygen, the whole
lobe could get out of control, not unlike what happens in an
epileptic seizure.

If this is the cause, it still needs to be explained why memories
come quickly, clearly and in chronological order. There are
differences between epileptic seizures and life review in NDEs.
The characteristic emotion in seizures is very different from the
calm, peace and tranquillity of NDEs. In a seizure:

The reliving of past events involves a random, single event of no
significance, but in the NDE it consists of multiple, single events
experienced in rapid succession.

Sabom, p.238

Psychological explanations of the experience also lead to difficulties. It has been suggested that a dying child has an attachment to

memories, that happy childhood memories help to obscure the threat of death, that a review of one's life occurs naturally to people. Not everyone will find these explanations convincing. On the other hand, those who believe that a life review is a genuine religious experience know that self-knowledge and self-acceptance are a vital part of spiritual maturation. Many religions hold that there is a life review after death, and this may be a foretaste of it.

The Decision to Return

Usually, people on an NDE want to stay. More than anything, they want to stay, but they realise that this is impossible, because it is not yet their time to go. Sometimes they make the decision to return themselves, usually because they realise that they are still needed by their families on earth. Sometimes the decision is made for them: they are sent back by the Being of Light or by relatives whom they have met. Often they are given the impression that they have unfinished business to complete before they are permitted to cross the barrier. Once the decision is made, it is immediately put into effect. My illustrations are taken from the responses to Dr Fenwick's questionnaire.

> Then in a moment of despair, I realised that I could not go on. No words were spoken but my predicament was completely understood. I loved my wife more dearly than life itself and I could not leave her like this... The journey back was desperate. Leaving was the worst experience of my existence and it will affect me as long as I live. I have no regrets. (p.108)

> All I knew was that I was under orders to go back and complete an unspecified task. I had no idea what that task was, but I knew that sometime something would happen and I would know what was required of me. (p.106)

> I was so happy but then the shadow of what looked like a man suddenly appeared in this light and waved at me to go back, but again I felt compelled to go towards this lovely light and again I was waved back. (p.105)

To someone who holds that an NDE is due to anoxia, the reason for the sensation of returning to the physical body would be that a sufficient supply of oxygen was reaching the brain, and anoxia had ceased. To someone who believes that there are psychological reasons for NDEs, it could be held that the crisis of approaching death had passed, and the reason for a retreat from reality no longer existed. Those who believe in divine providence may presume that, under God and by the skills of doctors and nurses, a sick person was on the way to recovery, so that the spiritual journey must come to an end and the person concerned must return to the physical body to begin the difficult road to convalescence.

The Return

The return to the body is usually rapid. People often speak of shooting back down the tunnel at tremendous speed and 'snapping back' into their bodies as if they were at the end of an elastic cord. Here are some typical cases.

> For Audrey Organ it was like being 'pushed like a returning space rocket, or maybe how birth feels to a baby – and back I came'. Mrs Dawn Gillott says, '…then my whole body seemed to jump. I looked round and saw I was back in the ICU.' Anne Alcott describes her return as being poured back in her body. Other people said they were 'snapped back' or 'slammed back'.
>
> Fenwick and Fenwick, p.40

> At that time I thought about my family and all and I said, 'Maisie, I better go back.' It was just as if I went back and got into my body… That's when they brought me back and that's when I came back to my body.
>
> Sabom, p.56ff.

Those who believe that an NDE is due to anoxia must explain why there is such a sensation of haste in the return to the physical body. The re-establishment of a sufficient oxygen supply would be likely to be a gradual rather than a sudden process. Nor is it easy to understand why the fear of death should so suddenly cease, if a psychological cause of the experience is attempted.

Those who have experienced an NDE find that their lives have profoundly changed. The NDE continues to be vivid in their memories, and the fear of death has been removed. They can usually lead life more serenely and show more compassion to their fellow men and women, and it often deepens their faith in God, although it does not necessarily confirm their Christian orthodoxy. This abiding impression is hardly surprising. Whether it be real or hallucinatory, it is always an experience of profound significance to those who have had it. Some believe that after it they have been gifted with what they sense to be psychic powers, for example, of healing or precognition.

Assessment

I have tried to put as fairly as I can the views and explanations, so far as they go, both of those who hold that NDEs are genuine experiences of a spiritual journey and those who believe that they are hallucinations with psychological or physiological causes. The scientifically minded are likely to take the latter view, because they look for scientific causes. Those inclined to a spiritual view of life and who have an open mind about the paranormal are more likely to take the former view, as I do myself. As yet, there is no way of proving either one or the other explanation. If it could be shown (with witnesses who attest to it) that a person in an NDE, when experiencing an OBE, does indeed see objects that cannot be seen from the bed of sickness, that would favour the spiritual type of explanation; but as yet no conclusive proof is forthcoming.

How does one set about assessing probabilities in the absence of conclusive proof? The similarity of the pattern of people's NDEs, and the sincerity of those who testify, provide reasonable certainty about the kind of experiences that they have had. How does one decide whether these experiences are hallucinatory or the product of a genuine spiritual journey? Susan Blackmore makes some suggestions (Blackmore, p.194ff.).

Obviously a good theory must be coherent. I think that this applies to all the various kinds of explanation. She further affirms that a good theory must be specific, answering particular points, rather than accounting merely for generalities. But, as we have seen, it is not possible to account for all the experiences of NDE on the basis of anoxia, nor can all the various elements of an NDE be explained psychologically. On the other hand, a spiritual explanation can do this, although that in itself is no proof of its superiority. Blackmore also makes the point that a good theory does not posit extra realms without very good reason. The principle of Occam's razor would be generally agreed: *entia non sunt muliplicanda praeter necessitatem* (entities should not be unnecessarily multiplied). But if the spiritual realm does exist, it is not unreasonable to invoke it as an explanation, especially if there are inconsistencies and gaps in other explanations. And there *are* inconsistencies and gaps in psychological and physiological explanations.

Why should people in NDEs experience a barrier? Why should there be a Being of Light? Why should relatives be seen? Why should the return to consciousness in the earthly body be so sudden? Why should people in an OBE during an NDE seem to levitate to the ceiling? Until these and other questions are answered, these types of explanation are incomplete.

The third criterion for a good theory, according to Blackmore, is that it must provide testable predictions. There would be general agreement that this applies to scientific explanations. But a spiritual explanation is not open to testable predictions, so that on this ground this possibility can be ruled out without any examination. But testable prediction is not a criterion of excellence if an NDE is a genuine journey into another dimension or sphere of existence. To regard it as such is to engage in circular argument.

NDEs are very mysterious. There is a great variety of experiences. I hope I have given in this chapter representative quotations, relying for the most part on a few writers. But there is one presupposition on which the paranormal explanation rests that I have not even mentioned, because it is dealt with in an appendix of this book. I refer to the possibility that the mind can function without the brain, especially where memory is concerned.

Professor Swinburne, of the Oxford University Faculty of Divinity, has written about what people remember of their NDEs.

The principle of credulity might suggest that we ought to take such apparent memories seriously, especially in view of the considerable coincidences between them, as evidence that what subjects thought they had experienced they really did. But though the subjects referred these experiences to moments when the heart had stopped beating, etc., I do not know of any evidence that their brains had ceased to function. And if the brain was still functioning, then what the evidence would show is not that the soul may function when the brain does not, but only that its perceptual experiences (i.e., sensations and acquisitions of belief about faraway places) are not dependent on normal sensory output.

Swinburne, 1986

I think that Professor Swinburne's conclusion here is open to question. In the first place, brain activity cannot be measured unless it is known precisely when an NDE is taking place. Secondly, what is at stake is not whether the brain is functioning, but whether a person is in a conscious or unconscious state. The brain is functioning (in the sense that it would register in an electrocardiogram) when a person is in a deep and dreamless sleep, but there is no consciousness. In a similar way, the brain may be functioning when a person is experiencing an NDE, but that person may be completely unconscious so far as the brain is concerned. If so, the conscious experiences of an NDE will be mediated not through the brain, but through the soul. Of course, this depends not only on whether during an NDE the soul is parted from the brain, but also on whether the soul can function without the brain. For this crucial point the reader is referred to the appendix in this book about the mind/brain relationship.

It would be wise to listen to someone who has had direct experience of people who have had NDEs. There follows an interview with such a person.

Chapter VII

DIALOGUE WITH A NEUROPSYCHIATRIST

Dr Peter Fenwick is Consultant Neuropsychiatrist at the Maudsley Hospital in London, a Fellow of the Royal College of Psychiatrists, holding appointments at the Radcliffe Hospital at Oxford and the Broadmoor Special Hospital for Violent Offenders. He is a Senior Lecturer at the Institute of Psychiatry in London, and an Honorary Consultant at St Thomas's Hospital in London. More importantly for our purposes, he is also chairman of the British branch of the International Association for Near Death Studies.

ME: Dr Fenwick, I'd like to ask you at the beginning how you came to be interested in the near-death experience. Was it because of your own presuppositions, or was it as a clinician, or what? Perhaps I may make so bold as to ask you how it all began?

FENWICK: My mother was a surgeon, so I've always had an interest in medicine, but I also had an interest in mind and consciousness. The real difficulty was that in the late 1950s and early 1960s none of the textbooks said anything about consciousness at all. But I retained that interest. When I had just been appointed as a consultant at St Thomas's in the early 1960s, a colleague of mine came up and asked whether I would advise a student on a thesis. The thesis was on NDEs. I said I would be delighted to help, really to see if the stories in America which are common there carry across the Atlantic, because many of them didn't. But this one did; and she found a lot of them. And when I started up I found them here as well.

ME: Do you find that most of the NDEs occur after some sudden catastrophe that people have had, or just generally when they are ill?

FENWICK: It's very variable. Some people have had them after a catastrophe like myocardial infarct; some people have had them when they are very ill, for example with meningitis, and birth is very common as well; also one can get them in situations where one is afraid like sitting in a car on the motorway, without any terrible trauma, or falling off mountains when you don't hurt yourself, or you can get them when you are very sad. You can get them sometimes when you are asleep, in dreams. So it's very, very wide.

ME: When I wrote to you some couple of years ago, you told me that you didn't think very much of the anoxia explanation. Is that right?

FENWICK: That's correct.

ME: Do you still feel that?

FENWICK: I still feel that, and that is because if you starve the brain of oxygen, what happens is that you become confused and then lose consciousness; memory is affected, so you won't remember what's happened and any experiences that you have are confused.

ME: What about the feelings of peace that people have? Do you think that they are caused by beta endorphins and ACTH? Presumably, they come through the brain, the brain is still active, presumably, while these are happening; or do you think that they are something entirely different?

FENWICK: There are two theories. The first theory is that they are all brain phenomena, in which case you would look around for chemical messengers which could be involved in this type of experience. The second hypothesis would be that they are in some sense transmitted; or I suppose the third hypothesis is that it is a combination of both. So I think that if I were to try for a chemical explanation, the idea of a beta endorphin for this sense of calmness would be an extremely good one, but on the other hand they wouldn't explain anything else in the experience, because many people are given injections of morphine every day in this country, and don't have the experience. It would account for only a small part of it.

ME: Obviously, there are various kinds of OBEs, not merely NDEs, but out-of-body experiences for many reasons, drug-induced or whatever. Do you there is any difference in NDE OBEs?

FENWICK: Yes, I think there probably is. It's a little difficult to draw a difference in phenomenology. The NDE ones are certainly imposed on you, and they also seem to be rather more specific. The other ones can occur at any time. You usually don't just go up to the ceiling in the other ones, you go through the ceiling and out into the universe, as it were. So there are some differences, but there are a lot of similarities as well.

ME: What do you think about the explanation that OBEs are really a sort of means of escape from psychological or physical pain? It seems to me a very easy suggestion to make, but it doesn't seem to me to have much basis on which you can really try to corroborate it. Am I right?

FENWICK: That's correct, but there is little doubt that some people who have very, very severe pain do dissociate, and in the dissociation they may feel that they leave their body. Those ones, I think, seem to be different from the NDE OBEs. They also have a very clear stimulus. The OBEs in NDEs can occur sometimes without any pain at all, so you can't argue that it's just a dissociative experience in response to pain.

ME: Now, I'd like to ask you what you make of OBEs. I mean, do you think the brain constructs an alternative model, as it were, from the different perspective of the ceiling, or do you feel that it is really an out-of-body experience, not just experience, but actually out of the body? If so, I wonder if you could tell me why you think that? I don't think there is any independent evidence of OBEs as yet, is there? You know, people who have seen things which they could not have seen from their beds, and so on.

FENWICK: You can play it either way. The evidence is interesting. As for its being just another model, in one of the OBEs that we had, there's a lovely description of a woman during childbirth who left her body and watched them doing a Caesarean on her to deliver her child, with the clip going into her tummy; she saw the whole thing. She came round hearing the midwife saying, 'Push now, it's time for your baby to be delivered.' The argument is that that one was an OBE that wasn't veridical in any sense. On the other hand, there are OBEs which occur in NDEs which have a large veridical component to them. They report what is going on and Karl Sabom has looked at this and he's produced some quite compelling evidence that what they saw they could not have seen had they been lying on the bed where they were. So at the moment there is anecdotal evidence which supports the fact that they may be veridical. There is still a sufficient amount of evidence to suggest that they probably bear comparison with the veridical. I suspect it's going to be like most parapsychological experiences. The subject falls into that domain, I would think.

ME: I wonder what you make of the tunnel, or whatever it is, something like a tunnel, that people see. It's suggested by the sceptics that it's due to the inhibition and excitation of the brain cells in the visual cortex, and a sort of rundown of firing at the centre leading to the outside giving the impression of light getting nearer; or some psychological explanation that it's a change of consciousness at the approach of death, or even a reliving of the birth canal. I wonder whether you have any ideas about this from your clinical experience.

FENWICK: The tunnel can appear when you are either near death, or when you are not near death, so you can't argue any hypothesis about brain malfunction; it won't work. So you then have to ask: what does the NDE as a whole mean? Then again we come on to the two hypotheses: either it's a function of the brain, or there is some way in which this experience is transmitted, and then you begin to deal with philosophy. Science, of course, will have nothing to do with philosophy, so you have to then argue that it is entirely constructed within the brain. But if you are prepared to envisage a wider interpretation of consciousness, for example, if you take the view that consciousness is universal, that everything occurs within consciousness, even that the models that we have of the brain are in fact occurring within consciousness, then it is possible to hold that although consciousness resides within the brain, it also resides without the brain, so one could have a different view of it.

ME: I wonder if the people you have talked to have had the full syndrome, as it were, or components of NDE, and whether many of them see what is sometimes called the Being of Light, whoever or whatever it may be?

FENWICK: Twenty-five per cent have all the components of

NDE, and I think about two-thirds see the Being of Light; the actual number is in our book which I haven't got with me at the moment.

ME: I wonder what you think the Being of Light is. I mean, it has been suggested that it is really the self by those who are sceptical, while others say it is some supernatural Being. I wonder if you have any views about that.

FENWICK: You must be clear that you can't mix your framework. If you are using a scientific framework, science will not allow any processes outside the brain, and that's because we are using a seventeenth-century model for our science, a model which was proposed by Galileo when he said it was a two-stuff universe of matter and energy. He said the universe has two sets of qualities, primary and secondary. The primary qualities are things that can be described mathematically like weight, movement, velocity and so on. The secondary qualities are things that are pursued by the senses like love, truth, beauty, etc. If you take a scientific view, it is a primary quality view that you are taking. You cannot have any experiential qualities in your description. You can only describe the brain in terms of neurons, etc. If you try to describe the subject of experience, you have to get it wrong; you can't do it in the scientific view.

ME: It seems to me as though you think that if you are going to interpret these things, perhaps science alone is not always sufficient. You may find it difficult to commit yourself on this point.

FENWICK: If one's going to interpret the experiences fully, and you want a full description of them, then science alone wouldn't be sufficient. It would give you a one-sided view only. If you want to talk about the validity and nature of subjective experience, then our science is not the right way to do it.

ME: Yes. Well, now, I'd like to ask you next what you think of the barrier which so often seems to appear. Science doesn't seem to give any experience of it as a phenomenon, so far as I can see, quite apart from any subjective interpretation.

FENWICK: The barrier is interesting. Most cultures have it, although it varies from culture to culture, but the actual fact of the barrier is transcultural. Sometimes it's a river among the Japanese. In our culture, sometimes there's no barrier at all; people just know if they go on that they won't be able to get back; sometimes in an English country garden it can be anything – it can be a small stream, a village. The actual thing that produces the barrier, it's difficult to say what it is, but it seems to be a fundamental part of the experience. We don't know what it means either, because nobody who has crossed the barrier has ever come back.

ME: Thank you very much. Going on from there, I wonder what you make of the pastoral scene. I mean, no one could say it's descriptive; there's no green grass in heaven! Is it symbolic, do you think, or what kind of explanation do you give?

FENWICK: The pastoral scene is very clearly cultural. In our country, we have a quintessential English landscape, with a lot of birdsong, very bright colours, wonderful flowers, little benches, honeysuckle-laden trellises, etc. There are very few birds that have been seen; the only animals that I've had reported are by somebody who reported all the dogs of his life! You will be pleased to hear that there are no gnats, snakes or negative creatures in this place. If you go to another culture, then you have quite a different scene. So I think it is essentially culturally determined. What I would like to see is if people from a rural environment have the most wonderful towns, and those from an urban environment have the most wonderful rural scenes. There's no data on it.

ME: Do you think it's symbolic of peacefulness?

FENWICK: I'm not sure that it's symbolic. I think that heaven, as we have the picture of heaven, is derived from this experience rather than vice versa.

ME: What about the relatives who sometimes appear? Some people say that it's a psychological comfort to the dying to see their relatives around them. Sometimes it's a relative who tells a person to go back to earth, isn't it? I wonder what you make of it all.

FENWICK: People who are seen in the experience are not always dead; you can have living people and you can have dead people. So it's clearly not just people who have died. Children tend to see more of their living friends than adults do. Usually it's the close relatives, but people can have the experience without any relatives being seen at all. I was interested in relatives coming to sick people who were dying, so I asked in hospices how common it was, and I've had two consultants in palliative care positions who run hospices, who have said that they think probably about 70 per cent of people before they die have a dead relative come to collect them, and they also said that it is not unusual for people to die out of bed and be found on the floor. He thinks that this is because some of them may have tried to get out of bed to go with the relative who has come to collect them. This is something which seems to be very fundamental.

ME: Do you think it's clearly hallucinatory, or is that beyond your competence?

FENWICK: No. Here you depend totally on the framework you are using. If you say, 'Is it hallucinatory,' then you are using primary Galilean qualities, and you are using our current science. Our current science says that everything is generated by the brain, so relatives coming, in our current science, is hallucination. If you use a wider frame of interpretation and argue for an interconnected universe, then you can ask the question whether these are truly relatives coming or not.

ME: Thank you. It does seem as though you are saying you take your choice according to which way you feel, after looking at the scientific evidence.

FENWICK: Yes. Once you have dealt with the scientific evidence. As we have as yet no explanation of consciousness and no accepted scientific theories of consciousness, it is something which we cannot fully understand; and so it is an open question.

ME: Thank you very much. Now, next, I wonder what you think about the life review, if there's a scientific explanation of that. I know that the temporal lobe, if prodded by an electrode, can produce a flashback, but you don't get a chronological life review that way. I wonder what you think.

FENWICK: There's a lot of difficulty with the life review. The first point is that if we talk now about near-death experiences that occur after a myocardiac infarct, then we are dealing with a brain that is essentially unconscious and as such it would not be able to access memory stores effectively. Any memories would be confusional, so there isn't a proper scientific explanation for it. Let's assume for a moment that you could access the memory stores. It's very unusual to get a complete memory experience like that, but even more unusual is the fact that the life review is moral, and you are in a position within the experience of judging whether you have done well or not; quite often you will yourself feel the pain of the other person if you have hit somebody in a fight. It's not straightforward memory; it's much more complex than that, and if it was straightforward memory, then I doubt we would have it because of the confusional aspect, because of the fact that the memory is so sensitive to anoxia or any other metabolic cause that we can name.

ME: How very interesting! So it's really quite different from what can happen to pilots or people when drowning?

FENWICK: I think it's quite different from the anoxia of pilots because in our series we had a pilot who lost his supply of oxygen when he was fighting in the war and knows exactly what an anoxic experience is like, and it's confusional. He's also had a near-death experience, and he says they are quite different.

ME: That *is* interesting! Now, about coming back to the body. Why is it so sudden? People seem to come back with a thump, almost, rather than a gradual return, which I presume it would be with anoxia.

FENWICK: Yes, the actual return itself is an interesting part of the near-death experience, and it is separated from the ordinary out-of-body experience, because in the ordinary experience you tend not to go back with a thump like that, and you tend to hover around trying to get back in. Often people are frightened that they will never be able to do so. So the near-death experience seems to be very different. Its mechanism I don't know; I don't know of any theories, and I can't think of any myself.

ME: Thank you. I wonder if you'd mind if I asked you for your own personal rather than scientific assessment of the whole near-death experience syndrome?

FENWICK: Well, it's a philosophical question, and it depends entirely on what philosophical point of view you come from. If one ignores science, and one ignores it because it's unable to deal with subjective questions, then one is left with a wider view of man. If you are going to answer questions like that, then you have to answer them from the experiences that people have. The near-death experience is very much like another set of experiences called the mystical experience. In the mystical experience, which is a transcendental experience, the individual sees through into the very structure of matter itself, and those people who have had these mystical experiences say it is composed of universal love. So they argue for the world being conscious and loving, and if you look at the near-death experience it seems to have the major characteristics of this as well. It's a form of heightened consciousness, and the light and the Being of Light are always surrounded by universal love. So it seems to me that the near-death experience is probably of the same dimension as the mystical experience. It then comes down to 'What does the mystical experience mean?' I think that what one is doing in the mystical experience is looking at or into the very fundamental structure of the universe. You might say, 'Well, how's that?' because we know that the universe is made up of atoms and molecules and there's no love there; but then you have to remember that a model of the scientific kind removes any secondary qualities. If you had a science of consciousness, then, of course, you would be in a much better position.

ME: When you say that consciousness is throughout the universe, well, it sounds a little like panpsychism, that everything is conscious in ways beyond our understanding, but I think that that's not actually quite what you mean?

FENWICK: No, I don't mean that at all. What I'm saying is that if you think of how we get our information, how we get our models, how we derive our sciences, how we relate to each other, the whole thing takes place in the bed of consciousness, and none of these things would happen if consciousness were not there first. There's the beginning of a scientific theory that every particle may have two faces, the conscious face and the material face. *It may be something like that,* I think. The other point, a very important point, is that in the near-death experience those people who have had the profoundest experience move towards a unity with naked energy, naked consciousness, naked love, call it what you like. It's the fusing of the individual with the whole in that sense. So I think that probably we just have far too limited a view of the universe really to understand the real nature of these experiences.

ME: Dr Fenwick, thank you very much indeed for the way in which you've answered these questions. Indeed, I rather wish that I had asked you them before and not after I had written the chapter on the near-death experience!

Chapter VIII
REINCARNATION

In considering paranormal phenomena in relation to religion, we cannot ignore the question of reincarnation. Many readers will think it wrong for a Christian, especially a bishop, even to research the question of reincarnation. But we must search for the truth, wherever the path may lead us and at whatever cost. But is this not a subject forbidden to Christians? Reincarnation as such has never been officially condemned by the Church, even if the Councils of Lyons (1274) and Florence (1439) implied this by affirming that souls go immediately to heaven, hell or purgatory. Does not reincarnation involve the importation of foreign ideas from Eastern religions into Christianity? Not necessarily. Reincarnation is found in the Jewish Cabbala; it was held by Plato, Pythagoras and the later Platonists, who used the Greek word *metempsychosis* to express the idea. It may even, I shall suggest, be found in the New Testament. Influential people in Europe have subscribed to it, including Goethe, Herder, Ibsen, Maerterlink and the philosophers James Ward and J M E McTaggart.

Eastern faiths hold that reincarnation is the result of *karma*, according to which people receive the just desserts of their present life in the circumstances of the next. But it is possible to hold a view of reincarnation without *karma*. Nor is it necessary to hold that everyone is reincarnated, or that the process goes on eternally unless and until a soul receives true liberation from the world of desires.

This is a book about the paranormal, and the primary aim of this chapter is not to prove that reincarnation does take place, but to try to understand just what would be involved if it does, and to look at the evidence in favour of it as well as against it.

What Would Reincarnation Involve?

Just what would reincarnation involve? It must entail a continuity of some kind between one life and the next. John Hick has suggested that for a person to identify with an earlier period of this present life, continuity of memory, physical body and character disposition are required (Hick, p.305ff.). Most people have some memories of their early childhood to enable them to identify with what they were like then, even if they cannot recognise themselves from a photograph at that early age. (Even birthmarks, if there are any, may alter as a person grows). As for reincarnation, it is rare to claim memories of an earlier life (although a few do claim this). But it is hard to understand how the concept of reincarnation would ever have gained currency had there been no memories of an earlier existence. When such memories are claimed, some are derived from dreams, some from a sense of déjà vu, some through mediums, some through hypnotic trance, while some are apparently simply memories.

Children may claim detailed knowledge of an earlier life, starting from the age of two, and they are also said to manifest 'behavioural memories'; but these have all faded by time they are ten. There are also claims of birthmarks and birth defects deriving from an earlier existence. Because these memories of an earlier life usually fade, and because the physical body of an earlier life is obviously different from the present one, character disposition must always be a necessary sign of continuity. The basic character of people remains as they develop from childhood to adulthood. Most mothers would claim that their children have certain characteristics and dispositions from birth. Is continuity of character sufficient if there is no longer any conscious memory of an earlier life (although this may be buried in the unconscious mind)?

> The question of identity is one which philosophers have long debated, but never resolved.
>
> Beloff, p.214

If the whole goal of reincarnation is the eventual integration of personality so as to make people fit to appear in the presence of God, then continuity of character disposition would seem prerequisite.

If reincarnation does take place, there must be some carrier of personality from one body to the other, which can exist during the interregnum between the two. What this entity might be must remain unknown. Some have called it the 'astral body' or 'etheric body' or even 'dream body'. For others, these have distasteful overtones of spiritualism and New Age philosophy. The best way of referring to it, I believe, is the soul. The word *psychophore* has also been used, but this merely denotes a carrier without specifying its nature. In some way the memory, which is strongly connected with the physical brain (although no one knows its nature), must be transferred to this psychic entity, whatever it be called, if it be accepted that people can remember a past life; and this memory in turn must be embodied in or transferred to the brain of the later life. Clearly, those who believe in reincarnation must hold a dualist view of body and soul, and posit an unknown entity capable of this transference. Dualism, which is discussed in Appendix I, is for some people so improbable that they reject the idea of reincarnation outright without waiting to examine any evidence that it does indeed take place.

Genetics and Reincarnation

To what extent are people dependent for their character on the nature of their physical bodies? Recent scientific research suggests that the heart is the centre of a person's emotions (as traditional belief has always held). A change of tastes and character with new characteristics similar to those of the heart donor has been claimed after a heart transplant operation. Claire Sylvia met the family of Tim, the young man who was killed on a motor bicycle and whose heart was donated to her.

> 'Was he a beer drinker?' I asked.
> His sisters nodded... When I told them I wanted a beer soon after the operation there were smiles all round...
> 'He hardly ever got sick,' somebody said, 'and when he did he got over it fast.'

Not much doubt about that answer. Maybe I really had inherited his resilience. I asked if he liked green peppers.

'Are you kidding? He loved them,' a sister told me. 'He used to fry them up with a whole kielbasa sausage.'

I explained that I had never liked green peppers before the transplant.

'But what he really liked were chicken nuggets,' said Annie.

'Oh, my God!'

'What is it, Claire?'

'I just remembered something I never told anyone. After the transplant, when I was finally allowed to drive again, the first place I went to was Kentucky Fried Chicken. I had this craving for chicken nuggets which I'd never had before.'

Everybody laughed. John said that after Tim's accident, they had had to remove a container of chicken nuggets from under his jacket. He was carrying them when he died.

Sylvia and Novak, p.184ff.

No doubt, as anecdotal evidence such a conversation does not rate very high, especially as the story was admittedly ghostwritten. But other similar cases have been reported after heart transplants (Sylvia and Novak, p.214). Another instance of apparent cellular memory (on a very different subject) is reported by McConnell, who, having trained earthworms to curl up in the face of a flashing light, minced them up and fed them to other worms which he alleged acquired the former earthworms' memories (McConnell, pp.465–68).

Whether or not there are cellular memories that can cause changes of taste and character, questions need to be asked in the light of our modern knowledge of genetics whether it is possible for a person to be reincarnated with a character disposition similar to that of a previous existence. We know that tendencies towards many characteristics are likely to be genetically determined at the moment of conception; for example, it has recently been claimed that a gene on a particular chromosome predisposes a person to depression and suicide. Biologists, I think, are inclined to be dogmatic neo-Darwinists, assuming that an embryo is pre-programmed by its genes in all aspects of its development, while other people are inclined to put more emphasis on environment than on heredity. We do not understand exactly how the foetus develops, especially its brain. The variation in the occurrence of physical disabilities which arise from similar defects suggests that other factors are involved as well. In particular, the well-attested phenomenon of 'maternal impression', when a baby shows those very defects of which the pregnant mother was scared that her baby would have, shows that the environment can play a major part. (There is the case of a woman who was so shocked to find that her brother's penis had been amputated that her own baby was born without one.)

It would not seem impossible that, if there is a discarnate entity that is to be united with a foetus, it could affect that foetus at a sensitive time of its development, with resulting birthmarks and memories, cognitive and/or behavioural. But I find it impossible to imagine an impersonal process by which this could occur. One of the grave objections to Hindu and Buddhist concepts of reincarnation is that the *linga sharira* of Hinduism and the *vinnana* (karmic deposit) of Buddhism become reincarnated by some impersonal process into a physical body whose dispositions are to a large extent predetermined. In these Eastern cultures, there may be 'departing dreams' and 'announcing dreams' in which a discarnate entity foretells a future reincarnated existence. This suggests that the discarnate entity may choose the parents and sex of its future existence. But it is not easy to imagine how such an entity could determine whether a foetus has a Y chromosome, knowledge of which is needed if it is to retain or change its sex. In Burma, one quarter of the cases investigated by Professor Stevenson involve a sex change.

Whether or not the choice lies with the entity concerned, the process of reincarnation, if it happens, would be as mysterious as is the process of 'maternal impression'. Not all reincarnations, if they take place, need be the result of the personal choice of the previous personality, although the considerable number that are alleged to occur within the same family might point to the view that this does occur. A scanning of embryos would be needed to ensure a suitable body for reincarnation, and it would seem that this would have to be done by some discarnate entity far more knowledgeable than the previous personality.

We may perhaps conclude that these considerations render the concept of reincarnation difficult, but not absolutely impossible.

Reincarnation and Christian Doctrine

Many Christians find it difficult to look at cases of alleged incarnation objectively, because they are prejudiced against the concept. It is therefore necessary to look at doctrinal objections to the concept (and also at any advantages) before proceeding to consider particular cases.

There are those who feel a distaste for the idea because their goal is set on heaven, and anything that impedes the face-to-face vision of God immediately after death meets with their disfavour (Perry, 1984, p.188). This objection disappears once it is conceded that not everyone is reincarnated, and that humanity needs further opportunities for development before we can all appear before the face of God.

Four further objections have been noted (Hick, pp.366–72). The first of these concerns the lack of such a doctrine in the New Testament. We shall look further into this in the next section when certain New Testament texts are examined. The second argument is that Christianity has traditionally attributed an absolute importance to this present life as the period of grace in which our eternal destiny is determined. But the concept of purgatory has already modified this belief. It is not denied that the individual in this life may decide to take the fundamental option for evil, and this would indeed determine that individual's eternal fate. Such a final and irrevocable choice of evil, however, seems improbable in this life, and it is to be hoped that no one has ever made it. Very few people indeed are saints. Most of us are a mixture of good and evil. It is perhaps helpful, in thinking about the future destiny of humanity, to make use of the type of theology often dubbed 'Irenaean' which has a time-honoured history. According to this way of thinking, our journey towards heaven is seen as a pilgrimage, a long and slow process of sanctification, and with this type of theology the concept of reincarnation seems more congruent.

Another argument against reincarnation, according to Hick, takes its stand on the doctrine of the resurrection of the body. But

Hick points out that the two doctrines, resurrection and reincarnation, although formally at variance, 'agree more deeply in their view of man as a psycho-physical unity, so that life after death must be in a body', without which a soul remains passive and unable to communicate. If reincarnation be a fact, a person who is reincarnated is not resurrected in his old physical body, which has disintegrated at death, nor is such a person resurrected in a spiritual kind of body. He is reborn or reincarnated in a new material body, before he goes on later to receive a spiritual body.

The final argument against reincarnation which Hick mentions is that it seems incompatible with the doctrine of the atonement according to which Christ wrought 'a full, perfect and sufficient sacrifice for the sins of the whole world'. I have discussed the doctrine of the atonement in an earlier book, together with my understanding of it, and it would not be appropriate to repeat it now (Montefiore, 1993, pp.97–115). But here it should be stated that there is no conflict between the concept of reincarnation and the once-for-all nature of what God has done through Christ. As Hick puts it, 'There is no logical connection between the idea that Christ died once only, for the sins of the world, and the idea that men have only one life in which to accept the benefits of that atoning death.' Our urgent need of repentance is not due to the belief that our one and only chance of response is in our present existence, but to the intrinsic urgency of the call.

The objections on Christian grounds to the idea of reincarnation do not seem to be well founded. Are there any arguments in favour of it? It may be useful to clear away at the outset some misconceptions. Acceptance of the belief that reincarnation occurs to some people should not imply that it happens to all. Nor does it imply that there is an unending cycle of reincarnation until the soul can at last achieve freedom from desire so that it can enter into the blessed state of *Nirvana*. Nor does it demand the acceptance of *karma*, that we all get what we deserve and that we are, as it were, punished for our evil deeds in this life by being reincarnated in a less pleasant form of existence. In other words, a Christian view of reincarnation could be very different from those held by Eastern religions.

As for positive advantages that the doctrine would bring, it seems clear that some people who are cut off by a violent death before they reach maturity have no chance of developing their character. Children who die young are quite undeveloped. The seeds of character are there, but they has not been able to grow and develop during adolescence and adult life. Further, there may be some developed souls that are not so evil that they prefer darkness to light, but who need further opportunities to develop their preference for the light. There are those too who have lived lives so grossly disadvantaged that they too have been unable to develop their potentialities. There may be others who have advanced sufficiently to be sent back to help people of a later generation.

In all these cases it would seem a positive advantage to believe in the possibility of reincarnation, without as yet committing oneself to the belief that it does exist. Catholic beliefs have traditionally included the doctrine of the limbo, the abode of souls excluded from the blessedness of the beatific vision, but not condemned to punishment; the *limbus patrum* where the saints of the Old Covenant awaited the coming of Christ, and the *limbus infantium*, the abode of unbaptised infants who suffered from original sin, but who have not committed any actual sins. Such a doctrine of the limbo is abhorrent to many people today. What then does happen to those who have died in infancy? Of course, we cannot know, but if they are insufficiently developed in their present existence, it seems reasonable, and even congruous with sound doctrine, that they should have another earthly existence in which they could develop.

There are those who still believe with St Augustine that the decision made for or against Christ at the moment of death decides whether a person goes to heaven or to hell. This, however, is not New Testament teaching. The belief that Christ, after he was dead, preached to disobedient spirits in prison (1 Peter 3:19) suggests that there is a chance of repentance after death. When Jesus said to the penitent thief, 'Today you will be with me in Paradise' (Luke 23:43), he was not speaking of heaven; he was making use of the image of the garden so often employed by those recounting NDEs which they do not associate with heaven itself. The word translated 'paradise' is in fact the Greek for garden. The idea that our eternal fate is determined in this life by a decision for or against Christ is no longer acceptable to Roman Catholic doctrine. According to the Second Vatican Council, those who hold in good faith the tenets of another faith may be granted the gift of eternal life.

What then does decide a person's destiny? There are theologians who speak of taking the 'fundamental option' or basic disposition to what a person conceives of as good (Mahoney, p.221). A person may make a fundamental choice of light or darkness. But this is not to say that those who opt for the light go straight to the beatific vision into the very presence of God himself. We are all still faulty and flawed when we die. God in his overflowing grace accepts us as we are. But, *pace* the Reformers, we are not yet fit for heaven, even though we may have matured greatly in the course of our earthly life. We shall not be able to stand eternally in God's presence until we have become the persons God intends us to be. It would be immoral for God suddenly to transform our characters at the moment of death so that we are miraculously perfected. We need further opportunities for the development of character. Purgatory has been traditionally conceived as the place or state of temporal punishment where those who have died in the grace of God are expiating their venial faults and such pains as are still due for mortal sins that have already been forgiven. But it is better to think of purgatory as a sphere (I cannot call it a place) where our characters are purged, purified, further developed, and are advancing towards perfection. If this be the case, those who are thought likely to benefit from a further earthly existence might be reincarnated, as a kind of purgatory, or pre-purgatory, to help them towards the beatific vision. If we hold to this kind of reformed belief in purgatory, there can hardly be an objection to a limited reincarnation for some souls; indeed, there could actually be advantages.

Reincarnation in the New Testament?

Traces of reincarnation have been alleged within the New Testament itself (Leggett, 1987, p.83). According to Mark's Gospel (followed by St Matthew's Gospel), when Jesus came down from the Mountain of Transfiguration, where he was reported to have conversed with Elijah, his disciples asked him why the scribes taught that Elijah must come first, referring to the prophecy in Malachi to the effect that Elijah would come before the Day of the Lord. Jesus is reported to have replied, 'Yes, Elijah does come first, to set everything right... I tell you that Elijah has already come, and they have worked their will upon him, as the Scriptures say of him' (Mark 9:12ff.; Matthew 17:11ff.).

Commentators do not comment much on the meaning of this remark.

> There is no reason to doubt the main point, the identification of the Baptist with Elijah.
>
> Rawlinson, p.121

> The saying implicitly identifies Elijah with John the Baptist.
>
> Vincent Taylor, p.395

> In fact Elijah has already come in the person of John the Baptist.
>
> Nineham, p.239

Jesus did not say that the function of John the Baptist was to carry out the prophesy of Malachi about Elijah, although this is how commentators have understood the verse. He did not say that the Baptist was merely carrying out the role of Elijah. By saying that he had already come, he surely meant that Elijah had returned to earth.

It is true that Elijah was believed to have been carried up to heaven in a chariot of fire and so, unlike the rest of us, he never died (and later Judaism held similar ideas about Jeremiah and other canonical prophets). However, in Jesus's time, most Jews, except for the Sadducees, believed that there is life after death for all, so that the difference between Elijah and the rest of us is not all that great, other than that he was to return to earth with a physical body, whereas we shall have a spiritual body after death. But his was not a sudden descent from heaven like the earlier sudden ascent into heaven: John was conceived, he grew in his (new) mother's womb and was born. Furthermore, Elijah was a different person from the Baptist. We know that John was a man of his time, a cousin of Jesus, born of elderly parents with a mother who had yearned for a child for many years, and that in the early days of his ministry, before he began his public ministry, he had spent his early days in the desert regions of Judaea, possibly in contact with Qumran. Elijah and John the Baptist were different persons, shaped by different cultures and different environments. All they had in common was character disposition. Yet Jesus identified the two. Maybe Jesus was speaking only figuratively, but the plain meaning of his reported words is that Elijah was reincarnated in the person of John the Baptist. It is interesting that the commentators do not seem to envisage this possibility.

Moreover, this is not the only occasion in the gospels when Jesus identified Elijah with John the Baptist. He is reported to have said, 'All the prophets and the law prophesied until John, and if you are willing to receive it, he is Elijah who is to come' (Matthew 11:13ff.). Some people thought that Jesus himself was Elijah (Mark 6:15; Luke 9:8) and the first question that the priestly delegation from Jerusalem asked him when they cross-examined him was, 'Are you Elijah?' (John 1:21). The fact that Herod thought that the Baptist had risen from the dead, that his mighty power was manifest in Jesus (Mark 6:16) and that others thought that Jesus was one of the prophets (Mark 6:15; 8:28; Matthew 16:14; Luke 9:19) is evidence that the idea of reincarnation was not far from people's minds. It cannot be said to be totally alien to the New Testament.

Adult Memories of Earlier Lives

After considering what reincarnation would entail (and concluding that it is a difficult concept, but not absolutely impossible) and after examining the New Testament for traces of the doctrine, we must next examine such positive evidence as there is in favour of it.

In some families, a child may have an absorbing interest in a different culture. I have a friend whose daughter in her childhood had an unaccountable obsession with and love for all things

Indian. This is very feeble evidence for reincarnation.

Occasionally, adults become convinced that they have lived former lives. Two such instances may be quoted here. Edward Ryall, in 1970, claimed extensive memories of a previous life as a seventeenth-century West Country farmer by the name of John Fletcher. Although in his book (Ryall, 1974), he evidently shows considerable knowledge of his time and period, the parish records of Weston Zoyland, where he claimed to have lived, show no mention of any John Fletcher, neither his marriage nor his parents' deaths nor the baptism of his children; and, moreover, doubts have been cast about the alleged location of his house, which, it is claimed, was marshland until 1800 (Wilson, 1982, pp.87–95). This in itself is hardly convincing evidence for reincarnation.

The second instance concerns Dr Arthur Guirdham, a former senior consultant psychiatrist in the NHS. A patient who was referred to him claimed to have memories of an earlier life among the Cathars, a medieval sect of the Albigensian heresy persecuted by the Roman Catholic Church (Wilson, 1982, pp.36–40). Guirdham became convinced that he, too, had once been a Cathar, with whom the lady had been in love in her earlier life. Two more ladies convinced him that they had been Cathars as well. Guirdham already had considerable knowledge of the Cathars, and had written a novel about them. Interviews with any of the women concerned were refused (on professional grounds) and he refused also to reveal their names, even after they were dead, or to produce the photograph of the scar on one of them said to correspond to her earlier injuries when persecuted as a Cathar. Despite considerable knowledge of the period, including what seemed like authentic jottings from a Cathar childhood notebook, this is hardly convincing evidence of reincarnation.

Dreams and Déjà Vu

Knowledge of reincarnation might come from dreams. If dreams can produce precognition (see p.28), flashbacks might also occur of previous lives. But there is much controversy about dreams. Some think that they represent the flushing of the cerebral system, others that they give entry to a person's unconscious, others that they draw on the collective unconscious. For these reasons it would be foolish to rely on dreams for evidence of reincarnation.

The sensation of déjà vu is very common. Raynor Johnson cites John Buchan and D G Rosetti (Johnson, p.386). 'I find myself,' wrote Buchan, 'in some scene which I cannot have visited before, and which is yet perfectly familiar: I know it was the stage of an action in which I once took part, and am about to take part again.' Rosetti wrote in her poem, *Sudden Light*:

> I have been here before,
> But when or how I cannot tell:
> I know the grass beyond the door,
> The sweet keen smell,
> The sighing sound, the lights around the shore.

Although such sensations may be convincing to those who experience them, they can be explained on physiological grounds.

> The feeling of similarity, like many other feelings, appears to be controlled by neural activity in the limbic system. It is likely that when events really are familiar the hippocampus is activated and signifies the fact. However, the same mechanism can be set off in abnormal (neural) activity and give rise to the sensation of familiarity without any actual recognition having taken place... But, you might object, I am not epileptic, and have often experienced déjà vu. This is because many people have occasional spurious activity in these parts of the brain and research is only just beginning to reveal its implications.
>
> Blackmore, p.206ff.

Clearly, these observations make it unwise to regard déjà vu as anything but supporting evidence for reincarnation. Similarly, it would imprudent to invoke the evidence of mediums in this connection, because although at times they do seem to impart genuine information, very often they do not (see p.43).

Memories from Hypnotic Trance

There is a basic problem about alleged recollections of earlier lives given in hypnotic trance. A person who is hypnotised feels under an obligation to carry out the wishes of the hypnotist, and for this reason evidence derived from hypnotic trance is suspect in a court of law (Beloff, p.206). It may well be manufactured from subconscious memories in an effort to obey the hypnotist.

Some instances of knowledge of earlier lives obtained by hypnotic trance may be given. The first (and most famous) concerns Virginia Tighe, a twenty-five-year-old married lady from Colorado (Wilson, 1982, pp.82–94). In 1949, under hypnotic trance she began to speak in a soft Irish brogue of her earlier life in Cork in the first two thirds of the last century. She used words reminiscent of that time and area, and claimed to have been Bridey Murphy who was married to a barrister, living an ordinary life in a cottage and dying after breaking her hip in a fall in 1864. The case aroused great publicity, but none of her details of Cork in the last century could be corroborated. Although Mrs Tighe produced detailed accounts of neighbours, shops, etc., none of these details could be authenticated as historical. Mrs Tighe had a Scottish Irish aunt who had lived in the family home in the USA when she was eighteen, but it is doubtful whether all the details she recalled of nineteenth-century Ireland could have been derived from her. They might have been the result of books she had read but had long forgotten, with details spun into memories in obedience to the wishes expressed by her hypnotist. While it is possible that they are genuine, they are very flimsy evidence on which to accept reincarnation.

Another case with which Wilson deals concerns a young girl from Merseyside who, when hypnotised, flashed back to an earlier life as Joan Waterford who, with her mother, was tried as a witch at Chelmsford in the sixteenth century. There is one contemporary record of this trial in Lambeth Palace library, and all the details given correspond to this account, with one exception. The girl, under hypnosis, insisted that the trial took place in the reign of Queen Mary in 1566. But in fact Elizabeth was queen by then. The Lambeth library copy, however, gives the year of the trial as 1556, when Mary was queen. Copies of the original transcript of the trial were printed later, and by inadvertence the date given was 1566, when Elizabeth was queen. Evidently the girl had once read one of these, and forgotten all about it; and in a desire to obey her hypnotist about a former life, she became Joan Waterford, and even gave a passable imitation of sixteenth-century speech. Of course, when she came out of her trance she, like others, had no idea of what she had said.

A further case probed by Wilson concerned a highly educated woman, who was sceptical of reincarnation, but agreed to be hypnotised and 'regressed' to several earlier lives. (This is not uncommon in such cases: one person 'regressed' to no less than fifteen previous existences!) In one of them, she claimed to have been a seventeenth-century Jesuit by the name of Anthony Bennet (Wilson, 1982). The Jesuits, however, keep very accurate records and there is no record of an Anthony Bennet to be found. Furthermore, when challenged by Eysenk to say the *Pater noster*, 'he' could not get beyond the first two Latin words. How, then, could she have given a plausible impression of a seventeenth-century Jesuit? There seems to be a faculty of the human mind that has a very accurate (unconscious) memory of what has been read in the past, and which can be very creative in filling in gaps in order to construct a coherent story. It is not unlike the phenomenon of 'multiple personality', in which a person may suddenly switch into another personality (or into various personalities) with no memory of what that person has been formerly. Because of this, it is imprudent to rely on alleged memories of earlier lives disclosed under trance as evidence for reincarnation.

The Bloxham Tapes

Scepticism about the value of apparently genuine memories revealed under hypnotic trance is supported by an examination of some transcriptions of the many tapes made by a respected hypnotherapist near Cardiff. A selection of these tapes has been published (Iverson, 1976). I give here just one example of a person under Bloxham's hypnosis.

Jane Evans, born in 1934, became, under hypnotic trance, successively the wife of the tutor of Constantius's son, better known as Constantine the Great, when the family was in England in A.D. 286; Rebecca, a wealthy Jewess in York who died in the massacre of Jews there in 1190; Alison, servant to Jacques Coeur in medieval France, who died in 1451; Anna, servant to Catherine of Aragon who lived 1485–1536; Ann, London sewing girl in the reign of Queen Anne (1665–1714); Sister Grace, a nun in Maryland, USA, who died around 1920.

The earlier lives were told in great detail by Jane Evans when unconscious under hypnotic trance. Subsequent research has revealed that details of the time of Constantine bear remarkable resemblances (even including names) to a historical novel, *The Living Wood*, published in 1947 and republished in 1970 under the title, *Princess Helena*. Again, the story about Catherine of Aragon's servant has been shown to be dependent on a historical novel called *The Virgin Widow*. The story of the York massacre can be found in a couple of histories I have on my own shelves. If Jane Evans was telling the truth when she said she could not remember reading these books about these subjects, she must have been suffering from cryptomnesia, a not unknown condition, when the conscious mind forgets and the unconscious memory retains clear details.

Children's Memories

So far, alleged evidence in favour of reincarnation has been shown to have little value. Rather different is the case of children's memories which have been investigated over the years by Professor Ian Stevenson, a professor at the University of Virginia, USA, who has examined over two and a half thousand alleged cases in various non-European cultures and has published case histories of what he considers the more convincing cases in different cultures (Stevenson, 2001). Unfortunately, until recently, he has ploughed a solitary furrow. It would obviously be more satisfactory if there were others; but those who have now entered the field formerly worked under him.

Professor Stevenson has attempted to investigate alleged cases of childhood memories with academic detachment and thoroughness, although, by the nature of the subject, by the time he heard of a case to investigate, some time had usually passed since the beginning of these alleged memories. I list here the headings of his introduction to each case history.

After an extensive discussion of the case, he begins with a summary, then lists the persons interviewed during the investigation. He next lists the relevant facts of geography and possibilities for normal means of communication between the two families concerned. There follows an account of the life and death of the person whom a child claims to have been in an earlier life. He then records statements and recognitions made by the child concerned, and with each item is given the name of the informant, the verification (often made by Professor Stevenson himself), and comments. After that he goes on to consider whether there is a birthmark allegedly relating to the former life, and the attitudes of parents to their son's memories of his alleged former life. He then considers the attitude of the parents of the person the child was alleged to be in the former life towards the boy making the claim, and ends by considering any extrasensory perception on the part of the child concerned, and passes comments on the paranormal processes apparently at work in the case. He concludes with a consideration of the boy's later development. I mention all these to show the professional thoroughness that characterises his investigations.

Stevenson has investigated 2,500 alleged reincarnations and published case histories of children in India (1975), Sri Lanka (1977), Turkey and Lebanon (1980), Burma and Thailand (1983), and among the Tlingit Indians of South East Alaska (1966) and the Igbo of Nigeria (1986). The children are between the ages of two and eight, occasionally older, but usually younger than eight. He has published accounts of what he believes to be behavioural memories, image memories, 'announcing dreams' (in which a deceased person informs members of his family of the family he will be reincarnated into in the future), and 'departing dreams' (when a deceased person informs members of his family, into what family he or she will reincarnate) (Stevenson, 1997, p.6ff.).

Behavioural memories occur when a child who remembers a former existence seems to behave in a way unsuited to his present family, but appropriate to the earlier one. Phobias relating to the child's death in an earlier existence take place in 35 per cent of Stevenson's investigated cases, and philias often occur (for example, a desire for foods unusual in the child's present family).

When there is an alleged sex change, there is cross-dressing, and a desire for the kind of games suited to the other sex. Behavioural change is particularly noticeable with children in Burma who believe that they were formerly British or Japanese. Behavioural memory may involve a child who believes that she was formerly a teacher organising her playmates in a game of being at school. These memories gradually fade and the child as it grows up adopts the culture, tastes and way of life of its present family.

In speaking of their previous lives, children may use the present tense: 'I have a wife and two sons.' They tend to speak about what they believe to have been their earlier life with an intensity and emotion that may astonish adults who hear them. They usually remember their previous death, especially if it were violent. Professor Stevenson records that 51 per cent of the deaths among the children he has investigated were violent, far more than the average. They may conceive hatred and a feeling of vengefulness against those whom they believe to have been their murderers in a previous existence.

As an example of cases that Professor Stevenson has investigated, I choose one from an earlier published volume (Stevenson, 1975). His own description of the case is too lengthy to be given here, so I am quoting an admirable summary of the case given by Dr and Mrs Badham:

> At the age of four and a half, a boy named Prakesh began to declare that his 'real' name was Nirmal, and that his 'real' home was in Kosi Kalan. He named 'his' father and sisters, and talked of 'his' father's shops in detail and longing, and the names of many neighbours. He insisted that he be called Nirmal, and night after night he tried to run off towards Kosi Kalan, 'his' home. He went on and on until his parents beat him to stop his chatter. However, unknown to his parents, Prakesh's alleged memories exactly corresponded to the life situation of a boy called Nirmal who had died shortly before Prakesh's birth. This was not discovered until five years later, when Nirmal's father happened to be in Prakesh's village. Prakesh immediately recognised 'his' father and begged to be taken 'home'. The meeting led to further reunions and an eventual visit to Nirmal's former home. Prakesh recognised by name all Nirmal's brothers and sisters and friends. He showed intimate knowledge of the house and all its fittings, save that his

knowledge was geared to the situation ten years previously so that he was puzzled by features that had been altered in the intervening decade. Stevenson came across this case three weeks after the first 'reunion', and has set out in tabulated form 34 of Prakesh's claimed memories, the names of those who remembered him making these claimed memories prior to the 'reunion', and the names in the other family who could verify the accuracy of each alleged memory as a fact pertaining to the actual life-situation of Nirmal. Moreover, every member of the family testified that, before the 'reunion', they had had no knowledge whatever of each other's memories.

Badham and Badham, p.99ff.

In this particular case, very little time elapsed between the 'reunion' and Stevenson's questioning of those involved. Of course, it is not possible to guarantee the honesty of all those questioned; nor is it possible to ascertain whether there had been any earlier contact between Prakesh and people in Kosi Kalan. There is, I suppose, a possibility that Prakesh may have picked up memories of Nirmal by telepathy from members of Nirmal's family, and that his unconscious mind spun them into a consistent whole which enabled him to believe that he had been Nirmal in a previous existence, but if this were the case, why did his memories not reflect the present situation? His was certainly a coherent story. Readers must judge for themselves whether or not they find reincarnation the simplest solution of the case.

Another case concerned Ravi Shanker, born in Uttar Pradesh in India. When he was between two and three years old, he kept asking for the toys that he claimed he had had in his previous life. He said he was the son of a barber, Sri Jageshwar, in another district of Uttar Pradesh, and that he had been murdered. This came to the ears of Jageshwar, and it transpired that his only son, Munni, a six-year-old, had indeed been murdered by two relatives, a washerman and a barber, who had hoped to gain his inheritance. Ravi was born some six months after the death of Munni. Ravi's father was angry with his son and refused to allow him to visit Jageshwar, as he feared that the boy would be taken away from him. But a meeting was arranged in 1955 when the boy was six years old. He correctly identified toys and possessions he claimed he had had, and he gave an account of his murder which seemed accurate to Jageshwar; how he was enticed away while eating guavas, taken to the riverside, had his throat cut in an orchard, and was buried in the sand. Ravi was afraid of his father who strongly disapproved of these tales, and afraid too of the two murderers (who, in the absence of witnesses, had not been found guilty) and of all washermen and barbers. He said he did not know that the two were his murderers, but when he saw them he was filled with fear. Ravi's mother testified that he had a linear mark resembling closely the scar of a long knife wound across the neck. She said she first noticed the mark when he was three to four months old. The mark was apparently congenital. As he grew, it gradually changed position until it was just below his chin; and it faded. There had been no contact, it was said, between the two families previously: they lived in different districts (Stevenson, 1975, pp.99–104).

In this case there was a longer period before the case was investigated; and, of course, there might have been some chance contact between the two districts unknown to the investigators. The birthmark might be a mere coincidence. Again, telepathy might account for the apparent knowledge of Munni on the part of Ravi. Or it might be a case of reincarnation.

The Druse religion in the Lebanon is an offshoot of the unorthodox Ismaili sect of Islam. Its adherents believe in reincarnation. One of the cases that Stevenson investigated there concern Suleyman Andary, who was brought up by his paternal grandmother. As a small child, he claimed to remember that he had lived before, remembering the names of some of his children, and he knew the village called Gharife where he had lived, and that he had owned olive trees and an oil press near a water fountain. When he was five or six, his family heard him talking in his sleep, mentioning the names of people. Suleyman did not remember dreaming, but when he woke up and his family told him of this, he recognised them as the names of some of his children in a former life. He later remembered that he had owned some religious books, and this stimulated other memories. He had been *mukhtar* (mayor) in his village, and he remembered his full name, Abdullah Abu Hamdan. He did not mention this to adults until he was thirteen, and preferred not to talk about it at all, for fear of being teased. It turned out that there had been an Abdullah Abu Hamdan in the village of Gharife, who had had a large family, whose names Suleyman had mostly remembered. He had been deposed from being *mukhtar* because of a falsification that he had made; perhaps this was one of the reasons why he did not want to talk about his previous life. There had been no communication, the investigators were assured, between the family of Suleyman Andary who was born in 1954 and that of Abdullah Abu Hamdan, who died a natural death near the beginning of 1942 (Stevenson, 1980, pp.52–76). Once again, alternative explanations could be given for this story; or once again it may have been a case of reincarnation.

A further characteristic of many such cases of alleged reincarnation is that of birthmarks or birth defects said to relate to wounds or marks on the dying or dead body of the alleged previous personality. These are important in as much as they might seem to provide objective evidence, which may be photographed and checked with post-mortem accounts, hospital reports, etc., relating to the earlier death (Stevenson, 1997, p.43ff.). It might be said that these marks correspond through mere chance, as birthmarks and birth defects are not uncommon. Stevenson claims that the chance of birthmarks appearing in the same part of two bodies have been calculated at 160:1. In some cases, however, two marks are to be found on the two bodies, in which case the odds are said to be 25,000:1. Stevenson has published pictures of a remarkable case where two birthmarks on a child correspond exactly to the places where a bullet entered the head of the previous personality beneath the chin and exited at the top of the scalp, with the top mark larger than the lower one, as a bullet makes a larger hole when leaving a body than when entering it (Stevenson, 1997, figures 15 and 16).

These birthmarks tend to disappear, and even to move, as the child grows up. They are usually different in various ways from ordinary moles or *nevi*, being hairless and raised above the skin or sunk below it.

There are also differences of pigmentation (darker in the case of 'former' Indians and lighter in the case of 'former' Europeans) among Burmese children who claim earlier lives of different nationalities, as well as some differences from the normal physiognomy that would be expected in the child's country of origin. Stevenson also notes some twenty-five cases of internal disease suffered by the alleged previous personality which have left their mark on the child (Stevenson, 1997, p.149ff.).

Stevenson also mentions birth defects in children who claim an earlier life similar to defects in the previous personality. Some 2 per cent of all children are born with birth defects of some kind, due to various causes – uterine conditions, teratogenic drugs, or genetic factors such as chromosomal abnormalities. Many – some say as many as 70 per cent – are said to be due to unknown causes. The evidence suggests that more than one factor may be involved. For example, cleft palate and lip are not concordant in most cases when they occur in identical twins. Stevenson suggests that reincarnation may be one factor involved in these birth defects. He cites cases of defects in the extremities (hands or toes) and in the neck, and defects concerning two or more regions of the body. In each case, defects at birth exactly match those at the death of the previous personality (Stevenson, 1997, pp.115–44). In one case, there are malformed fingers corresponding to the amputation of fingers made with a sword on a previous personality (Stevenson, 1997, figure 24). Stevenson also mentions birth defects in sub-Saharan West Africa, when parents, believing that children are responsible for their own deaths, may mutilate a dead child in the hope that the child will not return to them after an ensuing pregnancy, only to die once more prematurely. These mutilations nonetheless may turn up in a later child (Stevenson, 1997, p.145ff.). This might be due, however, to the phenomenon known as maternal impression, when a mother produces a child with the very defect which she most fears (see p.173).

These birthmarks and birth defects deserve rigorous scrutiny because, while it may be possible to find alternative explanations of other alleged signs of reincarnation, it is very difficult to explain birthmarks and birth defects in this way. The odds against them appearing by chance are very large, and (apart from maternal impression in a few cases) it is very difficult to account for them other than by the hypothesis of reincarnation. Even then we can only surmise how they have occurred. In Appendix I, we argue for a theory of interactive dualism binding together both body and soul. We must presume, if the cause of these birthmarks is reincarnation of a soul conjoined with a body that has been subject to violence or mutilation, or suffers from some internal disease, that that soul has been affected by this close interaction. When it is first conjoined to another body, it may, we must surmise, still carry traces of that earlier body, just as it may carry behavioural traces of the previous personality. We must go further and surmise that it imprints these physical characteristics as well as the behavioural memory and the conscious memory of the previous personality on the foetus at an impressionable stage of its development, and that these may become apparent a few years after birth and for a few years thereafter. It seems likely that these memories were never intended to happen, and when they do occur, they fade away as the soul and the new body become linked in a new close and interactive embrace. However, actual bodily defects cannot fade away in this way, so that a person born without fingers cannot subsequently grow them, since this kind of regeneration, which can take place in certain species, cannot occur in human beings.

I have spent some time on these birthmarks and birth defects because they are of importance to anyone who is trying to assess whether reincarnation is real or imagined. What of the other factors of the syndrome: 'announcing dreams', 'departing dreams', claimed behavioural memories including phobias and philias and behaviour inappropriate to a child's present existence, and claimed memories of a former life, including names of people and even details unknown to members of the earlier family? Those who oppose the idea of reincarnation seek to explain these in various ways.

It has been suggested that insufficient time has been given to investigating cases of alleged reincarnation; that there has been communication between the two families unknown to the investigators; that there has been insufficient anthropological study of the culture in which children make these claims; that in many cases too much time has elapsed before any investigation has been able to be made; and that while Professor Stevenson is a person of undoubted integrity, the investigators working for him have been biased in favour of reincarnation (Edwards, p.256ff.). It is alleged that parents, perhaps as a result of fantasies in their dreams, have brought up their children to believe that they have been born before in a previous existence, and encourage them to behave in a way consonant with these beliefs. Even so, this would hardly account for their knowledge of things that their previous parents did not know; and in any case a survey of Indian parents has shown that 41 per cent of parents discourage their children from believing that they have had a previous existence, perhaps frightened that this might lead to their losing them to their claimed former parents.

It is alleged that children may have made up accounts of their earlier lives for the sake of gain, since many who make such claims look back to a higher social status than their present one. In one case, Wilson has claimed that four such claimants 'look like four rather unpleasant little boys putting on a thinly disguised act to earn themselves better food and an exemption from drudgery' (Wilson, 1982, p.215). But what about others who have 'gone up in the world'?

Is it possible that knowledge about claimed earlier families are not the result of reincarnation, but the result of the subconscious construction of a previous personality from telepathic communication with members of these families? But in no case have the children concerned shown any signs of psychic behaviour other than their alleged memories of a previous life. Such a theory seems less credible than the hypothesis of reincarnation, and it cannot account for evidence from birthmarks and birth defects. Multiple personality seems unlikely in children so young, if only because at that age they would not have memories buried in the unconscious from which they could construct stories of an earlier existence.

Other difficulties remain. Why does one Druse boy claim an earlier life with detailed knowledge of people, while another claims the same earlier life with only sketchy knowledge about it (Stemman, p.191)? There must be telepathy and/or fantasy at work in at least one of the boys. Why do alleged memories of reincarnation usually occur in cultures where there is already widespread acceptance of reincarnation? Is it really sufficient to explain this by positing that in other cultures such memories in childhood are suppressed by parents, or that there is a tendency to remember the dead more than in our Western cultures, or that the closer bonds within the family in Eastern countries result in the retention of family memories, or that a different sense of temporality, gives more space for reflection and memories (Stevenson, 1987, p.165ff.)?

Why are there more memories among boys than girls? It has been suggested that they would be more likely to suffer violent deaths than girls, and that former lives are more likely to be remembered by those whose lives had been blighted by the trauma of a violent death; but it may be doubted whether this is a sufficient explanation. Again, why do only a few claim memories of an earlier existence? It may be that, if reincarnation does take place, we are not meant to remember a previous existence, and those who do are suffering from some fault which corrects itself as they grow older. It must be remembered that it is not necessary for those who do believe in reincarnation to hold that this happens to everyone.

These are difficulties to be faced by those who believe in reincarnation; but it must be emphasised that they are not decisive for withholding belief in the same way as we noted near the beginning of this chapter that the idea of reincarnation itself, although it may seem in some ways improbable, is not impossible. This chapter is not intended to sway the reader one way or the other; it is intended to demonstrate that the idea of reincarnation is worthy of further consideration and that evidence that claims to favour it deserves far more attention than is at present given to it.

Perhaps I may add a personal word at the conclusion of this chapter. Although I am inclined to accept reincarnation, it is of little importance to me whether we are reincarnated or not. Jesus taught his disciples to pray, 'Thy kingdom come on earth as in heaven', and our prime duty (as I understand it) is to live in this world according to God's will so as to fit ourselves to be with him in heaven. We are intended neither to look back to the past nor to look forward to the future, but to live in the present, and the 'sacrament of the present moment' provides us with all the grace we need to live according to the will of God (de Caussade, p.33). It is the present that matters. Reincarnation is important for our search for the truth about life, not for living it.

I turn next to an interview with the only person, to my knowledge, who has researched deeply into this subject and therefore has earned a right to be heard.

Chapter IX

QUESTIONS TO A PROFESSOR OF PSYCHIATRY

Professor Stevenson of the University of Virginia has written widely on reincarnation, and has done extensive field work in various parts of the world, concentrating on young children with memories of former lives. He is widely respected for his academic approach to the subject.

ME: First, I'd like to thank you very much for coming and talking with me while you are over here. I suppose you are in England looking at some alleged cases of reincarnation?

STEVENSON: Yes, that's right. There are two in particular I'm going to study. One I studied several years ago and the other one has been studied by a young colleague of mine, and I've not actually met the people concerned myself. I am writing a book on European cases.

ME: Yes, you promised a book some time ago about that, didn't you?

STEVENSON: Well, my books are always promised! It is finally going to come, I hope.

ME: What aroused your interest in the subject of reincarnation? Was it mental disorder, or your medical interest, or interest in the paranormal, or what? Originally, I mean. I know you've been in this field a long time.

STEVENSON: Yes, I have. There were two phases to my interest. My mother was very interested in Asian religions and in theosophy, which is a kind of Buddhism, and I grew up with a very extensive library that she had assembled on these topics.

ME: Madam Blavatsky and that sort of thing?

STEVENSON: That's right, yes. My mother was too independent ever to become a full adherent of any of those groups, but she had a keen interest in them. Then my interest lapsed, or at least went into the background, until after I'd finished my training in medicine and psychiatry. I became dissatisfied with current theories of personality. I didn't think that psychoanalysis or behaviourism or neuroscience answered all the questions that I had about differences between people. So that reanimated my interest in looking into paranormal phenomena, particularly cases suggestive of rebirth.

ME: Thank you. Now, I want to ask you, since you accept reincarnation, whether you see it as a blind phenomenon, or is there a purpose behind it? Do you see evidence of a Creator who produced it? It presumably doesn't just happen that people are reincarnated. Or are you agnostic about this? Are you just examining the phenomena?

STEVENSON: I think that probably at this stage I couldn't say more than that I examine the phenomena. But I do brood about ulterior meanings and where they might lead without any satisfactory or even tentative conclusion that I can communicate about it. I suppose I think of ourselves as being here in some sort of school, elementary school, to learn, to profit, to improve; and I think that if we are evolving, then possibly God is evolving, maybe experimenting with us.

ME: Yes, I know there are people who hold those views. Do you think that, if reincarnation really exists, dead people choose a foetus to which, as it were, to join themselves, or do you think it's chosen for them? I know there are 'announcing dreams' and 'departing dreams' which suggest that they might choose their foetus; but do you suggest that, if they do choose their foetus, they have a particular knowledge of which one will genetically suit them?

STEVENSON: There are some cases in which that claim is made, notably among tribes in north-west North America and also among the Tibetans. Both these groups sometimes select parents *ante mortem*. In the tribes of north-west North America, for example, an older man or woman who sees death approaching will go down the list of family members because there they believe they must come back in the same family. He or she rejects so-and-so because she's an alcoholic and rejects another one who hasn't really cared well for children, and selects, say, Susan, and says, 'Susan, I'm going to come back with you.'

ME: But that suggests, doesn't it, that a reincarnate person can affect a foetus that has a different genetic inheritance? Or if it didn't affect it, then there wouldn't be any continuity of any kind. I find that puzzling, and I wonder if you had thought about that, whether it's possible.

STEVENSON: I don't think that at that stage it is affecting the foetus. I think such a person has to take what foetus is available in their family, if they choose their family. I do think that sometimes the foetus can be affected, and then we get into the subject of birthmarks.

ME: Yes, but what continuity is there? I know there seem to be behavioural memories sometimes, as well as memories of families and so on. After all, our genetic make-up does determine, or at any rate has the potentiality of determining, our character. If there's no continuity of memory and if there's no continuity of body, and if they had chosen a foetus different from themselves, where lies the continuity?

STEVENSON: Much of the continuity might be subconscious; the form of an individuality that would be capable of developing some capacity if it took the trouble. As I mention in one of my books, I can speak French and German pretty well; at one time I used to speak Spanish as well, but I've let it go. I don't have that much need for it, but it remains, I think, part of my individuality, so that if I were to die and be reborn, and take up Spanish again, I think I would be a bit ahead than would be the case if I had never touched Spanish.

ME: Yes, I can see that, but I should have thought that there would be differences of character between the two persons, in the former life and in the later life. As for those differences of character, although they are not entirely caused by genetic factors, genetic factors do enter into them. And I'm puzzled where the continuity lies. I can see that there would be latent potentialities from a former life, but differences of character seem to me a little more difficult.

STEVENSON: Well, I don't think that the main essentials of our character are genetically based. I just don't believe that. Our physical form and our resistance to diseases have a strong genetical factor, but I'm doubtful about character. Of course, if you have a disabled brain, then that's bound to affect your ability to say whatever you wish to say. But I don't think that character is genetic.

ME: One of the things that puzzles me is how a person who has died exists before reincarnation. I mean, do you think of a bare soul, a kind of ground of being, or an astral body that is affected by the previous physical body to which it belonged, or again, is this an area about which you really don't want to say anything?

STEVENSON: Well, I don't think we can avoid saying something about it. Some of the subjects whose cases we have studied say something about another existence between death and presumably rebirth in some other plane of existence. And some of them recount events that they have observed in the family they have left.

ME: I can see that observations might be made, but that suggests a purely passive kind of existence.

STEVENSON: Yes, it does. Two at least, or three I've studied, claim to have intervened in terrestrial life, sort of like a discarnate poltergeist. That suggests that they have some powers and are not merely passive.

ME: How do you picture the continuity of the person or personality – or whatever you may call it – from one life to another? There isn't always continuity of memory, and never of body: we saw there might be latent potentialities, for example, of a reincarnated person learning Spanish, but where do you find the continuity? Simply in such memories as there are, including behavioural memories?

STEVENSON: Yes, I think so. There is continuity there of the emotions and the passions, the personal attractions. The children, for example, say, 'You are not my real mother. I want to go to my real mother, and she's in X village, take me there.' This is nostalgia. And then there's also the sense of incompleteness of events in which the deceased participated. A child of that type may say, 'Who's feeding my babies? Who's looking after my children? It's five o'clock, they'll be coming home from school and I've got to feed them.' And when it's a case of murder, there are often great feelings of vengeance: 'I'm going to kill them. I may be small now, but wait till I'm grown up.' There's a great deal of continuity in the affective dimension.

ME: I suppose it's not necessary to hold, if you believe in reincarnation, that everyone is reincarnated. A lot of cases that you have recorded say that they have suffered violent deaths, often of young people, whose lives have been cut short. In any case, there's the 'population problem' if everyone is re-incarnated. Presumably there's no reason, if you accept reincarnation, why everyone should be?

STEVENSON: No. I have nothing to say about that, really. Although I must just mention that a young epidemiologist at John Hopkins University, who was at the University of Virginia recently, gave a paper in which he showed that the so-called population explosion is not in fact an argument against reincarnation. I am encouraging him to publish his paper.

ME: I hope he will, because it would seem to be important, at first sight. Would you say that there is a sense in which a person begins all over again at rebirth? That the wisdom which we might hope to achieve after many years in this personality, that all that is lost? You did say that there was a latent potentiality. But most of us feel that we are a little wiser than when we were born and it seems to me that at rebirth you would almost start all over again with the innocence of youth and you would have to learn your way around all over again.

STEVENSON: It certainly seems to be true in my case. I can look back on my childhood and find aspects of it that I now find odious! I don't understand how I became what I am now, or think I am. On the other hand, there are children who show a remarkable precocity towards violence and crime and stealing that corresponds to previous behaviour, and equally remarkable and equally numerous are young children who are precociously generous and affectionate, as if they were born that way. And they often remember – they are mostly women, young girls, but some men too – they remember the lives of elderly women who were unusually generous and pious. So there is a continuity in some cases.

ME: Now, here is something that puzzles me that I would like to ask you. If memory and consciousness are not dependent on the physical brain, how are they transmitted from one life to another? Is it through a kind of astral body, with our brain communicating to an astral body, and then the astral body communicating to the new brain after rebirth; or in some other way? It's puzzling.

STEVENSON: It is puzzling, and, of course, one can do no more than offer the most tentative of conjectures; but I think there must be some kind of vehicle which I have called the *psychophore* – that's just the Greek for 'soul-bearing'. I got that with the guidance of one of our classicists because I didn't want to be associated with the idea of an astral body, much popularised, I think, with immature ideas about *karma* and New Age doctrines.

ME: Yes, but nonetheless, what you're thinking of as a *psychophore* is some kind of spiritual entity which somehow bears the imprint of the physical body and then communicates it to the next physical body.

STEVENSON: I think so, yes. Some of that goes back even to St Paul who talked about the physical body and the spirit body.

ME: Yes, I used the phrase astral body as shorthand. I don't want to press you to that particular phrase because of all its connotations. Now, I want to ask you whether you think that hypnosis can give us any genuine memories of earlier lives, or whether you think that it is more likely to be the unconscious making it up out of memories of what has been read in the past. I refer to what we know over here as the Bloxham Tapes, and to the famous Bridey Murphy case. Are you suspicious about these?

STEVENSON: Yes, I am. Most of them are worthless, absolutely worthless. There are a few cases – I refer to a couple of cases I've studied which include the feature of speaking a foreign language.

ME: That's not uncommon, is it?

STEVENSON: Yes, it *is* uncommon. I mean a true foreign language, not just 'speaking in tongues'. Most of what comes out under hypnosis comes from fantasies, or is based on forgotten knowledge.

ME: How about people who remember as adults, not as children? I mean people, for instance, like Guirdham, the psychoanalyst. Someone came to see him – who had memories of being a Cathar – and he decided he had been a Cathar himself together with four or five other people – this was an adult – are you suspicious of those?

STEVENSON: Yes, I am, because I think those persons can be loaded with information it is very difficult to exclude. That's why I prefer the cases of young children.

ME: I can understand that. Well, now, obviously you wouldn't be in such a controversial field unless you had critics. It seems to me that many of your critics were associated with you in your early days, in the 1970s and so on. And now things may well be somewhat different. For instance, you had an assistant called Ransom once: he had a lot of negative critiques to make. I daresay you've answered them.

STEVENSON: He made his criticisms and I replied to them. That was just private between us. And then he asked me if I objected to his showing them to others; and I said no. The only condition I made was that he should also show my reply. But he didn't do that. He disappointed me in that.

ME: It must be very difficult when you are in a foreign country to ensure that there's no communication between the family in an alleged former life and the family of the person now living. And it must take a lot of time to make a proper examination of the case. I know you publish very clearly what you've done; but do you feel sure that your safeguards are sufficient to prevent fraud and to detect fantasy? I mean, there is always the danger of fraud, and people's memories are sometimes – how shall I put it? – affected by their culture.

STEVENSON: Yes. I was never more than ninety per cent certain that something may have escaped me. I did publish with colleagues seven cases in which I had detected fraud or self-deception on the part of the informants. I have tried to check what one informant said against what another said. Frequently, we've brought in to interview not just members of the family, but perhaps the local monk or schoolteachers or the headman of the village and tried to get an appraisal of the value of the testimony of the main informants. I should think that on the whole we've done pretty well in that. I've been lucky often to have had with me the same interpreters, and they get to know the subject well and they get to know me and my methods.

ME: But then some of your interpreters strongly believe in reincarnation. I am thinking of Dr Prasad.

STEVENSON: They all would be, one way or another.

ME: But you trust them?

STEVENSON: I do; yes, I do. U Win Maung in Burma, for example, was one of them: he figures in my book on Burma.

ME: Then I think you hired a chap called Barker, didn't you?

STEVENSON: Yes.

ME: And he said that the cases were more due to Indian culture than evidence of reincarnation. There again, you were able to answer that, I presume?

STEVENSON: I think so, yes. Barker didn't have much experience with the cases. He was a disappointment to me in the field. He didn't take many notes. He took a sort of anthropologist's perspective of the cases.

ME: Here's a rather different sort of question. Do you think it possible that some cases of reincarnation are really cases of possession?

STEVENSON: Yes, we have several cases – I've published two and I'm going to publish another three – in which the subject was born before the person he remembered had died. In one case, the interval was three years, in another seventeen years, and in another case about two days. Those are cases of apparent possession: one presumes there was a tenant who was extruded in some way and the body was taken over by another personality. Those are cases of apparent possession.

ME: Why do you think it is that memories fade in young children? They start at two and go on usually until five or six, exceptionally until later. It's been said by critics that they get tired of telling their story all over again, which seems to me rather feeble. But there must be a reason why memories fade.

STEVENSON: Yes, but the reason may be the same as the reason why we forget memories of our infancy and early childhood. I can remember very little of my own life before the age of six. Some people say they remember nothing. I think the memories of early childhood become covered. The first five years of life in Asia are largely undemanding ones in which the mother in a sense is sovereign, and she gives a lot of attention to the child and shields it from experiences that may be difficult for it; and then, at four or five, the child usually does go out, if not to school at least out into the village and there it will encounter other persons and will be required to adapt to a different social situation. I think that the memories of all these events may simply become layered on top of the earlier memories. Behavioural memories often persist after the imaged memories have gone.

ME. Why do you think it is that so few people have memories of earlier lives? Do you think it's because they haven't had previous lives?

STEVENSON: The memory of previous lives may well be a defect. It's not necessarily a gift. The children are often in a state of considerable turmoil, with a sense of being loyal to two different families, a feeling of being isolated and different, a stranger in their own family. I don't think it's a gift at all.

ME: When you say it's a defect, what do you mean?

STEVENSON: The deceased person might not have drunk sufficiently of the waters of Lethe. Maybe we have to go back to Plato for that.

ME: Yes, but it was a myth in Plato, wasn't it? Presumably, if it's a defect, then something's gone wrong in the transfer of memories in what you call the *psychophore*.

STEVENSON: Right. But when the death is violent, then that barrier may be broken by the intensity of the emotions.

ME: Now, I'm going to ask what I'm sure you expect me to ask: why is it that the greater proportion of these memories occur in cultures where reincarnation is commonly believed? I can't believe that it is because our culture is against it and so our children are not allowed to speak of their memories, because children nowadays are encouraged to speak about things they used to be very quiet about – child abuse and suchlike. It seems to me more likely to be some other reason.

STEVENSON: I quite agree: I think that that's a superficial explanation. Indeed, in India, 40 per cent of parents actually suppress their children's memories of a former life. It must be something else that accounts for it. There are many, many cases among the Druses in Lebanon.

ME: They believe in reincarnation, don't they?

STEVENSON: They do. But when you go into a Christian village, or into a mixed village with Christians and Druses, the Christians just think you are engaged in some ridiculous enterprise. It's all nonsense from their perspective. It's possible that there's a genetic factor there that allows the memories to escape repression.

ME: I believe you've collected some 120 cases in the

USA and also some cases in England. Some are very suspect, like the Ryall case. And there's the Pollock twins. You're quite convinced about them, aren't you?

STEVENSON: Yes, I am; but as for Ryall's case, I remain baffled by it because, after he died, we tried to search out records and we didn't find a single member of his family identified anywhere and yet he had an amazing richness of detail, not just about major events, but also lesser details about which he was quite accurate.

ME: I suppose it is possible that there was some kind of telepathic communication with people who knew the facts.

STEVENSON: I suppose so; but he didn't show any signs of that. He did read rather widely. Even so, I do not understand how he developed such a large store of accurate knowledge about often obscure details of life in seventeenth-century England.

ME: One of your most interesting finds concerns birth defects and birthmarks. I don't know why they move or disappear. I would like to ask you what kind of mechanism could possibly reproduce them. Again, I suppose you will say it's the *psychophore*, but that only suggests to me that you don't know!

STEVENSON: Well, that's right, we don't know. I don't claim that we do. The movement of birthmarks, however, with the growth of the child, is understandable, because of the changes in the proportions of the different parts of the body as we grow from infancy to adulthood.

ME: All you claim is the fact?

STEVENSON: Yes, that's right.

ME: Why do you think that people are unwilling in our culture to envisage the possibility of reincarnation?

STEVENSON: First of all, some 20 to 30 per cent in some countries – of Westerners do believe in reincarnation. One of my French friends says it's 25 per cent in France now. But that's beside the point. The percentage of people among scientists who attach any importance to it is negligible – perhaps 3 or 4 per cent – and that is largely because of personal experience, not because of some research report that they've read. But then a lot of them are ignorant of the subject. They've never even bothered to look at what evidence is available. In the end, I think it comes down to this: paranormal phenomena are subversive of current materialism and the idea that personality is merely a function of the brain. The neuroscientists have a hegemony now, and any form of dualism is very much frowned upon.

ME: But even so, the vast majority in this country don't take warmly to the idea. Do you think that it's because of materialism and, of course, the inherited Christian tradition against it?

STEVENSON: Yes, I think that the Christian churches are very chary of paranormal phenomena in general, even among their saints and other gifted people.

ME: Tell me, is there anything else you would like to tell me, now that we have had the opportunity to speak?

STEVENSON: The important development, I think, in recent years, is that I have finally persuaded some colleagues to look at these cases independently. For about thirty years, the research was entirely in my hands or with my assistants whom I recruited in different parts of the world. Beginning about ten years ago, I was able to interest some other investigators and they have published various reports. This isn't ideal, because so far they are all my friends and they were to a great extent funded out of resources made available to me. So I'm still looking for other investigators who would be totally independent.

ME: Good. It is extraordinary to me that no one else but yourself has attempted an academic investigation into these cases.

STEVENSON: But you have to remember that they have been very little known; my books have not been widely reviewed. My last monograph, a two-volume monograph, on birthmarks and birth defects, has been totally ignored by the conventional journals.

ME: Professor Stevenson, thank you very much indeed. I know you don't often give interviews, and I am really indebted to you for speaking with me.

STEVENSON: It was a pleasure to talk with you because, unlike many people who wish to interview me, you have taken the trouble to inform yourself about what I have been doing.

PART THREE
The Paranormal and Christianity

Chapter X
CHRISTIAN VISIONS

So far, I have considered paranormal experiences that concern religions in general. In the closing three chapters, I shall look at aspects of the paranormal in connection with the Christian faith in particular. I daresay, if I was knowledgeable enough, I could also write about these aspects in other faiths; but I can write only about that with which I am familiar. I begin with Christian visions. Obviously, they are hallucinatory. But is that all that can be said?

Hallucination is the apparent perception of an external object not actually present. It is not an uncommon phenomenon, and it may be caused for a variety of reasons, some of them psychological. For example, a person who has been recently bereaved may have a hallucination of his or her dead spouse. This recently happened to a close relative of mine. Hallucinations may also accompany certain mental disorders. A person in extreme physical conditions (for instance, alone and cold on the Arctic ice cap) may easily hallucinate.

Some people have religious visions. Some of these are hallucinations caused for the reasons mentioned above. It would be generally agreed that some religious visions are mere hallucinations. Materialists would say that all religious visions are of this kind. But such a view is open to question. Well-balanced people may have them. Religious visions happen to people who are not living in extreme conditions, nor mourning the death of a loved one. The possibility must be investigated that these visions are genuinely religious and even divinely inspired.

Most worshippers are aware of the numinous to a greater or lesser extent when they worship, and they feel the spiritual presence of Christ. But a visionary experience is different: it suggests physical presence. In the past, many have had a vision of Christ; to mention a few of the better known, Gregory the Great, Francis of Assisi, Teresa of Avila, Lady Julian of Norwich, and Ignatius Loyola. It is perhaps not surprising that religious visions have been experienced more frequently by monks and nuns, since there are thousands of such men and women in the religious orders of the Roman Catholic and Orthodox Churches; and, in the contemplative orders, lives are wholly given over to the service of God in worship and contemplation. However, a sceptic might say that this makes the religious all the more prone to imagining spiritual realities and hallucinating about them. Religious visions appear to have been experienced more by women than by men, but that says nothing whatsoever about their authenticity, although it may conceivably be connected with the cerebral differences between men and women. Visions have also been claimed by children, for example, at Fatima and Medjugorje. In writing about visions, Karl Rahner has pointed out that between 1945 and 1952 no less than two thousand cases of alleged miraculous visions were investigated by the Roman Catholic church, and in Western Europe between 1930 and 1950 the Church investigated thirty cases of alleged apparitions of the Virgin Mary, and about 300 cases of individual apparitions to children, both girls and boys (Rahner, p.8). So religious visions are claimed in the present as much as in the past.

Roman Catholic Views on Religious Visions

The Roman Catholic Church has always shown a certain reserve about such apparitions. In recent decades, only three of many visions have been officially recognised as authentic: two in Belgium, at Banneaux and at Beauraing, and at Fatima. Rahner has listed twenty-seven places, 'scenes of alleged apparitions', where during the last two decades before his book was published in 1963, the Roman Catholic Church had actually condemned apparitions or refrained from approving them. Medjugorje in what used to be Yugoslavia should be added to them.

Furthermore, it is not incumbent upon any Roman Catholic to accept any vision as genuine. In 1877, in *Acta Apostolicae Sedis*, it was declared that 'the Holy See has neither approved nor condemned such apparitions or revelations but merely permits Catholics to believe in them – where they have the support of credible witnesses and documents – with a purely human faith'. Even the institution of the Feast of the Apparition at Lourdes does not conflict with this liberty. As Benedict XIV wrote:

> Without prejudice to the integrity of the Catholic faith a person may withhold his consent from such revelations provided he does so with due modesty, and not without reasons.
>
> Rahner, p.12

Visions fall into three categories – corporeal, imaginative and purely spiritual.

These categories need some explanation. Spiritual visions are imageless, and so it is impossible to communicate them to others. There can, therefore, be no external criteria for their authenticity. They belong to the *via negativa* tradition in mystical theology, and so it is hardly surprising that St John of the Cross, who wrote about his experience of mystical union with God, should have thought that intellectual visions are the only kind of vision worthy of credit. But, as Evelyn Underhill remarked, since these are imageless, it is hard to regard them as visions (Underhill, p.338).

Corporeal visions are not, strictly speaking, visions: they are bodily appearances of the dead. According to traditional theology, the appearances of the risen Christ to his Apostles after his resurrection were of this kind. This type of vision is, of course, claimed by some mediums (see p.48), but Rahner was thinking of religious visions when he wrote:

> The possibility of corporeal visions (even apart from the 'apparitions' of the risen Christ to the Apostles) can hardly be disputed; but conclusive proof of such an occurrence will rarely be possible in a concrete case.

The reason for this is that it is difficult to distinguish corporeal visions from imaginative visions, which may also include speech, movement and even touch.

The word 'imaginative' is used of the third category of

religious visions, not because they are to be regarded merely as the work of the imagination, like the hallucination of a mentally disordered person: they are the work of God impacting on the visual cortex of the brain, so that the image of a person who is truly present in the spiritual sense may be acknowledged by the senses. They are to be distinguished from other visions of this kind in as much as they are to be regarded as sent by God. Although in dreams people can speak, move and be touched, an imaginative vision should be differentiated from visions that occur in dreams when people are asleep, (although dreams also may be a channel of communication (see p.34)).

Imaginative visions are usually acknowledged to be the most important. St Teresa of Avila, the recipient of many visions of Christ, held that all hers were imaginative, which is hardly surprising since she believed that (apart from Christ's appearances to St Paul) Christ had not left heaven since his Ascension. Visions used to be believed to take place through the agency of angels; in other words, not directly through the agency of God. Although today most would doubt the work of angels as intermediaries, they would want to agree that God does not effect visionary experiences by direct agency and that they are mediated by some mode unknown to us. It is likely that this mode is not so much supernatural as paranormal, the more so because it is not always easy to distinguish imaginative visions from other kinds of paranormal experiences. The vision of St Teresa on 26 June 1570 is a case in point. Rahner comments on this:

> She saw the martyrdom of 40 Brazilian martyrs at the very moment when it happened. The process was so like profane clairvoyance that this latter must be presumed to be the proximate cause, the more so as a relative of St Teresa was among the martyrs.
>
> Rahner, p.38

More than one person may be the recipient of an imaginative vision, and some may hear or see what others cannot. (The various accounts of the conversion of St Paul illustrate this.) Rahner compared this phenomenon with what can happen in a mass hypnosis, indicating that there may well be an element of suggestion when crowds are eagerly awaiting a new revelation, as must have been the case when expectant crowds saw the sun rushing towards them at Fatima.

This small town in the middle of Portugal has become famous as a place of pilgrimage to the Shrine of Our Lady of Fatima. On 13 May 1917, three illiterate children between the ages of ten and thirteen saw a vision of a lady who reappeared on five subsequent occasions, and on the last occasion she revealed herself as 'Our Lady of the Rosary'. Francisco did not even see the lips of the apparition moving: Luci and Jacinta did not seem to have heard the same words. The apparitions disappeared piecemeal: the head, followed by the trunk, and then the feet.

Since God's grace works through natural events, can he not also work through paranormal events, so that God's use of man's paranormal faculties may be claimed as channels of divine revelation? This can happen with religious visions, which are clearly hallucinatory, such as a vision of the infant Christ. It can be a channel of divine grace, even though Christ himself is obviously no longer an infant. In the same way, it is possible to have imaginative visions of the various scenes of Christ's passion, as many saints have experienced. It is to be noted that all these visions have a subjective aspect. In them, Christ would have both a traditional visual appearance and would be clothed in the style in which he was customarily pictured at the time of the vision.

If this be granted, then it becomes possible to accept the authenticity of such a vision as that at Fatima and at the same time to hold that the 'sun miracle' was caused by mass expectation of a miracle, and to believe that the words that were heard were influenced by the psychic structure and cultural framework of the world in which the recipients lived. (This would enable Anglicans, who do not use the rosary or commit themselves to the Sacred Heart of Mary (as commanded by the Fatima disclosure) nonetheless to regard the occasion as a channel of divine grace.) The divine influence operates at a very deep level of the personality, but it functions within the personality, stimulating the visual cortex, and so it is bound to include a subjective element because it passes into consciousness through the human brain. Rahner wrote:

> For a vision to be truly the spiritual reality of a given person, it must be, metaphysically speaking, the true act of this person, not only an act produced in him by God, but also an act really performed by the person himself. This is to say that the act must express the laws of the person's ontological structure, because otherwise there would be no vision at all.
>
> ...the content of the imaginative vision – although the varying proportions of the different elements will be very difficult to determine in any concrete case – will inevitably represent the joint effect of divine influence plus the subjective dispositions of the visionary.
>
> Rahner, p.43

He admitted that:

> Even in the case of canonised Saints and Beati – that is, of people whose honesty, great sanctity and true mystical experience is beyond dispute – they can exhibit an abundance of errors and distortions, historical, theological and aesthetic.
>
> Rahner, p.64

One of the reasons why Roman Catholics have always exercised extreme caution over visions is their belief that some of them may be caused by the agency of evil spirits or by mental illness. Today, such visions would be more likely to be regarded as hallucinations caused by emotions and attitudes that have been repressed from consciousness. On the other hand, if we posit the existence of discarnate spirits, some could be evil in character, just as some people are evil. This leaves open the possibility of evil spirits as the cause of some visionary experiences.

The Churches of the Reformation and Religious Visions

'The Bible and the Bible only is the religion of Protestants.' While this well-known quotation is not entirely true, it is certainly the case that Reformed Churches make their primary appeal to the

Scriptures, and therefore they tend to be intellectual in outlook. They are therefore inclined to look askance at any kind of alleged revelation, whether public or private, that takes the form of visual images and that has no direct contact with the Scriptures. According to *The Encyclopaedia of the Lutheran Church*, 'The Reformation accorded no value to post-biblical visions... It should be noted that the appearances of the risen Christ are never described in the New Testament as visions. They are in a class by themselves.' Generally speaking, in Reformed theology, there is no systematic treatment of visions. There is reticence, caution, even suspicion about the subject.

Luther himself applied a threefold distinction to visions, but, unlike those of Augustine, his were biblically based – dreams, apparitions and face-to-face speech. Calvin likewise viewed visions with suspicion. He noted that the Lord himself does not appear in visions, but he did not rule out the possibility that angels might visit us and confirm the truth.

> How shall we know true visions of angels from false, true apparitions and miracles from counterfeit, but by the Scripture of God which is the rule and true measure by which we must try all things?
>
> Calvin, 7.31

Contemporary Visions of Jesus

Down the centuries, many people report having been given visions of Jesus. This applies both to ordinary laymen and women as well as to the greatest Christian saints. It must not be thought that these visions have been confined to Catholics. William Booth could hardly be counted in that camp, but he was vouchsafed a vision of Christ.

We need not doubt that people have been telling the truth when they report that they have had a vision of Christ. But the vision is unprovable, if it was not shared by others with the recipient, and it is difficult to assess if the person who claimed the vision is long dead. She or he is not available for questioning, and it is therefore hard to judge whether the vision is to be accepted as genuine, or regarded as the effect of some physical or mental dysfunction. There is insufficient material to judge whether the vision was entirely subjective, a symptom of stress or some related disorder, or the result of divine grace. For this reason, contemporary visions, in which the recipient is available for questioning, are more open to investigation. A few years ago, Professor Wiebe, to whom I am greatly indebted in this chapter, placed advertisements in his native Canada, and in Great Britain and Australia, soliciting evidence of visions of the risen Christ. He has given an account of thirty 'contemporary Christic visions and apparitions' as a result of interviews which he conducted with the recipients between 1988 and 1993:

> I do not know whether any of them would accept the designation 'visionary', for most were quite mystified by having such an experience, and none is in monastic life, although some are very active in their religious communities. None of them, moreover, seems to have deliberately induced the visionary experience(s), and most appear to think of them as quite ordinary. All of them were quite committed in their faith, although a number intimated that this commitment has fluctuated in their lives, even after the visionary experience(s)... I realise that the group of cases I have assembled is neither large nor randomly selected, and a study of this kind should be regarded as only exploratory. Quite a number of the percipients live in my home province of British Columbia and the fact that I found as many as I did living near me suggests that many more such experiences have never been documented.
>
> Wiebe, p.40ff.

Wiebe grouped these experiences into five categories. In the first group were people who fell into trancelike states. In the second group, the percipients were aware of a significant change in their physical environment. In the third group, their physical environment seemed to the percipients to be as they knew it to be, except for the visionary figure in it. In the fourth category, a visionary experience affected more than one percipient simultaneously, and in the fifth, there was a vision of some event in the life of Christ.

Wiebe's list of visionaries includes both men and women. They are predominantly lay. All of them had had some experience of Christianity, even if this was only in childhood and later rejected. Most of the visions, but not all of them, took place in response to spiritual needs. All resulted in increased Christian commitment. The fifth group (where there is a vision of some scene from Christ's life) is not uncommon among mystics, and so I defer consideration of it until the next chapter. To give a flavour of Wiebe's account of these contemporary visions of Christ, I shall give an excerpt from the account by one person from each of the other four categories, although to form a proper judgement the whole accounts should be read in Wiebe's book.

Trance and Dreamlike Experiences

The instance cited below is the only occasion when powers of evil appeared in visions of Jesus recounted to Wiebe. John Wheeler was thirty-six and he had only occasionally attended worship. Both he and his wife had indulged in occult practices earlier in their lives. His wife became a Christian as a result of a neighbour's influence, which annoyed her husband. Trying to go to sleep one night, he had what he described as a battle with an evil spirit, which he unsuccessfully tried to fight off. Just to his right stood a man in a brown robe with a sash. Robin could not see his face, but he considered him to have been Jesus. He tried to tie up the monster with Jesus's sash, but failed. Jesus reappeared and this happened several times.

> His wife was with him while this struggle was taking place. She told me that he levitated for long periods of the time that coincided with his troubles, and seemed to go in and out of consciousness. She says Robin floated in mid-air about a foot above the bed. His body was in a perfectly rigid position, and all the veins in his body were bulging. His head was bent so far back, she said, that she thought it would break. Although she could not see the figures which appeared to him, she could ask him what was happening, and he could describe the events taking place. She estimates that the various struggles occurred over a six-hour period, but he had no sense of the passing of time. When a fight sequence came to an end, he would drop back onto the bed and would relax until a new struggle began. During the struggle he could see his wife as well as two other beings, and they seemed as real as ordinary persons. The place he seemed to be in did not

accord with the physical description of the bedroom. However, Jesus would appear in Roman sandals with his feet first, as though he had descended from above. The struggle finally ended when Robin found that his struggles to tie up the monster did not succeed, and he requested help from Jesus who bound the monster for him.

p.44ff.

The vision could be described as a pictorialisation of the battle going on in Robin's soul, giving rise to vivid hallucinations. The presence of paranormal phenomena, attested to by his wife (but by no one else), suggests that this is not the whole answer. Levitation is a phenomenon occasionally associated with visionary experiences. The apparitions suggest an imaginative vision into which subjective elements have been intruded. The couple's previous dallying with occultism has certainly affected the form of the vision; but it may have laid Robin open to the spiritual forces of evil that manifested themselves in the form of evil creatures. The presence of Jesus in a brown robe and wearing Roman sandals suggests that he appeared in the kind of clothes in which Robin would have imagined him.

Cases of an Altered Environment

Marion Gallife told Professor Wiebe of extraordinary events that had happened to her two years earlier. She had been devastated by the death of her son, Joel. One afternoon, her anger overflowed and she complained bitterly to God. She fell asleep, and at about 9 p.m. she woke up, feeling that she must go downstairs for a Bible reading with her family. As she opened the Bible, she sensed that she must stand up, and they all did. The back door flew open and a gust of wind moved through the room.

A painful sensation creased Marion's chest, and she wondered aloud how much pain she would have to bear. Then a light brighter than she had ever seen exploded upon her and filled the room. The light gradually faded and a man dressed in white came into view. It was Jesus. He appeared to be transparent rather than solid, and his long hair caught her attention. She first saw his profile, and he turned to her, stretched out his hand and commanded her (so it seemed) to look down the length of his arm. As he did so, his body disappeared from sight until she could see only his hand. From the end of his hand a hill covered with green grass began to form. As her attention was directed towards the hill, she saw Joe running towards her with three other children. Joe was wearing his favourite chequered shirt, blue jeans, a jacket, and the belt with the big brass Harley Davidson buckle. She kept saying, 'Look at our Joe. Our Joe's coming.' But the command came to her, 'Look past Joe. Haven't you forgotten them? They are with me.' Then she realised who the smaller children were. One was her child from a pregnancy which had been terminated because of fibroids in her womb, and the two other children were twins she had lost because of the effect of the terminated pregnancy. The twins would have been fourteen if they had lived, and the other child sixteen, and the three children who appeared with Joe appeared to be these ages. Marion's sorrow turned to joy at the realisation who the children were. In response to encouragement from Joe, she began to sing in praise to God. Marion's husband did not see any of the things she reported, but he observed she was in an extraordinary ecstasy as these events unfolded.

p.50

After this vision, Marion's attitude towards her dead son changed – she knew he was alive. The story reads like a dream, but Marion was fully awake if in a seemingly ecstatic state. Her experience could be dismissed as purely hallucinatory, due to stress at the loss of her fourth child. But there are again some paranormal phenomena, for example, the ecstasy noted by her husband. The hill covered with green suggests comparison with some near-death experiences (see p.149). Joe's wearing of his favourite clothes (which she subsequently found lying in a drawer in his room) shows subjective input, unless he 'chose' to appear thus in order to facilitate recognition. The size of the other children also suggests subjective input, as they had died in infancy or as a foetus, and could not be expected to grow in their spirit body as they would have done if alive. If this is a genuine imaginative vision given by Christ in response to her spiritual distress, then we would expect it to contain subjective elements.

Private Experiences

Deby Stamm-Loya had had a difficult childhood and adolescence in Arizona, with mental and physical abuse. By thirteen she was a thief and compulsive runaway. She experimented with drugs, mostly LSD, which magnified or distorted her physical perceptions, but the images she saw were always of things that were actually there and not hallucinations. She experienced flashbacks, which filled her with feelings of dread and even of paralysis. She tired of this kind of life, acquired a Bible and began to read it a lot. One day, she sensed the presence of God, and surrendered to that presence. She became a Christian. One evening, after watching a movie, she felt a desire to know God better. She went to bed to think about this.

She lay on her back for some time with her eyes closed, thinking about these things, and when she opened them some minutes later a man she instantly identified with Jesus stood at the end of her bed some five or six feet away. His arms were stretched out as though he were reaching for her. He stood there for a moment, appearing much as he does in traditional portraits of him, and in a manner similar to that in which a normal man would appear, and then he began to change. A radiance enveloped him in pure white light that gradually increased in intensity. As this radiance intensified, it extended farther and farther beyond him, so that it finally consisted of pure white light nearest to him, and various shades of yellow, orange and amber beyond the whiteness. As this transformation took place, Deby became conscious of being drawn into the immense universe of which he seemed a part, and had the sense of being far removed from her parents' home. Then she lost natural consciousness and became aware only of his voice and the things that he said to her. In reflecting back on the experience, Deby says that the things that he said had the greatest significance to her. He told her that he had everything in the universe under his control, including her life, and that he had many things to teach her. He said that he loved her, and that she could keep her attention fixed on him. How long this experience lasted she does not know, for when she regained natural consciousness, she was lying in her bed, and it was morning. She firmly believes that she had not fallen asleep at the time when the vision (her term) began, because she does not fall asleep when lying on her back. Moreover, the bedroom door was open to the adjacent room, and she saw the figure standing at the end of her bed against the background of that room.

p.55ff.

Once again, this experience could be dismissed as a purely dreamlike experience, despite Deby's insistence on her wakefulness, the more so as there could have been, by the nature of the case, no witnesses other than herself. It could be said to be a response brought on by herself through her sense of need. On the other hand, it could be accepted as Christ acting through an imaginative vision to meet Deby's spiritual awakening and search. It could be said to have been influenced by Deby's experience with drugs, despite her emphasis that the difference between her earlier LSD experiences and this vision was 'like the difference between night and day'. She was not able to describe the figure in the vision in detail, but the fact that it was dressed as Jesus would have been traditionally pictured suggests some subjective input. The great light she saw and its whiteness are characteristic of a genuine vision. At the time, she did not know anyone else who had had a visionary experience of Christ. Whatever the nature of the vision, it certainly had a profound effect on Deby's future lifestyle.

Cases with Observable Effects

Here is a story that is so remarkable that it deserves to be told in full as Professor Wiebe has recorded it. Strange things are alleged to have happened in California, but this one seems to beggar belief.

Kenneth Logie's life had been marked by a number of extraordinary experiences. He had been minister of a Pentecost Holiness church in Oakland, California, for about forty years, and reports events that rival the New Testament in kind and number. Among these are various Christic encounters, including several claims of group experiences.

When Kenneth and his wife moved to Oakland, the church was not capable of fully supporting them financially, so he sold bread to supplement his income. His work meant that he was often late for the evening service, but the small congregation accepted that. He would begin his preaching a little later than usual when this happened. On a Sunday night in April 1954 he again arrived late and, as a result, was still preaching at 9.15, when he saw a shadow on the exterior glass doors, made by someone standing outside. He wondered who might be arriving so late in the evening. He reported that 'the door opened up, and Jesus started walking down the aisle, just as plain as you are'. He turned to the people on one side of the aisle, and then to the people on the other side of the aisle, smiling as he went. He walked up to the platform where Kenneth was preaching, but instead of walking around the pulpit, moved right through it. When he placed his left hand on Kenneth's shoulder, Kenneth collapsed to the floor. Jesus then knelt down alongside him, and spoke to him in another language. Kenneth responded in English, believing that he was interpreting what was being said to him. He says that this event was witnessed by the congregation of about fifty people present on that occasion.

Kenneth reported another incident which took place in May 1959 in the same church. A woman in the congregation described a vision she said she had when she was in hospital and was thought dead. Mrs Lucero reported that Jesus had appeared wearing the clerical robe of a Catholic priest. He told her to have faith in God. She explained that, because she was of a Catholic background, this apparel somehow assisted her in making the identification of the figure as Jesus.

Kenneth says that when Mrs Lucero got up to tell her story, she was wearing a black raincoat because the weather had been rainy that day. As she spoke, she disappeared from view, and in her place stood a figure taken to be Jesus. He wore sandals, a glistening white robe, and had nail prints in his hands – hands that dripped with oil. Kenneth reports that this figure was seen by virtually everyone in the congregation, which he estimated at two hundred people. He also reports that the figure was filmed (in colour) by a member of the congregation with the kind of eight-millimetre movie camera popular at the time. Kenneth said that the photographer was so awestruck that he placed the camera on top of the organ to keep it steady.

The appearance was much like Salman's *Head of Christ*. Kenneth said that the effect on the people in the church was electrifying. After several minutes Jesus disappeared and Mrs Lucero was visible again.

p.77

Professor Wiebe first heard this extraordinary story in 1965 from Kenneth Logie and his wife when he was an undergraduate, and saw the film, but did not think to investigate it further. But in 1991 he spoke to Kenneth again, by which time his first wife had died; and he spoke to four or five people who had been present at the incident in 1965, all of whom supported the account given above. He asked to see the film again, but was told that unfortunately it had been stolen from the apartment where Kenneth lived. He remembers in the film a figure which looked like the traditional image of Jesus with his glistening white robe and outstretched arm, but he cannot remember the full face; and while one person corroborated this, there were differences in the memories of others, as one might expect after a lapse of over a quarter of a century. At the time when Professor Wiebe saw the film in 1965, opinions differed about it. Some thought it was fraudulent; but it is unlikely that the sophisticated techniques of film enhancement had made much progress by 1965. The film, it was said, bore the marks of amateur photography.

It might seem strange that a person was in church with a home movie camera during a service of worship, but Kenneth explained to Wiebe that the church had been the scene of much paranormal activity, including healings, exorcism, prophecies, speaking in tongues and resuscitation. On one occasion, the church was said to have been bathed in visible but unconsuming fire, causing neighbours to call the fire brigade. Images such as crucifixes appeared on walls with liquid oil flowing from them, with fragrant aromas; and one person who had been sceptical about the film reported that he had seen this happen, and had examined the walls when the church was being rebuilt and could find no sign that the images had been contrived. In 1991, Kenneth showed Wiebe black and white pictures of these images, and photographs of the stigmata on his hands and a white cross on his forehead.

It seems likely that Kenneth himself was a person with psychic gifts and that through him (as is said to happen occasionally with a medium) the paranormal phenomena in the church occurred. What of the vision of Christ? Critics might well dismiss it as merely hallucinatory. There are aspects that are clearly subjective, such as the appearance of Christ. It almost surpasses belief that the film that showed him could have been 'lost'. If it had been stolen as alleged, to what purpose? One would have thought that a film about which such claims could be made, when its loss became known, would have caused a great furore. Professor Wiebe did not find many witnesses to events that had occurred thirty years previously, and one would want a search for more witnesses and verbatim statements by those before coming to any judgement about the nature of the vision. This is a tale that might contain an account of two genuinely imaginative visions of Christ; but without better evidence about phenomena that had happened so long before the witnesses described it, it cannot be accepted as hard evidence by any serious enquirer. More research is required on such tales.

The Physical Mechanisms Involved in Visions and Hallucinations

How is it possible for a person to see a vision that others cannot share? Even if it originates through divine initiative, it surely uses the same mechanisms as those that produce dreams or hallucinations, the difference being that an imaginative vision is divinely originated. Semir Zeki, Professor of Neurobiology at the University of London, is one of the foremost researchers into the visual cortex, and the discoverer of those areas of the brain that detect colour and motion. He admits:

> Dreams and hallucinations are not subjects which most neurobiologists would wish to concern themselves with. But any theory of integration must take them into account, for both consist of integrated visual images, with the difference that they are entirely centrally generated.
>
> Zeki, p.325

He has explained what happens when there is a visual hallucination as follows:

> These may be defined as perceptions in the absence of a visual stimulus. It is common to find that objects and people in a hallucinatory episode are somewhat distorted, being for example much

smaller (micropsia) or much larger (macropsia) than in real life. But otherwise their hallmark is that of a visually normal scene, indeed one that is commonly, though not always, reported as a pleasant one... They are commonly in vivid colours. Their normality is such that Aldous Huxley wrote, 'There can be no doubt that exactly those parts of (the) retina which would be affected by the image of a cat... or the portions of the sensorium with which those organs of sense are connected, were thrown into a corresponding state of activity by some internal cause.' Hallucinations, like dreams, are therefore *visually normal*.

The visual normality of dreams and hallucinations, their sense of reality, is so intense and compelling that all of us have experienced situations which we subsequently find difficult to ascribe to dreams or to reality. It is difficult not to conceive of them as internally generated images which are fed back into the cortex as if they were coming from outside. If this were so, one would naturally expect that the primary visual cortex might be involved, if only because in normal vision (to which dreams bear such a striking resemblance) the first cortical stage which the incoming signals enter is area VI (in the visual areas of the striate cortex). Indeed, evidence suggests that during dreaming there is a massive increase in cerebral blood flow not only in the visual areas of the pre-striate cortex, but also in the striate cortex itself.

Zeki, p.326

Presumably, it is not possible to discover whether there is also a massive increase in blood flow during hallucinations (or in visions), as these cannot be produced to order for scientific investigation. If this is the way that hallucinations take place, we may assume that it would be the same in visions, except that in genuine visions (including those that use psychic mechanisms) the apparition is not psychogenic, but divinely initiated.

Psychological Explanations of Visionary Experiences

So far in this chapter, it has been assumed that imaginative visions of Christ can indeed occur, being initiated by divine grace, and probably mediated in some paranormal way. But this is by no means generally accepted. Two other types of explanation have been given. One of these falls into the psychological or mental category, especially among those who equate the mind with the brain and who do not believe that people have souls. I am grateful to Wiebe for his systematic analysis of these theories, which I am following in the remainder of this chapter. It is necessary to examine these other explanations before one can be convinced that a vision of Christ is indeed authentic.

It has been suggested that apparitions, including religious apparitions, occur as a result of wish fulfilment (Murphy, 1945, p.2ff.). It is difficult to rebut such an argument, because no one can make a window into another person's unconscious, and so disprove such a theory. On the other hand, this explanation can be shown to be exceedingly improbable in some cases (and even one such case is sufficient to discredit the theory); certainly in my own, as I shall show later in this chapter. Such a theory does not explain the paranormal phenomena that may accompany a visionary experience. Like all psychological theories, it is unable to account for shared experiences of visions.

Another attempted explanation concerns stress. At first sight, this appears much more probable. It is suggested that stress brings on hallucinatory experiences, including religious visions (Jaynes, p.93). This may well be the reason for an apparition of a former spouse occurring to a grieving widow or widower who cannot come to terms with the death of a well-loved partner. But it cannot cover those cases where the percipient did not know that a death had taken place (Perry, 1959, p.141). Similarly, it cannot cover all religious visions, because not all percipients of this kind of vision are under stress. In any case, such a theory would have to demonstrate that stress alone is insufficient to trigger hallucinations, since most people who experience very considerable stress do not have hallucinatory experiences. The theory would have to presuppose that only people with a tendency to hallucinate have visionary experiences. While some people who have religious visions are indeed stressed and worried, many more who have had them did not seem stressed at all.

There are others who do not believe that spiritual visions of Jesus are in any way activated by God, but are on a par with ghosts and apparitions. F W H Myers, way back near the start of the twentieth century, believed that a vision takes place when the percipient becomes aware by telepathy of the condition of the person concerned, and that this knowledge is communicated to the conscious mind in the form of a vision (Myers, p.191). Those who believe in an afterlife can extend the theory so that the percipient becomes aware of the soul of someone who has died. Visions of Jesus, however, do not fall easily into this category. Why does he appear as a commanding figure, radiant with light and brimming with life, rather than as a person who has passed through death? Visions of Jesus almost invariably have a profound effect on percipients, filling them joy and happiness, quite different from that of ghosts and apparitions of the dead. Wiebe commented on this theory.

> No version of this theory adequately explains those experiences in which the physical location of the percipient seems to change. Nor does this theory account for the capacity of some percipients to grab hold of the figure which appeared to them. Moreover neither those experiences involving groups or observable changes, nor those in which Jesus is seen as a child or as crucified, appear to be adequately explained... Finally the theory seems to suppose that the disembodied soul of a person retains a fixed appearance and on this supposition it cannot explain the variety of Christic figures seen by the percipients.
>
> Wiebe, p.176

Other attempted psychological explanations of visions focus on the unconscious mind either working on its own, or in telepathic communication with the spirit of the apparition. There are further theories which involve the unconscious. Freud believed that hallucinations are thoughts turned into images from repressed or unconscious memories. These might be suppressed erotic thoughts, which could account for a mystic's raptures of union with God. Eroticism may indeed enter into some religious experiences. Samuel Rutherford, for example, a leading Presbyterian minister of the seventeenth century (after whom the American right-wing Rutherford Trust is named), once consoled the widowed Lady Kilmuir with the words:

Since you be alone in your bed let Christ be as a bundle of myrrh,

to sleep and be all night between your breasts, and then your bed
is better filled than before.

Coffrey, p.105

But there is no eroticism in the visions of the saints. As Evelyn
Underhill pointed out, the 'spiritual marriage' of Teresa of Avila
was entirely un-erotic (Underhill, p.95). Teresa was not interested
in the pleasurable feelings of rapture: she was concerned with the
fact of union in relation to her adoration of God.

Jung differed from his former master, Freud, in many ways
and especially in regarding the unconscious not merely as a sink
but also as a window into higher things. He believed that there is a
collective unconscious, which does not belong to the ego itself,
but is common to all humanity; and because it is dissociated from
the ego, he believed that it may be externalised and appear in
symbolic form in a vision. Whether or not there is some truth in
this theory, it cannot be the whole truth, if only because it cannot
account for collective visionary experiences.

Neurological Explanations of Visionary Experiences

Hallucination, as we have noted above, is an omnibus term for the
perception of an object or person not actually present. It may have
many physiological causes, such as sensory deprivation, fasting,
brain disease, *delirium tremens*, delirium caused by physical illness
and psychopathological states of mind, such as are experienced by
those suffering from hysteria or schizophrenia. In all these cases,
the hallucinatory phenomena have neurophysiological origins.
The question arises: are there neurophysiological explanations
that can fully account for religious visions? There are those who
say there are, and their arguments need to be examined.

Electrical stimulation of the left temporal lobe can produce
vivid recall of past memories (see p.151), and tumours and lesions
of the temporal lobe are said to be able to produce hallucinations,
as can gentle electrical stimulation of the lobe. But this hardly
provides an explanation of the content of religious visions. Why
these visions and not some other hallucinations? Certainly, there
is the illness called religious mania, but in that case the patient can

think of little else except religion. Why should an apparently normally balanced person have a religious vision? Hartmann has produced a 'perceptual release theory'.

> Hartmann suggests that the essential mechanism of hallucinations consists of 'releasing into consciousness' various pieces of information, originally derived from sensory experience, that have been stored and altered. The neurophysiological activities thought to be involved are those in the brain stem, including some that originate in the pontine brain stem that bombard the physical cortex, possibly the visual area. Hartmann further speculates that defects in the norepinephrine systems involved in neurotransmission could account for some forms of hallucination, and believes that the chemical substructure of such functions as reality testing might be found in the ascending norepinephrine systems that extend to the cerebral cortex.
>
> Wiebe, p.202

This sounds very impressive to those of us not conversant with the neurophysiology of the brain, but in fact it is mere speculation, and it does not seem able to account for all forms of religious visionary experience. Other writers, however, have built upon the theory. When considering the phenomenon of light at the end of the tunnel in connection with near-death experiences, we considered the disinhibition of cerebral function (see p.144ff.). Disinhibition has also been suggested as the real cause of visual hallucination. Normally, there are sensory inputs into the visual system, but this does not occur when we are asleep. The absence of these permits image formation in dreams. When the sensory input falls below a certain threshold, there is disinhibition, and previous memories may be perceived, it is claimed, as hallucinations. If the total system is inactive, fantasies will arise. If the system is active, these fantasies, it is claimed, turn into hallucinations.

Once again, it is not clear why such fantasies should be specifically religious, especially as in religious visions there is often no connection with previous memories. Nor do neurophysiological explanations (or, for that matter, psychological explanations) account for collective experiences and the psychokinetic phenomena that have been claimed to accompany some of these.

A Personal Observation

The present writer has a personal interest in the subject of religious visions, since he became a Christian as a result of a vision of Jesus. This occurred one winter afternoon when he was sixteen years old, during term time in a residential school. Sitting alone in my study, I saw a figure in white approach me, and I heard in my mind's ear the words, 'Follow me.' I knew that this was Jesus. How did I know? I have not the slightest idea. I had no knowledge of Christianity whatsoever – it had intentionally been kept from me. My parents were both Jewish – my father was president of his synagogue. I had never been to a church service. I had never read the New Testament. I had never discussed Christianity with my friends. The only manifestation of Christianity that I had witnessed was that a few boys knelt beside their bed to say their prayers at night in the dormitory. (Jews do not kneel to pray.) Apart from at school, all my friends and acquaintances were Jewish. I had been barmitzvahed at my synagogue, and at school I did not attend chapel or religious education lessons. Far from attending them, someone from outside the school came to give me lessons in Judaism. I had not been searching for a faith: indeed, I had even thought of becoming a rabbi. Yet I immediately recognised the figure I saw as Jesus. How I knew this, I have no idea. He was not a person who had crossed my conscious mind. (Naturally I do not know what happens in my unconscious, or it would not be unconscious.) In my vision, Jesus was clothed in white, although I cannot remember the nature of his clothes, nor yet his face, and I doubt if I ever knew them. I feel sure that if anyone had been present with a tape recorder or a camcorder, nothing would have registered. The experience filled me, as conversions often do, with a very deep and abiding sense of joy and happiness.

I do not often speak of this experience, partly because it is a private matter and partly because I do not wish to claim any special standing by coming to Christianity in this way. Indeed, it is an easier way than most, because the decision was, as it were, made for me. Although I feel sure that the visual cortex and the auditory cortex were in some way involved, I couldn't doubt that it was divinely initiated, although probably it was mediated through some unknown paranormal process. It was certainly not caused by stress: I was in good health, a happy schoolboy with good friends, leading an enthusiastic life and keen on sport as well as work. I do not recall any need to suppress erotic fantasies! I am equally sure that it had nothing to do with my memories, for I had no memories about Jesus. Again, I am sure it was not wish fulfilment. I was (and still am) proud to be Jewish. I am at a loss to know how it could be psychogenic, although I accept that my brain was the channel through which the experience came about. My sensory input at the time was not at a low ebb. I think it unlikely that the collective unconscious, if it manifested itself in a hallucination, would have taken what for me would have been an alien form. I cannot believe that I was in contact with a ghost, for the figure I saw was alive and life giving.

I cannot account for my vision of Jesus by any of the psychological or neurophysiological explanations on offer. That does not of itself prove that it was of divine origin, but my experience over the last sixty plus years of Christian life confirms my belief that it was.

Criteria for the Authenticity of Religious Visions

My own experience, while self-authenticating to me, hardly provides objective criteria for judging the authenticity of religious visions. However, Rahner has produced some (Rahner, pp.76–88). Piety and personal honesty, he insists, are prerequisite. Personal honesty, yes; but piety I would question. I cannot pretend that I was a particularly pious boy when I was favoured with a vision, although my religion was certainly real. As we have seen in the instances given earlier in this chapter, few of the percipients could be called pious. It is a pity that Rahner seems to reserve his criteria for religious visions for those experienced people who are already on the mystic path, presumably monks or nuns. He does not seem to consider genuine visions that come to ordinary and not particularly pious people.

Secondly, Rahner affirmed the need for bodily and mental health. This needs some qualification. When we consider the physical phenomena of mysticism, we shall find that some traits shown by the mystics have affinities with hysteria in the wider sense of that term. Mental health is a very difficult phrase to define with accuracy. Mental imbalance is better: if a mentally imbalanced person claimed a vision, that indeed would invite suspicion.

Rahner affirmed that neither charity nor stability nor apparent objectivity prove that a vision is authentic; and that paranormal phenomena do not in themselves constitute decisive criteria. Again, the impression of real sensory perception is no adequate criterion: it is of the nature of hallucinations that they appear real. Nor can popular support be regarded as decisive. In Lublin, for example, a weeping Madonna is said to have been visited by 100,000 people in one day, yet the apparition was condemned by the Church.

Rahner asserted, I believe rightly, that it would be improbable that important divine communications would come by means of visions, whether public or private. He also affirmed that the content of a vision, to be authentic, must accord with Christian doctrine (meaning, of course, the dogmas of the Roman Catholic Church). Writing as one who greatly respects that Church, but who cannot accept all its dogmas, I am not so sure about his definition. It seems too narrow. But it certainly seems unlikely that new insights into doctrine will come by means of visions; for, as I believe, God has revealed himself in Christ as fully as human personality can disclose him, and he has given us minds to reflect on what he has done, and the Holy Spirit to illuminate our minds and that of the Church as a whole, to lead us into truth. At the same time, it seems probable that God would accommodate religious visions to the images and perceptions of those who belong to other faiths; but I can write about only what I know, and my knowledge of other faiths is not, alas, very extensive.

A decision about the authenticity of any particular vision is never easy. Certitude may be attained, but not certainty. In any case, religious visions are of secondary importance compared with the spiritual life of an individual and of the Church as a whole, although they can be of great significance to an individual, as I have found in my own case.

Finally, I must repeat my conviction that in genuine visions God does not act directly on the percipient. I think it unlikely that he acts through angels. It seems more likely to me that he uses some paranormal mode to communicate to us a vision of Christ, although of course it would spring from the divine initiative and be of divine origin. It also seems probable that any transcendental message is clothed unconsciously by percipients in whatever contemporary and earthly imagery as is natural for them.

Lest this should seem too abstract, I pass next to an interview with a Christian visionary.

Chapter XI

QUESTIONS TO A CHRISTIAN VISIONARY

I found 'Joan' as a result of a weekly column I was then writing for the Church Times. *After a column on parapsychology, I received a letter from a lady who was a church organist and her husband a churchwarden. She told me that her family had psychic gifts. This had included her father, a priest now dead with whom the family is still in touch; her nephew and particularly her niece are also gifted. On following this up, I met the niece, a retiring girl in her mid-thirties who lives in a remote village, and as a trained nurse commutes to work in a hospital. 'Joan,' as I shall call her, does not wish to be identified. Among her gifts, like those of her brother, is an ability to contact earthbound departed spirits. On visiting a psychic lady, she was told that her psychic gifts also included healing. On a parish pilgrimage to Walsingham, she had an overwhelming vision of the Mother of Our Lord in the course of which she was told to work within the Church and that she, Mary, was her psychic and spiritual guide. Since then, her gifts have further developed, and she has a considerable healing ministry. I sought the advice of a spiritual guide and psychically gifted priest, and he replied that he had 'enquired' into the family and found that they are personally impeccable.*

ME: Tell me, Joan, all this started with a visit of yours to Walsingham. Is that right? Did you have a vision there of Our Lady?

JOAN: Yes, I did.

ME: And ever since that, you seemed to be close to her?

JOAN: Yes.

ME: When you felt close to her, she began to speak to you?

JOAN: Yes.

ME: Was it that that put into your mind the idea of healing? Was it because you are a nurse?

JOAN: No, I found this out after I had seen the psychic lady, and she told me I had a gift of healing.

ME: And why did you go and see this psychic lady? Because, after all, psychic things are all in your family?

JOAN: I've always been interested in it.

ME: But it is in your family, isn't it?

JOAN: Yes, my grandfather was psychic and he was a healer. He was a priest, too. And my brother can see spirit forms, and sometimes my mum can see things that happened years ago.

ME: Really?

JOAN: Sometimes she's driving along the road, and she can see things hundreds of years ago, there's a sort of flash of light.

ME: You mean she goes back across the centuries?

JOAN: Yes.

ME: So it's almost the whole family who are psychic. It looks as though it might be something genetic, doesn't it?

JOAN: Passed down, I suppose.

ME: Very interesting. Passed down the generations. You've been to a psychic, but psychics aren't necessarily Christian, are they? But you yourself have been brought up as a Christian?

JOAN: Yes. I wouldn't have gone to Walsingham otherwise!

ME: What sort of difference did it make to your healing? Did you do it by the laying on of hands or by prayer, or by what?

JOAN: By the laying on of hands, and by praying. I was doing it before. I knew I had a spiritual guide, for we all have a spiritual guide. I always wondered who mine was.

ME: How did you know we have a spiritual guide?

JOAN: The psychic lady told me.

ME: And then you found that your spiritual guide was the Blessed Virgin Mary?

JOAN: Yes, but I didn't know until that day when I went to Walsingham, and she made herself known to me.

ME: Can you remember her in her vision to you?

JOAN: She had a white dress and a blue robe on and I had a flash of blinding light in front of me and I felt this tremendous power round me and then Our Lady spoke to me.

ME: And when she spoke to you, was it in your inner ear? You didn't actually hear words? I daresay if you had had a recording machine there, you wouldn't have got anything on it.

JOAN: No, but I did hear her voice. It was different from my own.

ME: And then?

JOAN: I went on with my healing.

ME: And how did the ministry of deliverance get started?

JOAN: My Lady told me to go to certain places, and that there was a soul there that needed to be sent to the Father, and she told me what to do.

ME: So you have your own way of doing it which I'm not going to ask you about because I think it's very personal and private to you.

JOAN: She told me to go to a lot of places, first to a lot of old churches.

ME: I'm very puzzled about this, because I think it might be very frightening to people to think that there are a lot of earthbound spirits that have not gone on towards the Light. What do you think makes them earthbound? Do you think it's because they haven't had a proper burial or what?

JOAN: A lot of it is that they have died traumatically, and they don't know they've been killed, or they are not ready to go, they've got other things they want to do. When I've spoken to some who are trapped, before I take them on, they often say that they were murdered or something like that, or that they've got a lot to do, and they couldn't leave.

ME: So they didn't realise they were dead?

JOAN: No, not all. Some do know they are dead.

ME: That's a funny position to be in, isn't it, not to know you are dead?

JOAN: Sometimes they've been murdered in the back, or from the back, a lot of the olden day ones.

ME: So they didn't know they were dead?

JOAN: It was the shock of it. For some reason, they get trapped.

ME: It's a very funny business to me. I mean, when you're dead, you're dead, but for some reason you may remain earthbound.

JOAN: Most of them are olden day people.

ME: Are there any of them who have died recently?

JOAN: There were some people from the 1960s. They were killed in a car accident, and they were on their honeymoon – they just sort of wander round in a void.

ME: They are lost: they don't know that they ought to go on?

JOAN: They can't seem to find the Light, a lot of them. A lot of them say they look for the Light, but it doesn't come.

ME: It's odd. It's not for me to question the ways of God, but you'd have thought they would be able to find the Light. Of course, some spirits are bad, they are evil – they don't want to go to the Light.

JOAN: No. They have to go back to the dark world.

ME: But you manage to persuade them, sometimes?

JOAN: Yes.

ME: But if they are very evil, then you can't cope with that, presumably? Really evil spirits have to be left alone, don't they?

JOAN: Well, I have sent them through.

ME: But I thought you met some in a haunted house, your aunt told me, very, very evil spirits.

JOAN: In that house, where that couple were, I was given the power to send them on.

ME: Do they change their evil habits when they go on?

JOAN: No, they go back to the dark world.

ME: Will they ever get out of that?

JOAN: Well, I was told that they have to change their ways.

ME: They won't get out of it until they have changed their ways? Someone's got to change them; but surely, until they had changed, you wouldn't have been able to send them on?

JOAN: There are some that are not in human form. I have seen some – well, it's difficult to describe – more like creature types.

ME: You've seen them in your mind's eye?

JOAN: No, I've seen them.

ME: You've actually seen them! They're not human any more?

JOAN: Well, there are some.

ME: Have they lost their humanity, or weren't they ever human?

JOAN: Oh, I don't think they were ever human.

ME: So you think there are evil spirits. Do you also see angels?

JOAN: Yes, they're very beautiful.

ME: I'm sure they are. Do you see them with wings, or not?

JOAN: Yes.

ME: Do we also have guardian angels?

JOAN: Yes. I have seen some angels in a white light, and some are golden. They are very beautiful. Some of them have a golden face and blue eyes.

ME: Tell me, when you think of Our Lady, you think of her as your guide? Or more than that?

JOAN: More than that.

ME: It's difficult to put it into words, isn't it?

JOAN: It is, really.

ME: You often see her with her Son, don't you?

JOAN: Yes.

ME: So you feel that they work very closely together?

JOAN: Yes. One day in church when I saw them, they were standing at the altar, speaking to me about the sacrament, and Jesus put his arm round her shoulder, and they looked so close. They're very loving.

ME: Do you think that Our Lady's main job is to look after people on earth?

JOAN: It's the job of all spiritual guides.

ME: Is it? Presumably, some spirits go on into the Light, and they go on to wherever the future lies? Or not?

JOAN: Some of them stay back and help people who are on earth.

ME: Is there a choice whether they go on or stay and help?

JOAN: Yes, it's their choice what they do.

ME: But no way is better than the other? Or is it?

JOAN: I don't know really.

ME: What about children who have died very young – do they go on or are they reincarnated, do you think?

JOAN: I was told that all souls are reborn.

ME: What does that mean, I wonder?

JOAN: When our life ends, our souls go to the Light, and are then reborn into another body.

ME: Does that happen to all of us, or not necessarily?

JOAN: I'm told that some people have several lives.

ME: Do you know your previous lives?

JOAN: Yes.

ME: You do!

JOAN: I was told that I was a nun.

ME: So you were a nun, were you? Where? In this country?

JOAN: My Lady told me that I was a nun in both my other lives, and I am close to her now because I was close to her in both my other lives as well. She said that I was Bernadette and Catherine.

ME: Bernadette. You mean the one at Lourdes?

JOAN: Yes. She said that was why I am close to her in this life, because I was close to her in the other two lives.

ME: I have an idea that Bernadette didn't die all that time ago, did she? I must look it up. And before that you were a nun?

JOAN: Yes. My name was Catherine.

ME: Of Siena? Or Genoa? Or some other Catherine?

JOAN: I don't know where.

ME: It's very kind of you to tell me all this. I don't want in any way to get you to tell me things you don't want to say. You do understand that?

JOAN: Yes.

ME: Well then, you've had some further developments, haven't you, which your aunt told me about? You can look at someone, and you see blackness where there is something wrong with them. Is that right?

JOAN: I see it with my spiritual eyes.

ME: Have you had that gift for a long time?

JOAN: No, only quite recently.

ME: If you had looked at me before I had my kidney out, you would have seen blackness there?

JOAN: Where there's an illness, I see darkness. If I put my hand on them – it's difficult to describe – I can see inside the body with my spiritual eyes and where I can see the black, there is illness.

ME: Does this help you with your spiritual healing?

JOAN: Yes, it does.

ME: So you know just what you are looking for?

JOAN: Yes, and then I take the black away.

ME: How do you do that?

JOAN: I throw it out like that…

ME: What about people who are sickening?

JOAN: The start of an illness is grey. I've only had that gift about two or three weeks. When I take the bad area away, it has to be bathed with holy water. I do it with my spiritual hands. My human hands are outside, but my spiritual hands are inside, filled with holy water.

ME: Where do you get the holy water from?

JOAN: I don't know – it just appears. It's a phenomenon which we cannot understand.

ME: I think that's right.

JOAN: I bathe the area with the holy water, and then the golden light comes through and it goes over that area; and then, when that's done, it all closes back, and if My Lady tells me there's another area, my hands are over that other area, and it opens up.

ME: Now is it Our Lord who told you that, or his Mother, or what?

JOAN: Sometimes it's Jesus and sometimes it's Mary.

ME: So they both guide you, then?

JOAN: Yes. Mary does most of the time, but sometimes Jesus does it. I did a healing on a lady the other day – I get a bit nervous when I get someone new, they always expect so much from me, you know, and I never know if a person's going to get better or not, because I'm not told – and I had my hands on her, and He said, 'Do not be afraid because my hands are over yours,' and I looked down and saw his hands on top of mine, and He said, 'I am with you always.'

ME: How lovely!

JOAN: And He said, 'The Spirit will not abandon you.'

ME: Did the lady get better?

JOAN: She's only been once, she's coming back after Christmas; but she felt much better.

ME: Do you know what happens after your healing or not? I mean, do people come back or just walk out of your life?

JOAN: Most of them come back, and they get better. There are some who don't get a full healing.

ME: I think that's inevitable, don't you? But they may get a spiritual healing. Is that right?

JOAN: Yes. My Lady says that the healing of the soul is far more important than the healing of the body. And then, after the soul is healed, the body can be healed. Some get a full healing, some get a partial healing, and some can't be helped, but they will get peace and calm within. But this is not up to me. It's their power, and I am just the channel.

ME: I gather there have been some criticisms from local clergy about you. It's been said that you have passed messages from the dead to the living, and this is said to be unscriptural. Is that right?

JOAN: I don't ask them to send me messages. It doesn't happen very often. They come and say, 'Will you tell them that I'm all right?' I can't not pass on a message like that. Once they've got the message through, they don't come back any more. Their loved ones are greatly comforted, and they can get on with their lives.

ME: Then there was some criticism about a haunted house, which you continued to visit after a Requiem Mass had been held there, and you are said to have insisted on going on visiting there, and as a result you attracted many earthbound spirits.

JOAN: That's not true. I went to the house in the first place because the priest had asked to me go there. After the Mass, the couple who lived in the house found no help at all. The Mass was held, but the spirits didn't go.

ME: But I thought that they did go when you went there again.

JOAN: Yes, they did go when I went.

ME: But then a lot more came?

JOAN: The residents went. But not all of them had gone after the Mass. One or two had gone, but some were still there, and I had to talk to each one and make them go. It was only quiet for a couple of days, and then it all started up again. The couple who were living there called me back: I didn't ask them. You see, after the house was blessed at the Mass, there was a spiritual light around the house, and as a result there were spirit forms coming to the house from all over the place, because it was like a beacon. They were even in the barns and stables. They were coming from all over the place, even across the marshes.

ME: Why was the house like a beacon?

JOAN: Because it has the spiritual light around it, and they could see it. I asked My Lady what was happening and she said that this house had now become a stepping stone to the Father where all the lost souls could go, because they knew that was the house where they could go to the Light.

ME: And this was because the priest had blessed it?

JOAN: Yes. And she said I wasn't attracting them, and it was for me to send all those souls on. There were lots of them, and I used to talk to them in groups to send them on. My Lady said that this house was a learning step for me spiritually, and also for the couple that lived there. The man who lived there has developed spiritually, and he saw the light around the house as well.

ME: But the couple have moved out now?

JOAN: They only moved because his wife was ill and they'd got a lot of land and animals. They couldn't cope with it any more. That's the only reason they moved out. It's all quite peaceful now, and the light has gone.

ME: Do you have many such deliverances?

JOAN: I've had one or two people who have asked me to go to a house and send someone on, but mostly I just see the forms and the place.

ME: People are very puzzled about this. When you see the spirits, presumably they are dressed?

JOAN: Yes, they have the clothing which they had on in their time.

ME: Sometimes a ghost does the same things every night, you know, plonk, plonk, plonk, up the stairs; and I feel that's more like a print on the environment rather than an actual spirit; or do you think it's a spirit?

JOAN: They just go round and round in circles. Time has no meaning for them. Some of them have been trapped for about five hundred years, and when I tell them what year it is, they can't believe that time has moved on like that. They just can't understand because they don't see everything as it was in their time.

ME: All the spirits that you have sent on, have they all died a violent death?

JOAN: Sometimes they show me how they died, in a vision. Some of them are pretty horrific. It's usually a violent death, and very traumatic.

ME: It's very kind of you to tell me all this, and don't think I'm going to put anything into print which you haven't seen and approved. I must say, it is not for us to criticise, but it does seem strange to me that when God created the universe, he could have allowed souls to be trapped like this.

JOAN: Some of them seem to have been mad, or something like that. It's something that the human mind finds very difficult to understand. Some of them have killed themselves. Some of them feel that they've got to stay and look after the building. There were one or two priests who felt they couldn't go, they had to stay and look after their church.

ME: They were very possessive kind of people, I suppose?

JOAN: Yes.

ME: Is there anything else you would like to tell me?

JOAN: Well, I have quite a few visions of Jesus and Mary; sometimes they take me into the spirit world and they show me what it is like.

ME: What is it like? Or can't you tell?

JOAN: There's a garden area, which seems to be the place where people go when they want to speak; they speak to them in that garden, it seems to be a central area. There's a rock higher up where Jesus stands. The man who was in that haunted house, he had a vision and saw the garden, although I had not said anything to him about it.

ME: And they take you there to have a look at the garden sometimes?

JOAN: Yes.

ME: Is there anything else you would like to tell me?

JOAN: I seem to have another gift now. I visited a Second World War museum one day. I was shown a pilot's cap and as I held it I could see the pilot in the plane and I saw the German plane shoot it down. I could see and hear all his thoughts and emotions and his prayer to God, as he knew he was about to die. Then I saw him cross over into the Light. He was held by an angelic being from the moment of death, who carried him into the Light and to Jesus. I even saw the plane crash. It was quite incredible. I touched other items in the museum and the same thing happened. When I was walking in the forest I touched a tree and I could see the life force!

ME: Don't you do healing at a distance sometimes? Your aunt told me – she shouldn't have done so, I'm sure! – you used to see the countryside passing as you went in your spirit body...

JOAN: That was when I found I could fly in my spirit body.

When I first started, I could see the sea and everything beneath, but now, when I go, I go through this panel of white light and I'm there in a few seconds. If I don't know where I'm going, I always end up there, the Spirit knowing rather than me. Sometimes my (dead) grandfather comes with me.

ME: Is he a blessing to you?

JOAN: Yes, he helps me a lot. He watches over me.

ME: Do you know any other psychics? They're not all religious, are they? What do you make of that? How do you think of them?

JOAN: My Lady tells me to work with them, and they're beginning to see...

ME: That God is behind it all?

JOAN: Yes.

ME: That's lovely. I know you're religious. But some people have these gifts which don't seem to have anything to do with religion. They may have spirit guides – oh, someone who lived in China ages ago – isn't that right?

JOAN: Yes.

Unfortunately, the tape ran out at this point. I made some notes.

She said she actually hears Jesus's voice. Once she left a bit of blackness in a person she was healing, and she was told about it, and cast it out. She said she is told beforehand what to do: but if some person asks her to do a healing, she always asks permission first. When I pressed her about reincarnation, she said that if souls haven't achieved enough, they have to come back to earth. She made a distinction between a spiritual body and the soul which she described as like a blue globe. She said animals have souls as well as humans, and go to the animal afterworld.

I asked her about her journeys in her spiritual body. She said she looked different in her spiritual body, which was golden, and that she had been mistaken for an angel!

I asked her further about what she did about evil spirits. She said she held in her hand a spiritual gold crucifix. The evil spirits could not stand it, but fled screaming into the dark world which swallowed them up. She had been told never to be afraid, because she was under the personal protection of the Blessed Virgin Mary. She said that Jesus had told her that he was often pestered by evil spirits during his earthly life. She had been told that her part-time work would end when a great healing took place through her.

Chapter XII

THE PARANORMAL AMONG THE MYSTICS

We have already seen that many saints and mystics have been granted visionary experiences. But many other strange paranormal phenomena have also been noted in their lives. While there is a tendency for exaggeration in all hagiography, perhaps the strongest argument for the genuineness of these phenomena is that the saints and mystics to whom they occurred did not approve of these happenings, for they did not help them in their quest for that union with God for which they yearned. Mystics certainly do not perform to order! Their experiences are not the kind that can be tested under laboratory conditions. It is necessary to rely on what the saints themselves have written, and on reliable testimony (often sworn testimony) by those who witnessed the phenomena.

Who are mystics? They are those who claim immediate communion with God, the One Reality. They may try to recount their experiences in human language, but in a sense it always remains ineffable, for we have no words that do justice to the 'act of union' by which they try to fuse themselves with, and thus apprehend, the reality of their sought object.

And who are the saints? The word is used in the New Testament to designate members of the People of God. In common parlance, it is used to refer to people of outstanding holiness. Roman Catholics may use it in a more specialised sense. That Church has had a rigorous and complex procedure before a person is beatified (first step) and then canonised into sainthood. This has involved sworn testimony, which used to be critically examined by the 'Devil's Advocate'. A person does not have to be a priest or nun or monk to qualify for sainthood, although a cloistered life may make it easier for some to give themselves wholeheartedly to God. The Orthodox Churches also have procedures before a person is officially recognised as a saint. Other churches recognise saints in a more informal manner. If we think of saints as those who are specially gifted with love for God, there must be a great many saints of God who have escaped public recognition.

The Nature of Sanctity

Can sanctity be more fully described? William James described the saintly disposition as 'the character for which spiritual emotions are the habitual centre of the personal energy: and there is a composite photograph of universal sanctity, the same in all religions, in which the features can easily be traced'. He sees the fruits of sanctity as asceticism, strength of soul, purity and charity (James, p.274). Christians understand charity to mean loving God with the whole of our being, and loving our neighbours as ourselves. In a saint, these are no longer commandments to obey, but a delight and a joy by God's grace to achieve. I mention these dispositions of mystics and saints to show that paranormal phenomena have no part in their goals or ambitions. Although there must be some connection between the paranormal and sanctity, the two are distinct. No saint or mystic is the worse for not having paranormal experiences, nor do paranormal experiences in any way signify a saint or a mystic.

Saints and the Paranormal

There have been so many incredible miracles attributed by legend to the saints – like the Cornish saint who was said to have travelled over the Channel in a cabbage leaf – that it is easy to dismiss as legendary all paranormal phenomena attributed to them. Stories about weeping statues of the Virgin Mary, especially when these are found to be fraudulent or to have natural causes, hardly help. Accounts found in The Lives of the Saints (Baring-Gould, 1898) often abound in tales of the supernatural, of which the only attestation (if there be any) may well be a single witness in extreme old age who had heard the story when he was a young man from someone he could not remember.

> The reader is left in the dark, he has to take the narrator's word for it, and if he detects, as he often may, an underlying tendency to strain every point that can be made use of for the purpose of edification, it is hardly to be wondered at if the multiplication of astounding marvels leaves him unimpressed.
>
> Thurston, p.2

Even when we are convinced that we are not victims of fraud or pious exaggeration, and that something strange has indeed happened in the life of a saint, it is not always easy to distinguish paranormal characteristics from those more usually associated with neurotic disorders. Hysteria nowadays is used in a more extended sense. According to the *Oxford Companion to the Mind*, among its meanings is a state of dissociation, including trances, multiple personality and twilight states (Gregory, p.333ff.). Some of the physical phenomena of mysticism seem to be similar to, or possibly actually are, hysterical symptoms.

Herbert Thurston was a Jesuit priest of deep scholarship whose wide interests included the paranormal phenomena connected with the occult as well as the remarkable manifesta-tions that have often accompanied sanctity. He was a considerable scholar, of a somewhat sceptical bent, who set out to study, and to subject to critical analysis, some of the stranger manifestations of mysticism. He gave a number of lectures on these strange phenomena, covering a wide variety of Roman Catholic saints. These articles and lectures were collected after his death and edited by Dr J B Crehan, SJ (Thurston, 1952). As a result of his researches, Fr Thurston concluded:

> The evidence accumulated and relatively easy to access in the processes of beatification and canonization, printed with the sanction of the Congregation of Rites, is often more remarkable, and notably better attested, than any to be found in *The Proceedings of the Society for Psychical Research.*
>
> Thurston, p.2

With so much labour already expended on the subject and to such good effect, it seemed foolhardy to attempt original research into paranormal phenomena in the life of the mystics and saints. What follows is, for the most part, culled from the researches of Fr Thurston. Footnotes are given for ease of reference.

Levitation

Levitation is a phenomenon that has not only been attributed to some of the saints, but also to others who have been gifted with paranormal powers.

Here I am concerned only with the former, as their attestation is greatly superior. Levitation is important in the discussion of paranormal phenomena, because a vision of Jesus may be thought to be merely hallucinatory, and an apparently miraculous healing may be regarded as merely the result of an unexpectedly quick acceleration of the natural forces of rehabilitation; but levitation, if it takes place, cannot be either a natural process or merely a subjective state. For a person to find himself or herself involuntarily lifted off the ground and suspended in mid-air cannot be regarded as other than paranormal. It cannot be explained by any known force of physical attraction. Those who have been seen to levitate have usually been lifted off the ground a distance varying between a few inches to a few feet, but there are also a few well-attested cases (such as that of St Joseph of Copertino) where a person is alleged to have ascended to the level of a church roof or to treetop level.

In the case of St Teresa of Avila, the evidence seems conclusive. She wrote about it herself in the twentieth chapter of her *Life* in a passage where she distinguishes her mystical experience of rapture from that of union:

> In these raptures, the soul seems no longer to animate the body, and thus the natural heat of the body is felt to be sensibly diminished – it gradually becomes colder, though conscious of great sweetness and delight. No means of resistance is possible, whereas in union, where we are on our own ground, such a means exists – resistance may be painful and violent, but it can almost always be effected. But with rapture, as a rule, there is no

such possibility – it comes like a strong swift impulse, before your thought can forewarn you of it, or you can do anything to help yourself – you see or feel this cloud, or this powerful eagle, rising and bearing you up with you on its wings.

You realise, I repeat, and indeed see that you are being carried away, you know not whither... In such straits do I find myself at such a time that very often I should be glad to resist, and I exert all my power to do so, in particular at times when it happens in public and at many other times in private, when I am afraid I may be suffering deception. Occasionally I have been able to make some resistance, but at the cost of great exhaustion, for I would feel as weary afterwards as though I had been fighting with a giant. At other times resistance has been impossible: my soul has been born away, and often my head also, without my being able to prevent it, to the point of being raised from the ground.

Teresa goes on to give a particular instance when this happened:

This has happened only rarely; but once, when we were together in choir, and I was on my knees about to communicate, it caused me great distress. It seemed to me a most extraordinary thing and I thought there would be a good deal of talk about it, so I ordered the nuns (for it so happened I was appointed Prioress) not to speak of it. On another occasion, when I thought that the Lord was going to enrapture me (once it happened on our patronal festival, when some great ladies were present), I have lain on the ground and the sisters have come and held me down, but nonetheless the rapture has been observed. I besought the Lord earnestly not to grant me any more favours which had visible and exterior signs; for I was exhausted by having to endure such worries and after all, I said, His Majesty could grant me that favour without it becoming known. He seems to have been pleased of his goodness to hear me, for since making that prayer I have never again received such favours – it is true, however, that this happened not long since.[1]

This seems a manifestly true account, partly because Teresa had a sensitive conscience and an intellectually sharp mind and wrote accurately, and partly because she was writing her *Life*, not

---

[1] Peers, E A (ed.), *Life of St Theresa*, Chapter XX.

because she wanted to make these things known, but at the express command of her confessor. It was not by her wish that these experiences became public knowledge. What is more, there are independent attestations to her levitations. Fr Thurston cites Sister Anne of the Incarnation at Sogovia in her deposition under oath.

> On another occasion between one and two o'clock of the afternoon in the daytime I was in the choir waiting for the bell to ring when our Holy Mother entered and knelt down for perhaps a quarter of an hour. As I was looking on, she was raised about half a yard from the ground without her foot touching it. At this I was terrified, and she, for her part, was trembling all over. So I moved to where she was and I put my hands under her feet, over which I remained weeping for something like half an hour while the ecstasy lasted. Then suddenly she sank down and rested on her feet and turning her head round to me she asked me whether I had been there all the time. I said yes, and then she ordered me under obedience to say nothing of what I had seen, and I have in fact said nothing until the present moment.[2]

This is not the only attestation. Bishop Yepes, who knew her well, recalls in his *Life of Teresa* her attempting to resist ecstasy on one occasion after receiving Holy Communion. She clutched desperately at the bars of the grille as she rose in the air and in great distress cried out: 'Lord, for a thing of so little consequence as is my being bereft of this favour of Thine, do not permit a creature as vile as I am to be taken for a holy woman.' The bishop also remembered another occasion when an ecstasy came upon her, and she clutched at the mats of the floor which rose up in the air with her![3]

Archbishop Rowan Williams in his excellent study, *St Teresa of Avila* could not have known of these independent testimonies when he wrote:

> She clearly believed that she was physically levitating and needed to be held down, but most of what she says is compatible with

---

2 Mir, M, *Vida de Santa Teresa*, 1.286.

3 Yepes, *Vida, Virtudes y Milagros*, 1, Chapter XV.

strong vertiginous feelings generated by shock, by unusual or sudden changes of posture, and other factors, feelings reported by those whose ordinary physical rhythms have been unconsciously affected by profound absorption... I do not think that this passage or comparable passages have any clear evidence to offer about the phenomenon of levitation.

Williams, p.68

This scepticism seems unjustified. It would be hard to get stronger evidence of levitation both from Teresa herself and also independently from two witnesses.

There are a good number of other saints for whom there is excellent evidence of levitation. Many testimonies come from depositions made under oath. For example, Prospero Lambertini was *promotor fidei* (Devil's Advocate) in the case of Joseph of Copertino. Later, when Lambertini became Pope Benedict XIV, he said that the Congregation of Sacred Rites had heard 'witnesses of unchallengeable integrity who gave evidence of the famous upliftings from the ground and prolonged flights of the aforesaid Servant of God when rapt in ecstasy'.[4]

The theologian, Fr Francis Suarez, is the subject of a different kind of attestation. A paper, still extant, was found by chance that was written by a Br Jerome de Silva at the order of his confessor, to be kept sealed until the death of Fr Suarez. In this paper, Br de Silva attested to having on one occasion entered an inner room unexpectedly and seen Fr Suarez kneeling in ecstasy before a crucifix, his head uncovered, his hands joined, and his body in the air lifted three feet above the floor on the level on which the crucifix stood. 'I went out,' he wrote, 'my hair standing on end like bristles on a brush.' Fr Thurston noted that some of the best evidence can be found about people like Fr Suarez who have never been beatified. He went on to write:

There can be little doubt that St Richard of Chichester saw St Edmund, Archbishop of Canterbury, raised from the ground in ecstasy as he was praying in his chapel, while the evidence for St Catherine of Siena's levitations seems overwhelming.

Thurston, p.23

---

[4] Lambertini, *De Serv. Dei Beatificatione*, III, xlix, 9.

Fr Thurston was not always so definite. He regarded the evidence for the levitation of St Francis of Assisi, St Ignatius Loyola and St Francis Xavier as falling short of proof, although he did not deny that it might have occurred. In some cases, he has been able to show that later pious biographers have attributed testimony to earlier witnesses that in their recorded utterances they themselves never made. But the fact that some claims of levitation are the result of pious exaggeration does not invalidate the considerable number of people whose levitation may safely be regarded as having taken place.

In our present state of knowledge, the phenomenon is inexplicable. Levitation usually takes place in ecstasy. Trance is not to be equated with ecstasy, although ecstasy may be included among trance states because it involves a changed state of consciousness, for which trance is an omnibus term. Professor McDougall suggested that it should include a whole variety of states, such as catalepsy, comas, sleep, somnambulism, mystical ecstasies, hallucinations, hypnosis, mediumship and dual personality, to which he probably would have wished to add hysteria (Inglis, p.7ff.). Ecstasy may be a changed state of consciousness that is divinely given to enable union with God. A new study in depth of levitation is badly needed in the light of contemporary knowledge. Is the metabolism of the body changed? Is it a psychosomatic phenomenon, with the body, as St Teresa suggested, affected by the soaring of the soul towards the Transcendent? What do scientists think of levitation? We do not know. If they have heard of it, they tend to disbelieve it, or ignore it. Most theologians do the same.

The Stigmata and Other Bodily Effects

When Paul wrote to the Galatians 'I bear in my body the marks of the Lord Jesus' (Galatians 6:17), the word he used for 'marks' was 'stigmata'. Scholars have argued over whether he meant this literally. If so, he was not alone. Since the thirteenth century, there have been some fifty well-attested cases of those who have received the stigmata; that is to say, mysterious wounds that have appeared in their hands and feet corresponding to the wounds of

Jesus on the Cross. The exact details may differ from person to person. Some also manifest wounds in their side (corresponding to the spear thrust of the centurion to make sure that Jesus was dead) and marks on the head (corresponding to the crown of thorns placed on Jesus's head in mockery by soldiers after his trial before Pilate). It is noteworthy that these wounds correspond to places on Jesus's body where he was believed to have been wounded, not where he was actually wounded. The stigmatic wounds appear on the hands, but in fact Jesus was nailed to the Cross through his wrists, and his hands could not have borne the weight of his body. Again, the marks on the head represent those thought to have been made by a circlet of thorns, whereas it has been demonstrated that Jesus was far more likely to have been mocked with a radiate crown.

It seems probable that St Francis of Assisi was the first to be honoured with the stigmata. There are two reported instances of this happening a few years before Francis, but it seems probable that in both these cases the wounds were self-inflicted. The earliest account of St Francis's stigmata was written between two and four years of his death. Brother Leo wrote:

> The Blessed Francis, two years before his death, kept a Lent in the hermitage of the Alverna... And the hand of the Lord was upon him. After the vision and speech he had with a seraph and the impression on his body of the Stigmata of Christ, he made these praises which are written on the other side of the sheet...

Other early accounts differ about the exact nature of the stigmata. It seems probable that there appeared raised dark cicatrices or scarred wounds, circular on the inside and longer and oblong on the outside. These may well have given rise to the accounts that speak of black nails raised from the body and formed out of his flesh. During Lent, Francis would have been meditating profoundly on the Crucifixion of Jesus, and the appearance of the stigmata show the depth of his love for the Crucified, and how he was entering into the passion of Jesus, and, as Paul put it, 'completing what is lacking in Christ's afflictions' (Colossians 1:24).

Between Paul and the thirteenth century there are no recorded cases of stigmata; but what happened to Francis made an enormous impression on the mediaeval church, and Fr Thurston has suggested that from it there might have developed a 'crucifixion complex', and thereafter stigmata began to occur (often with bleeding), usually, but not uniquely, among those with a special devotion to Christ. In a very few instances, the stigmata were fraudulent: occasionally, they may have been self-inflicted. But in the vast majority of cases, the stigmata seem to have been genuine, and those who received them tried to hide them from the public gaze. Among them must be counted the most holy, but, as Fr Thurston has put it (p.70):

> Stigmatisation is a very wonderful thing, and it is generally associated with holiness, but it does not seem to constitute a guarantee of holiness.

There have been hundreds of cases of reported stigmata, but only about fifty of them seem to have been adequately documented. In most cases, the recipients were people of great devotion and piety, but it has to be admitted that most of them had earlier shown some symptoms of neurotic disorder; and in some cases there were strong symptoms of hysteria and split personality. Furthermore, if wounds bleed on Fridays, but not on other days of the week, the suspicion must arise that they do not originate from a manifestation of divine power so much as from psychological disturbance. To say this is not in any way to detract from the piety or devotion of the women concerned. Hysteria (the word is derived from the Greek word for womb) was originally thought to be an illness confined to women. We now know, from men's reactions to stress in the world wars, that this is not the case; but in normal circumstances it is women who are mostly associated with the condition. It is noteworthy that, apart from St Francis, Padre Pio and one other, stigmatics have all been female. The reception of the stigmata, like levitation, is associated with ecstasy; and the ecstasy of a mystic is not always easy to distinguish from the trance of a hysteric. Hysterics may be people of extreme piety despite apparently hysterical symptoms. As has been already noted, hysteria nowadays has an extended meaning. It is no longer associated only with people who suffer from hysterics, but with any who may go into a trance or have an abnormal and exaggerated tendency to suggestion. Such people show good sense and are level-headed, such as those who have received the stigmata.

The stigmata must be most striking to behold: they are extraordinary signs of devotion to Christ, and when they occur, the phenomenon is usually found among saints or mystics. It could be regarded as a psychosomatic phenomenon, an exterior manifestation of an interior identity with and devotion to the Crucified, differing among individuals according to temperament and character. Possibly the phenomenon is hysterical in origin, but no one can explain how it occurs. If there is a psychological or physiological process that explains it, we do not know it.

Fr Thurston noted one remarkable characteristic of a few stigmatics. St Veronica Giuliani, in the last years of her life, believed that her heart had in some marvellous way imprinted on itself marks of the holy things that had filled her thoughts during her lifetime; a chalice, a crown of thorns, three nails, etc. Some thirty hours after her death, her body was opened by two professors of medicine in the presence of the governor, and these medical witnesses drew up a formal statement to the effect that these symbols had been found in her heart in positions corresponding to the drawings she had made. Again, Caterina Savelli of Sezze, kneeling one day before the Reserved Sacrament, felt rays from it that wounded her hands, feet and side. No outward signs of these wounds appeared during her lifetime, but when she died the wounds on her hands were detected, and her heart had a long-standing and deep fissure, as attested to by her physician and surgeon.[5] Blessed Charles of Sezze is said to have had his body opened after death by order of the Pope, and a wound in the heart was found, formally attested to by doctors.[6] These cases call to mind that of St Teresa of Avila (not a stigmatic) who wrote in her *Life* of a glorious angel who thrust a gold spear into her heart.[7] (Cynics have regarded this as suggesting that her mystical

---

[5] Memmi, G B, SJ, *Vita della Serva de Dio Suor Caterina Savelli*, pp.132–42.

[6] Imbert-Gourbeyre, *La Stigmatisation*, 1.315ff.

[7] Peers, E A (ed.), *Life of St Teresa*, Chapter XXIX.

experiences were erotic in nature, but those who read her works could assure themselves that this is utterly untrue.) Her heart was indeed fissured (although conceivably the wound may have been made when the organ was removed). This fissured heart may still be seen today in the shrine at Alma de Tormes. It seems likely that these fissures were caused in the same way as the stigmata. They show the intimate relation between body and soul. How these organs continued to function with such wounds is not an easy question to answer.

The Capuchin friar Padre Pio de Pietrelcina is believed to have worked many miracles and to have experienced ecstasies and even bilocation. He was also a stigmatic. But the Holy Office made public its judgement in the *Acta Apostolicae Sedis* in 1923, namely that 'after due consideration the happenings associated with Padre Pio have not been proved to be supernatural in origin'. This does not actually deny their genuineness: it may even be read as an acknowledgement that they were paranormal. In 1997, Padre Pio was beatified in acknowledgement of his holiness and was declared a saint in 2002.

These are not the only remarkable effects of sanctity upon the human body. Some female saints, vowed to celibacy as 'brides of Christ', have occasionally received on their finger what seems to be a miraculous ring, a token of their espousal to Jesus Christ (Thurston, pp.130–40). The giving of the ring was often preceded by ecstasy and accompanied by the stigmata. The ring was, of course, visible to its recipient. Sometimes an onlooker could see a reddened circle around the finger, and at other times the ring was actually visible to an onlooker. Was this a hysterical symptom? The testimony of onlookers could be very strong, as in the case of Marie-Julie.[8] Could the recipient and the onlookers all have been hallucinating? It would seem more probable that this was another psychosomatic phenomenon, showing the close intimacy of body and soul.

Some holy persons have been impervious to fire and heat. St Polycarp is an outstanding example. His martyrdom in A.D. 155 is the earliest account of martyrdom in Christendom outside the

---

[8] Imbert-Gourbeyre, *La Stigmatisation*, II, p.116.

Bible, and it is generally agreed to be authentic. Polycarp was a holy man. Irenaeus could remember what he looked like and 'how he could discourse with John and with the rest of those who had seen the Lord, and how he would relate their words'.[9] He was condemned to be burnt alive. He was allowed time for prayer before the logs were lit.

> And when he had wafted up the Amen and finished the prayer, the men attending the fire lit it; and when a mighty flame shot up, we who were privileged to see it saw a wonderful thing and we have been spared to tell the tale. The fire produced the likeness of a vaulted chamber, like a ship's sail bellying to the breeze, and surrounded the martyr's body as with a wall, and he was in the centre of it, not a burning flesh but as bread that is baking or as gold or silver refined in a furnace. In fact we even caught an aroma such as the scent of incense or some other precious spice. At length, seeing that his body could not be consumed by fire, those impious people ordered an executioner to approach him and run a dagger through him, and when he had done this there came forth a great quantity of blood which extinguished the fire.[10]

There are one or two authenticated cases in the Middle Ages when imperviousness to fire was used as a test of authenticity. These are not isolated phenomena. From depositions given by eyewitnesses two years after his death, we learn that Blessed Giovanni Buona in the thirteenth century walked on embers. St Francis of Paula in the fifteenth century also walked on embers and held in his hand live coals. Four classifications of imperviousness to fire have been noted: cases associated with holiness of life; those in which an individual seems endowed with imperviousness to fire and heat; spiritualist sessions in which mediums show their imperviousness; and 'fire walks' associated usually with pagan rites in various parts of the world (Thurston, p.117). The same effect can be produced under hypnosis. We may compare Deliberately Imposed Bodily Damage (DIBD) phenomena among Sufi dervishes with imperviousness to pain, infection and haemorrhage.

---

[9] Eusebius, *Hist. Eccl.*, IV, 15.
[10] Anon., *Martyrdom of Polycarp*, 15.

There is no explanation for these phenomena.

The Odour of Sanctity

St Paul wrote to the Church at Corinth:

> Thanks be to God who in Christ always leads us in triumph, and through us spreads the fragrance of the knowledge of him everywhere. For we are an aroma of Christ among those who are being saved.
>
> 2 Corinthians 2:14, 15

It seems likely that he was writing metaphorically here rather than literally. In the account of the martyrdom of St Polycarp quoted above, there is mention of an odour like incense emanating from his body while he was on his martyr's pyre. Polycarp is not the only instance of such an odour in the early Church. Some twenty years later, Christians of Vienne and Lyon wrote to their fellow Christians in Asia Minor about those among them who had been martyred, and described them as 'fragrant with the sweet odour of Christ, so that some even supposed they had been anointed with earthly ointment'.[11] Later, Gregory the Great wrote about a certain Servulus who was known to him. When he died there was a 'pleasant and fragrant smell' and a monk attested that the perfume lasted until his funeral.[12]

St Teresa of Avila in Chapter XXVIII of her *Foundations* tells the story of the founding of her strict (discalced) Carmelite nunneries. She had founded one at Toledo, and this was visited by a particularly holy lady, Catalina of Cordova. She wrote:

> She went to Toledo where she stayed with our nuns. They have all assured me that there was such a fragrance about her, like that of relics, that it clung even to her habit and to her girdle, which, as they had taken them from her and given her fresh ones, she left behind. The fragrance was so sweet that it led them to praise Our Lord. And the nearer they came to her, the sweeter it was, though

---

[11] Eusebius, *Hist. Eccl.*, V, 1, 35.
[12] St Gregory, *Dialogues*, IV, 14.

her dress was of such a kind that, in the heat, which was very severe, one could have expected its odour to be offensive. (I know that they would not say anything that was not completely true.) So it inspired them with great devotion.[13]

I quote from St Teresa because she is such a lucid and honest writer. Catalina was by no means the only such nun. Such a powerful perfume came from the cell of another Carmelite, Mother Mary Clare, that three medical doctors made medical depositions about it. Another well-known case is that of St Catherine de Ricci. No less than twenty nuns in her convent in Prato bore witness on oath to the strange perfume, like that of violets (which were then out of season) which emanated from her dead body, and which was occasionally noted during her lifetime.[14] An even more remarkable case is that of Sister Giovanna Maria of the Cross who died in 1673. Her finger gave out an exquisite fragrance, so much so that anyone who kissed it retained its fragrance. The scent emanated not only from her body, but from the very clothes she wore, spreading throughout the house so that it marked out her movements. The scent is the more remarkable in that she had an allergy to any perfume.[15]

So one could go on citing well-authenticated cases. It must be recognised, however, that perfumes have also been noted in mediumistic séances. Fr Thurston noted the testimony of a psychic who found that perfume emanated from the top of his head (Thurston, p.225)!

Light and Heat

Light has always been associated with the divine. 'God is light, and in him is no darkness at all' (1 John 1:5). Divine truth illuminates the mind. The Prologue of St John's Gospel describes the Divine Word thus: 'In him was life; and the life was the light of men... *That* was the true Light, which lighteth every man that cometh into the world' (John 1:4, 9).

---

[13] *St Teresa of Avila, Foundations*, XXVIII.

[14] *Summarium super Virtutibus*, pp.321–29.

[15] Weber, B, *La V Jeanne Marie de la della Croce of Roveredo*, pp.373–75.

It is one thing to use the image of light to describe the divine: it is quite another to experience physical light as an accompaniment of holiness. Yet it happens. Prospero Lambertini's (Pope Benedict XIV's) *Treatise on the Beatification and Canonisation of Saints* allows that there may be a natural explanation of these luminous emanations. There have been those who claim that it is the result of fasting, where there may be produced in the body an excess of sulphides which become luminous as a result of ultraviolet rays. The circulation of these sulphides may, it has been suggested, explain the luminous phenomena associated with mystics. As a sufficient explanation of the phenomenon, it seems inadequate. There is no record of its connection with fasting.

Two instances may be cited from the seventeenth century. The first is from the records of the beatification of Blessed Bernardino Realini in 1621. A nobleman of rank who came to ask his counsel found his door shut with bright light shining through the cracks. He was surprised to see this at midday in April when there was no need for a fire. When he entered, he saw Fr Bernardino in ecstasy and levitating a couple of feet from the floor.[16] Others bore witness to having seen on other occasions sparks coming from all over his body, and one priest found him on another occasion praying in a dark room, his face so radiant that it lit up the room. St Thomas à Kempis recorded the case of St Lidwina of Schiedam, who:

> ...was discovered by her companions to be surrounded by so great a brightness that, seeing the splendour and struck with exceeding fear, they dared not approach near her. And though she always lay in darkness and material light was unbearable to her eyes, nevertheless the divine light was very agreeable to her, whereby her cell was often so wonderfully flooded by night that it seemed to the beholders that the cell itself appeared full of material lamps or fires.[17]

Several of those in whom this luminosity was noted also manifested other physical phenomena of mysticism. But it should be

---

[16] *Summarium super Virtutibus*, pp.187–90, 200–202.
[17] Kempis, Thomas à, *St Lidwina of Schiedam*, p.119.

remembered that luminosity has also been associated with mediumistic séances, and it is not merely a characteristic of some saints.

Sometimes heat rather than light was emitted, *incendium amoris* as it is called. Our emotions, as we know, can affect our bodies. Fear can make our hearts beat faster, and we can be warmed by the ardour of love. But some saints have been preternaturally heated by divine love. We talk of being inflamed by love: some saints have felt that this was literally the case.

St Francis de Sales in his book on the Love of God wrote:

> Stanislaus was so violently assailed by the love of our Saviour as often to faint and to suffer spasms in consequence, and he was obliged to apply cloths dipped in cold water to his breast in order to temper the violence of the love he felt.

Walking one night in the Novitiates' garden and asked by the Rector why he was there, he replied, 'I am burning, I am burning.'[18] Again, St Philip Neri at times felt so aflame with the love of God that in the coldest night of winter he had to open the windows, fan himself and cool his burning throat.[19] Padre Pio is said to have been so overheated by love that his temperature could not be measured by a clinical thermometer!

St Catherine of Genoa is an outstanding example of someone who showed *incendium amoris*, so much so that Baron von Hugel, who edited her *Life and Teaching* (first published in 1551, forty years after her death) could not believe all the accounts of her last illness and regarded some passages as interpolations into the text (von Hugel, I, p.214). During the months of this illness, she again and again suffered sensations of intense heat. 'There was a day when she suffered such intensity of burning that it was impossible to keep her in bed.' On one occasion, a cup of cold water was brought to her: after she had put her hands in it to cool them, even the stem was heated.[20]

Again, the *Life* of Serafina de Dio, which appears to have been

---

[18] Goldie, *Story of St Stanislaus Koska*, p.136ff.

[19] Bacci, *Life of St Philip Neri*, vol. I, pp.26, 141.

[20] St Catherine of Genoa, *Vitae Dottrina*, p.167.

written from the evidence given during the process of her beatification, recounts that her nuns reported that they were scorched if they touched her face; and she herself said she was consumed by a living fire and that her blood was boiling. The same work narrates how, after her death, her body retained such heat, in particular in the region of the heart, that one could warm one's hand by holding it there, and even in the cold month of March the warmth was still perceptible thirty-three hours after her death.[21] These accounts could be paralleled by depositions about other saints. It is hard to reject them all as pious exaggerations, especially as the depositions were sworn on oath. They seem to be instances of the strong connection between body and soul.

Telekinesis

There are rare, but quite well-attested accounts of the consecrated host making its own way into the mouth of a communicant. To take but one example in a sworn deposition about St Catherine of Siena, a priest told how he frequently gave her communion and that often in the course of so doing, he felt the Sacred Host agitated, as it were, in his fingers, and escape from him. 'That at first troubled me,' he said, 'for I feared lest the Sacred Host should fall to the ground; but it seemed to fly into her mouth.'[22] No doubt, more than this is required to prove that telekinesis does take place; it has been discussed in an earlier chapter in connection with poltergeists.

Food

The Gospel account of the feeding of the five thousand (Mark 6:32–44) is often met nowadays with incredulity. How much more the multiplication of loaves by the saints! Nonetheless, there are well-attested cases where this seems to have happened. Fr Thurston wrote that 'the number of such stories, many of them resting on direct and first-hand evidence, is surprisingly great'.

---

[21] Sguillante, and Pagani, *Vita della Serafina de Dio*, p.260.

[22] Drane, A T, *Life of St Catherine*, II, p.76.

(Thurston, p.389). St Andrew Fournet (canonised in 1933) had been a co-founder of the Congregation of the Daughters of the Cross in western France. In 1824, and on another occasion a year or two later, according to sworn statements, the grain in the granary was insufficient for the needs of the nuns, but the remaining heaps stayed constant in size, despite the grain being taken from them.[23] In another case, a witness testified of St Don Bosco:

> I found a place where I could overlook the scene, just behind St Don Bosco, who was preparing to distribute rolls to some 300 lads as they came up. I fixed my eyes upon the basket at once and I saw that it contained fifteen or twenty rolls at most. Meanwhile, Don Bosco carried out the distribution, and to my great surprise, I saw the same quantity remain as had been there at first, although no other rolls had been brought and the basket had not changed.[24]

At the beatification of St Germaine Cousin (she died in 1601, but was not beatified until 1854), two extraordinary occurrences were attested to as due to her intercession. In 1845, during an exceptionally hard winter, starvation stared a Bourges convent in the face. The grain was running out. The granary had a supply of flour that could last only two months. St Germaine Cousin was besought to intercede on the nuns' behalf. As a result, first the dough increased in the kneading troughs, and then the flour was multiplied. The nuns decided to measure it, and at the end of ten days it weighed the same as at the beginning, despite twelve bushels being used every twenty-five days.[25] Similarly, in 1829, the prayers of Jeanne-Marie Vianney, the famous Curé d'Ars, produced a flood of grain when sixty children were about to go without bread, and, on another occasion, probably during the drought in 1834, the kneading troughs were filled to the brim (Gheon, 1929). Fr Thurston noted that Prospero Lambertini (Pope Benedict XIV), in his *Treatise on the Beatification and Canonisation of Saints*, mentioned a number of cases where the multiplication of food took place, including St Clare of Assisi,

---

[23] *Summarium presented for beatification*, pp.376–77.
[24] Lemoyne, G B, *Vita del B Giovanni Bosco*, vol. II, pp.459–60.
[25] Veillot, *Ste Germaine Cousin*, pp.177–85.

St Richard of Chichester, St Mary Magdalen of Pazzi, and St Pius V; and he also referred to other cases connected with the names of St Thomas of Villanova, St Lewis Bertrand, St Rose of Lima, St Aloysius Gonzaga, St Francis Xavier, St Elizabeth, Queen of Portugal. While all such occurrences are hard to believe, they are said to have taken place a good many times in all.

Not only was food said to have been multiplied, but some refused it altogether. It seems to most of us a fact of life that if we do not eat, we will die. Not so with some! Fasting, uncommon these days, was taken seriously in the early Church. Egeria, who went on a pilgrimage to the Holy Land near the end of the fourth century A.D., recorded that there were those who during Lent took no food from Sunday evening until the following Saturday afternoon. The Desert Fathers in Egypt were well known for their prolonged fasts. But such abstinence pales into insignificance besides the experience of others. St Catherine of Genoa, for example, for twenty years went almost without food each Advent and Lent, a total of some seventy days annually. The reception of the Holy Communion sufficed her. During these periods, she could not eat: when people tried to persuade her to take food, her stomach repelled it. St Catherine of Siena similarly could swallow only small quantities of food, and that with much pain, and again her stomach returned it. Her case is particularly well attested. From September 1732 until Lent in the following year, she could take only the smallest amount of nourishment, and 'from Palm Sunday to Ascension Day, a space of fifty-five days, no food passed her lips, yet neither her weakness nor her suffering diminished her activity in good works'.[26] In more modern times, Louise Lateau (who died in 1883) was a humble devout French-woman who lived in a one-storied peasant cottage all her life. She received the stigmata and her distaste for food grew. In 1878, Dr Lefebre, vested with full powers by the bishop, said to her:

> Louise, since your strength is ebbing fast and you are near death, in the presence of God before whose tribunal you will soon be judged, tell me if you have eaten or drunk anything during the last seven years?

---

[26] Thiery, *Nouvelle Biographie*, vol. II, p.413.

To which she replied:

> In the presence of God who is to be my judge, and of the death
> that I am expecting, I assure you that I have neither eaten nor
> drunk for seven years.[27]

Other cases of prolonged fasting in church history could be
adduced. No doubt, a few were fraudulent. In some cases of split
personality or somnambulism, food might have been taken
without conscious awareness by the person concerned. But there
seem to be other cases that are genuine. No doubt, if a person is
inactive, a prolonged period without food, perhaps up to fifty
days, is possible, especially as those who do die suffer not so much
from lack of food as from the effects of hunger and fear.

It is not easy to discern the reason for such prolonged fasting.
Food 'is to be received with thanksgiving of them which believe
and know the truth' (1 Timothy 4:3). There are also cases where
people who are not particularly religious have gone without food
and drink for long periods. In ecstasy, the requirements of the
body may well be altered, as with animals during hibernation.
Contraction of the oesophagus, anorexia and rejection of food by
the stomach are well-known symptoms of neurosis.

> A considerable number of these cases of prolonged abstinence
> offer many points of analogy with the pathology of hysteria.
>
> Thurston, p.364

To say this in no way detracts from the saintly character of those
religious people who have experienced prolonged abstinence from
food. Their holiness can be freely acknowledged. At the same
time their continued existence without food seems paranormal.

Bodies of the Saints – Post-mortem

When a person dies, *rigor mortis* sets in, and when, after an
appropriate interval, the corpse has been interred in the ground, it
decomposes and disintegrates. This happens in the very great

---

[27] Thiery, *Nouvelle Biographie*, vol. II, p.413.

majority of cases, but not in all. In the case of St Francis of Assisi's corpse, for example, there was no rigidity of the cadaver. This is well attested. Fr Thurston assures his readers that he could give references to fifty saintly people in whose dead bodies the complete absence of *rigor mortis* has been observed. No natural explanation has been given of this strange phenomenon.

In some cases, this corporeal flexibility is accompanied by the well-attested effusion of red blood long after this could have been expected. In normal circumstances, blood coagulates in a few minutes after its exposure to the air. It may remain fluid in a dead body for not longer than twelve hours. Some of the cases where this has not happened, although well attested, are not very edifying, what with people cutting off small portions of the cadaver as relics and finding fresh red blood flowing from the wound that could not easily be staunched. In another instance, there was a dispute over the possession of the earthly remains of a dead bishop, and when the body was divided, some thirty-six days after his death, there was an effusion of red blood.

Some of the bodies seemed to exude perspiration and sweet perfume. In such cases, the corpse was found to be uncorrupted. The usual process of decomposition had not taken place. Fr Thurston distinguished several categories of corpses of this kind (p.233):

1. those which exhibited an extraordinary fragrance, sometimes lasting a long time;
2. total absence of *rigor mortis*;
3. immunity from decay, occasionally lasting for centuries;
4. bleeding of corpses after an interval of weeks, months, or even years since death;
5. occasionally the persistence of bodily warmth long after the extinction of life;
6. from some incorrupt cadavers an effusion of oil.

The incorruption of the bodies of the saints was noticed early in the course of the Church's history. A letter to St Augustine (in reality a memoir of Bishop Ambrose who died in A.D. 397) recounts that when the body of the martyr Nazarius was moved by Ambrose, some time later 'we saw the martyr's blood as fresh as if it had been shed that day. Further, his head, which the wretches had cut off, was so perfect and free from corruption, with all its hair and the beard, that it looked to us, at the time when we moved it, as if it had been washed and laid out for inspection in the tomb'.[28]

There are many factors influencing the rate of putrefaction of a corpse. The dry atmosphere of vaults can arrest decomposition: elsewhere, bodies have been known to become shrivelled and mummified. Nonetheless, the statistics that Fr Thurston has produced are arresting. Rather than trying to describe the hundreds of cases of incorruption, he looked at the post-mortem state of the corpses of the forty-two saints whose feast days are commemorated in the Roman Mass and who had lived within the last five centuries. In this selection of prominent saints, he found from the evidence that 'more than half had enjoyed some years, and often for vastly longer periods, the privilege of incorruption'. None of them had been canonised on this account. Some of them had lived not long ago (for example, the Curé d'Ars and Berna-dette). Of course, the bodies of saints are more likely to be disturbed than those of other people, so that we do not know what takes place in the generality of cases. But this high percent-age seems more than merely coincidental. It is puzzling, however, that not all the bodies of the greater saints (for example, Francis of Assisi, Ignatius Loyola, or Dominic) were found to have their bodies free from decomposition.

What happened to prevent putrefaction and to promote in-corruption? We do not know. Did the immune system of the bodies continue to prevent infestation? Did the process of sanctification give some special power to the body to avoid putrefaction? If so, why is not incorruption the fate of all dead bodies of saints? It seems that we are here in the presence of an inexplicable paranormal phenomenon.

---

[28] Migne, *Patrologia Latina*, XIV, p.38.

Extraordinary Healings

It is well known that some people seem to have an extraordinary gift of healing, which appears to function not through medication, placebos, hypnosis or by means of some form of meditation, but through the agency of a particularly gifted individual in an apparently non-material way. Such healing must be distinguished from that which is claimed from complementary or alternative therapies. There is even an association of so-called spiritual healers. Healing may take place through the laying on of hands, or simply through a one-to-one encounter. Alternatively, groups of individuals may pray for healing.

It is notoriously difficult to assess the effectiveness of 'spiritual healing', if only because there is great variability in human illness, and the possibility of remission through some unknown cause. A possible clue may be found in Polaroid photographs taken of Matthew Manning (Rhead, 2001). Manning, whose extraordinary paranormal powers have been described earlier in this book, now works as a healer. He reckons he has treated over 65,000 people with one-third cured and one-third helped in various ways (Manning, 1999). He has described the circumstances in which these photos were earlier taken. In the photographs, there appear to be diffraction rings (contrasting light and dark circular bands) centring on Manning's head. Diffraction is a phenomenon of all electromagnetic radiation. The wavelength has been calculated at about 2.2 mm, which corresponds to a frequency of about 140 GHz. It seems that Manning was directing very high frequency electromagnetic energy towards the camera at some hundred thousand million cycles per minute. It appears to have been sufficiently intense to have affected the film, although it would have been physically beyond the human senses. Two of the photographs are even more extraordinary. White patches with the same concentric rings touch both his head, and that of another person, outside their bodies. Manning said that, while the earlier photos were taken when he was meditating, these were taken when he imagined the transfer of white light to the other person. It has been suggested that for healing purposes the radiation might pass through soft tissue to denser structures such as bone, which could result in red blood cell production. Does this perhaps lie at the root of 'spiritual healing'?

Be that as it may, this chapter is concerned not with spiritual healing by otherwise ordinary people, but with mystics and saints. There are many stories of spiritual healing brought about through the agency of dead saints; some legendary, some exaggerated, but also some well attested. Sometimes one may wonder whether an illness was psychosomatic, so that when the emotional cause was diagnosed and dealt with, the physical symptoms disappeared. Sometimes one suspects that the expectation of healing actually effected a healing. At other times, people may only suppose that the healing of a person is through the intercession of a saint. At the same time, it could be that holy people acquire paranormal gifts of healing, and that these gifts persist after death. There is certainly a connection between sanctity and the paranormal, but it is very difficult to define. It should not be said that paranormal gifts promote sanctity, for sometimes they do the opposite; and all genuine mystics seem to wish that they were not burdened with such gifts. It may be that deep holiness involves the unfolding of potentialities of personality, including the gift of paranormal healing. This is difficult ground, and we can only speculate. But that extraordinary healings do take place seems undeniable. The Roman Catholic process of beatification requires a 'miracle' (attested to on oath when it has been witnessed) before anyone can be canonised as a saint.

I give an example of an extraordinary healing which took place this century. Fr Iweni Tansi was born in 1903, and died in 1964. He was a Nigerian, an Ibo, who became a Christian as a result of being sent to a Roman Catholic school, and he was one of the first ten Nigerian Roman Catholic priests. He was a very caring parish priest, ascetic and evangelistic, and he built two residential schools in his parish. In 1950, he was accepted for the novitiate by the Cistercians in England, and took the name of Cyprian. His deep holiness was recognised by the abbot, who was also Abbot General of the Cistercians; and after his death, the cause for his canonisation was promoted. His body was brought back from Mount St Bernard near Leicester to Nigeria. The following account of what happened on its return is well attested:

A young Nigerian woman, Philomena, not yet married, had contracted a serious disease. After an operation in Borromeo hospital in Onitsha, the doctors told the sisters who had brought her there that there was no hope. Sr Mary de Sales of the local congregation of the Immaculate Heart of Mary was dismayed at the diagnosis. 'If our daughter dies,' the distraught parents told her, 'you are responsible, because you are opposed to our consulting fortune tellers and using charm medicines.'

When she heard that Fr Tansi's remains were being brought to Onitsha, to be interred in the cemetery reserved for priests and religious near the cathedral, Sr Mary decided to take Philomena to the ceremony. By now the sick woman could not walk or stand up, and vomited every time she tried to eat.

Sr Mary lifted her into the car and took her to the cathedral. They were unable to get near the coffin because of the crowds, but the archbishop's secretary helped to make a way for them. As soon as Philomena touched the coffin, she stood up. 'Let's go to the Mass,' she said to Sister Mary. 'There is no need for anyone to help me. I can walk.'

During Mass, Philomena told her now incredulous companion, 'I'm hungry, I want to eat.' Taken to a nearby convent after the ceremony, she promptly ate two platefuls of food. Philomena declined assistance from some women who came to help her out of the car, and next day was as active as anyone else.

News of the miracle spread like wildfire. When the doctors at the hospital examined her, they could hardly believe it was the same person they had treated earlier, for the illness had completely gone. Philomena continued working for the sisters. Later she married, and now has three children.[29]

This is an account of only one extraordinary healing. There are many others that might be recounted, with sworn testimony. Are they to be regarded as miraculous interventions by God? Or might it be that the dead bodies of saints are not merely sometimes preserved from dissolution but are also endued with paranormal powers of healing?

---

[29] O'Connell, G, The Tablet, 1998, p.276.

Conclusion

It would be foolhardy to draw any certain conclusions from the remarkable phenomena recounted in this chapter. Certainly, many of them date from times when people were not so sceptical of the paranormal as they are today. What is certain, however, is that most of them cannot be dismissed as merely hagiographical tales or fraudulent stories. They are mostly well attested, indeed usually better attested than most accounts in the past, for they depend to a large extent on sworn depositions or eyewitness accounts by reputable and responsible people. Some of the phenomena may be of hysterical origin. Some can be paralleled in secular accounts of the paranormal. Some mystics were mediumistic, gifted with second sight, visionary experiences and precognition. Perhaps their sanctity developed their paranormal powers. We do not know. We value the saints, not for these extraordinary gifts, but for their devotion to Christ, for their commitment to God and for the sanctity of their lives. At the same time, if they had these extraordinary gifts, they should be properly investigated. The paranormal traits of saints and mystics deserve both sympathetic and informed enquiry and rigorous criticism. No ordinary explanation seems to have been found for them; in default of this, they may be regarded as paranormal.

Chapter XIII

THE PARANORMAL IN THE SCRIPTURES AND THE CHURCHES

I am by training a New Testament theologian, and as a result of my interest in the paranormal I have been forced to reconsider much of the so-called 'miraculous' in the New Testament which, it has been suggested, is shot through with the paranormal (Bretherton and Haddow, 1988). It is extraordinary that we theologians have tended to ignore the paranormal, and we have regarded it as improper to interest ourselves in such matters.

I use the word paranormal to signify that which cannot be explained by natural causation as we understand it, but which is not necessarily to be understood as indicating an act of God directly interfering with the regularities of nature. The paranormal may be caused by the operation of psychic laws about which we know very little and which override the normal regularities of existence, or it may be caused by an enlargement of human personality in ways unknown to us. God works through secondary causes. He can work through the paranormal, as well as through that which is natural; indeed, in some respects better.

It is now taken for granted by all the mainline churches that the Scriptures need to be read not only in faith, but also with critical acumen and understanding. Scholars have interpreted these passages without involving the paranormal. Because commentators usually ignore the paranormal, those events that I would put under that head are usually believed by them to be miracles due to the direct intervention of God (by fundamentalist or quasi-fundamentalist commentators) or viewed as myths and embellishments (by radical critics among those who engage in 'higher criticism' of the Bible).

My point can be illustrated from the beginning of the earliest

Gospel, St Mark. In the opening chapter, there is an account of Jesus's baptism.

> And when he came out of the water, immediately he saw the heavens opened, and the spirit descending upon him as a dove, and a voice came from heaven, 'Thou art my beloved Son: in thee I am well pleased.'
>
> Mark 1:10, 11

Commentators are chary of interpreting this literally. On the face of it, Jesus had had a visionary experience. Like other visions, it was hallucinatory (see p.213). There was no actual dove (pace Luke 3:22) and no actual voice that could be recorded. It was a divine vision (see p.235), and probably describes precisely what Jesus saw and heard; and its impact on him was so overwhelming that it gave him the impetus to end his thirty 'hidden years' of obscurity and to begin his public ministry.

Bultmann, however, considered this a 'faith legend' (Bultmann, p.264) while Dibelius called it a myth (Dibelius, p.271). Creed is sympathetic to E Meyer's view that the account is not historical, but 'we must take them to represent the pictures which believers formed of the beginning of his mission as Son of God' (Creed, p.56). Others regard the voice as the voice of God literally speaking to Jesus. Some see theological overtones, with the opening of the heavens signifying that the Last Days have begun, and the voice from heaven is the *bath quol*, the 'daughter of the voice', or the echo of the divine word, which is all that has been heard from God since the demise of prophecy. This may well be true and how Jesus himself interpreted it, but it does not tell us what actually happened.

Vincent Taylor admits the possibility of visionary elements. 'It seems best to explain the experience as inner and spiritual... It is by no means to be excluded that for Jesus himself the experience included visual and auditory elements' (Taylor, p.617). What the commentators have not done is to compare the event with paranormal visionary and auditory experiences that others have experienced. For Jesus it was a shattering experience of transcendence (the heavens opened) and of a voice sounding in his spiritual ears (which could not be literally the voice of God because God has no voice). Why could not Jesus in a divinely inspired vision have experienced the heavens opening, and actually heard a voice in his spiritual ears, and have seen the descent of the Spirit in the form of a dove? It is the obvious and simplest explanation. St Mark's account of Jesus's baptism, the earliest account, gives no indication that the voice or the vision was seen by bystanders. But Jesus's disciples would have been bound to ask him what impelled him into his public ministry, and surely he would have told them.

The baptism of Jesus should be considered in connection with his Transfiguration, because they are in some ways similar.

> And after six days Jesus took with him Peter and James and John, led them up a high mountain apart by themselves, and he was transfigured before them, and his garments became glittering, intensely white, as no fuller on earth could bleach them. And there appeared to them Elijah and Moses and they were talking to Jesus... And a cloud overshadowed them, and a voice came out of the cloud, 'This is my beloved Son, listen to him.' And suddenly looking round they no longer saw anyone with them but Jesus only.
>
> Mark 9:2–8

Loisy, Wellhausen and Bousset saw the story as a myth or legend, a post-resurrection story read back into the life of Jesus. Lohmeyer saw it as pure legend. Others have regarded it as a psychological experience following on from Peter's confession of faith at Caesarea Philippi. A more theological understanding is given by Ramsey, who believed that it showed that the Last Days had been anticipated and that the Messianic Age had begun (Ramsey, p.113). Nineham also gives a theological interpretation. A cloud-manifestation of God would have been expected at the end of the days, when supernatural figures might be expected.

> What was vouchsafed to the three disciples was a glimpse of Jesus in that final state of Lordship and glory to which he eventually would be exalted.
>
> Nineham, p.234

While all this may well be read into the story, it is not explicitly stated. We are simply told that Jesus (and his clothes) appeared unnaturally bright to his disciples. This can be paralleled in some well-attested stories of the saints (see p.268). The brightness was a paranormal phenomenon. The disciples, we are told, saw Jesus speaking with two people, whom they understood to be great figures from the past: in the account in St Matthew's Gospel, this is called a vision (Matthew 17:9). Is all this merely symbolic or should it be taken literally? Communication with apparitions of the dead is not unknown in psi experiences (see p.47). The voice that sounded in his spiritual ears was similar to that which Jesus experienced at his baptism. The cloud in which they were enveloped on the top of Mount Hermon (if that is where the vision took place) would have increased the mysteriousness of the experience. Was this a profound spiritual experience, mediated through paranormal phenomena? God can use the paranormal to further his purposes. Such an explanation of what happened on the Mount of Transfiguration in no way detracts from the spiritual importance of the story.

> A psychological interpretation of the phenomena does not at all preclude the view that such experiences, however subjectively determined as regards their form and visual content, may yet have been the vehicles, in particular cases, of genuinely spiritual intimations from on high.
>
> Rawlinson, p.119

Nor does such a view clash with the theological interpretations that have been placed on the experience. The sonship of Christ (that is to say, his uniquely intimate relationship to his heavenly Father as of a son to his father), which was communicated to him at his baptism, was also shown to his chosen three disciples at the Mount of Transfiguration. The appearance of Elijah and Moses shows that Jesus fulfilled all to which the Law and the Prophets were pointing. The fact of revelation is not diminished by the choice of medium in which it took place. But to ignore the medium – the paranormal – is to run the risk either of dismissing a story as legend and without historical basis, or of suggesting a direct intervention by God which many today do not believe to have occurred.

What is to be made of the story of Jesus's temptations in the wilderness for forty days (Matthew 4:2)? Most commentators regard it as a legend, not as a fact, but, as we have seen, much longer fasts were undertaken by saints (see p.272). St Matthew's and St Luke's Gospels give details of three temptations (Matthew 4:3–10; Luke 4:3–12). These represent temptations of social welfare (stones into bread), popularity through miracles (jumping from the Temple) and spiritual power (offer of world rule); and in each case Jesus overcame temptation by the use of biblical quotations. Are we to imagine that these temptations merely represent general classes of temptation to which Jesus was subject? Or that Jesus was prey to them only in imagination? Or that the gospels portray them as temptations that Jesus could have literally fulfilled? The latter is not impossible, if we bear in mind what can happen through paranormal powers.

Jesus was not only a visionary. He was also telepathic; that is to say, he knew without any auditory or visual communication what people were thinking. After Jesus had healed a blind and deaf man, both St Matthew's and St Luke's Gospels record that he knew without any word being spoken what the Pharisees were thinking, namely, that he was casting out demons through the power of Beelzebub, the prince of demons (Matthew 12:24; cf. Luke 11:14). On another occasion, when a paralysed man was being let down from the roof in the hope that Jesus would heal him, and Jesus had told him that his sins had been forgiven, all three synoptic gospels record that Jesus telepathically realised that his opponents, who were present, were asking themselves by what authority he was forgiving sins. In St Mark's Gospel, we are told that Jesus perceived this 'in his spirit' (Mark 2:8), St Luke merely recording that he perceived this (Luke 5:22), while St Matthew has the phrase 'perceiving their thoughts' (Matthew 9:4). This seems a case of extrasensory perception.

Another instance of this occurred when Jesus was watching people making their offerings in the treasury of the Temple in Jerusalem. He saw a poor widow putting in two copper coins. He exclaimed that, despite her poverty, she had put in all the money that she had. How did he know this? The widow did not tell him and none of the bystanders would have known. Jesus must have had telepathic knowledge of her financial situation. According to St John's Gospel, Jesus knew without being told about the past history of a Samaritan woman, that a nobleman's son was alive and that Lazarus had died. There is the more general statement of Jesus's intuitive knowledge about people. We are told that Jesus did not trust himself to the many who believed in him at the Passover feast because 'he knew what was in man' (John 2:25).

There are also cases of precognitive and clairvoyant ability in the gospels. Two may be mentioned from the beginning of Jesus's ministry. We are told that Nathanael expressed great surprise that Jesus knew who he was. 'Before Philip called you, when you were under the fig tree, I saw you,' Jesus replied (John 1:48). This disclosure so amazed Nathanael that he responded with the words: 'Rabbi, you are the Son of God, you are the King of Israel.' This was evidently no ordinary insight based on visual observation. Had that been so, it would not have had so momentous an effect on Nathanael. It was Jesus's clairvoyance that convinced him that Jesus was no ordinary person. It is a detail that is hardly likely to have been included unless it was based on an actual occurrence by some (unknown) fig tree, especially as Jesus suggested to him that this was a somewhat trivial reason for faith. A second instance concerns an event on the Sea of Galilee. After teaching the people from Simon Peter's boat, Jesus told Simon (who had had a fruitless night's fishing) to let down his nets for a catch; a huge haul of fish was taken, so that the nets were in danger of breaking. Jesus was no fisherman: he was a landsman whose family supplemented their earnings from the small plot of family land by working as carpenters. Landsman though he was, yet he saw without eyes where a large shoal of fish was situated.

At the other end of his ministry, two instances of his precognitive ability may be given. In the first of these, Jesus, according to all three synoptic gospels, told two of his disciples to fetch the colt on which he had to ride into Jerusalem (Mark 11:2). He told them what to say if anyone challenged them about taking the colt. Yet, there is no indication that any previous arrangements had been made about fetching the animal. It seems that Jesus simply knew what would happen; and it happened. The second instance occurred immediately before his arrest. He is remembered as having said: 'He that betrays me is at hand' (Matthew 26:46), and no sooner had he uttered these words than the crowd of people who arrested him appeared. It was Passover time and so there would have been a full moon; but the arresting party was not yet in sight. Yet, Jesus foresaw that their arrival was imminent. Again, it is hard to see why this statement of Jesus should have been included unless it was based on a memory of the occasion.

A striking instance of Jesus's ability to see without eyes can be found in his instructions to two of his disciples about making preparations for his last Passover meal in Jerusalem before his arrest. 'Go into the city, and a man carrying a jar will meet you; follow him, and wherever he enters, say to the householder, "The Teacher says, where is the guest room where I am to eat the Passover with my disciples?"' Again, it is unlikely that such a remark would have been included unless it was based on a historical event. How did Jesus know that they would meet a man carrying a jar? As he did not know who they were, it seems improbable that he was waiting for their arrival according to some secret plan. More probably it was due to Jesus's paranormal powers.

Not all cases are so probable. There are, for instance, some real difficulties in accepting at face value the account of Jesus foretelling that Peter would find a coin in a fish's mouth with which to pay the temple tax (Matthew 17:24–7). If he did, then this would have been a case of clairvoyance.

Jesus told Peter at the Mount of Olives before his arrest that he would deny him three times before the cock crowed twice (Mark 14:30). This remark is in all three synoptic gospels and it seems probable that it is based on an authentic memory of what Jesus actually said, especially in view of the account of Peter weeping bitterly when he found that the prophecy had come true (Mark 14:72). Again, Jesus had foreseen the future.

In the so-called 'Little Apocalypse' of Mark 13, and its equivalents in the two other two synoptic gospels, the coming fall of Jerusalem is prophesied. Undoubtedly, extra details have been added to these passages, and St Luke's Gospel draws on imagery different from that of the other two gospels. Since the chief accusation against Jesus at his trial was that he had spoken of the downfall of the Temple, it is likely that he did speak of the fall of Jerusalem. It might be said that he did not need special psychic powers to make this prediction at a time of growing tension between Jews and Romans. However, the Jewish Revolt was still more than a generation away. Most commentators on these passages regard them as *vaticinia ex eventu*, which is a polite way of using Latin to express the conviction that the prophecy took place after the event, that is, that it was made up from what happened later and written as a prediction of the future. They preferred not to entertain the idea that Jesus had made a genuine prediction of its coming fall. Why not? As we have seen, there are other instances of precognition in the annals of psychic research.

In the same way, is there any reason to cast doubt, as some have done, on Jesus's threefold prediction of his coming passion (Mark 8:31; 9:31; 10:33)? The actual language in which the predictions are now couched may have been embellished, but the prediction by Jesus of his coming death seems consonant with other apparent instances of his precognition.

Two categories of question arise from these predictions. Are they genuine prophecies, or not? Many scholars think not. If they are thought to be genuine prophecies, are they due to Jesus's divinity (which is presumed to include his omniscience) or to paranormal powers which he seemed to have possessed? There is difficulty in attaching to him omniscience, in view of his own confession of ignorance (Mark 13:32). It would seem they are signs of paranormal knowledge. To say this is in no way to depreciate the person of Jesus. According to Christian doctrine, he was fully a man, and therefore it may be assumed that he had the full range of human abilities, paranormal as well as normal.

It is not my object to argue that everything found in the gospels is descriptive history. Critical faculties must be used to the full in the study of the gospels. Of course, there have been alterations, additions and embellishments. These were customary in the days when the gospels were written. One has only to compare similar accounts of various sayings and incidents recorded in the three synoptic gospels to see how changes developed. It therefore should not be assumed that everything that can be considered as paranormal must have actually taken place. For example, passages in the birth stories in St Matthew's and St Luke's Gospels have not been cited here. This is because there are some contradictions in these stories which suggest that they may not be historical. I am not concerned here to probe into all the details of Jesus's historical ministry: all I want to do is point out that some passages are best understood by means of a paranormal explanation.

The Miracles of Jesus

In Jesus's day, miracles were regarded as common. If not fraudulent, many could be explained today in natural terms. Exaggeration was likely. What of Jesus's miracles? In the stories of healing in the gospels, different means are employed for different people. Some healings are recounted as though they were purely spiritual, as when Jesus heals by a word of command (Luke 13:12ff.). Others, such as the healing of the epileptic boy, can be achieved only through prayer (Mark 9:29). But not all healings seem to be of this kind. Some appear psychosomatic, as in the case of the paralysed man lowered through the roof whom Jesus healed after pronouncing the forgiveness of his sins (Mark 2:9–11). Others seem to be the result of an outflow of psychic power or spiritual energy from his person, as in the case of the woman with a gynaecological disorder (Mark 5:25ff.). I have myself experienced healing of this kind. I remember an occasion when I fell ill with gastric influenza on the eve of a great festival at which, as vicar of the church, I knew I had to be present. The chaplain of a local school came and laid hands on me, and I felt a flow of cold air from his hands, which caused convulsive movements of my stomach, after which I was able to get up and officiate. The chaplain assured me that his ability to heal had nothing specifically to do with religion: it was a paranormal power with which he happened to be endowed.

In addition to healings, there are also cases of exorcisms in the gospels. In those days, there was little concept of the real causes of illness, and sickness, disease and disablement were often thought to be caused by the infestation of demons. Hence, the comparative frequency of exorcism by Jesus, who naturally accepted the beliefs of his age in such matters. However, Jesus did distinguish between those diseases that he judged needed exorcism, and those for which he used other means of healing. What is important is that his exorcisms were effective. Nor should we necessarily suppose that there were no cases of possession in the particular mental illnesses that he encountered. For example, the madman who lived among the tombs, when asked his name, said it was Legion (Mark 5:2ff.). This has been variously interpreted to mean that he had suffered from abuse at the hands of Roman soldiers in the past, or that he suffered from a multiple personality disorder. But we cannot rule out the possibility of possession (see p.105).

The nature miracles have provided special difficulties to some. There are good arguments that can be deployed to show that these are not authentic historical records, but *haggadah*, pious tales made up to show moral or spiritual truths. The Matthaean addition to Mark's account of Jesus's appearance on the Sea of Galilee is often placed in this category. He is said to have raised Peter when he tried to walk on the water to touch him (Matthew 14:28–32); a story, it is said, told to illustrate the need for faith. Again, the account of Jesus turning water into wine (John 2:1–11) has been suspected by many to be an adaptation of a not uncommon legend from the Hellenistic world, which is used to show that Jesus turned the water of the Old Testament into the wine of the New.

Not all of the so-called nature miracles are of this kind, although they are often considered as such by biblical critics. For example, the feeding of the five thousand (Mark 6:41–4) and its duplicate, the feeding of the four thousand (Mark 8:7–9) are often considered to be unhistorical. Perhaps Jesus persuaded the crowds, it has been suggested, to share with one another their picnic lunches. Or perhaps the story arose as an allusion to the Christian Eucharist, of which it certainly has some overtones. It is thought impossible that Jesus did actually multiply the number of fish and loaves. But, as we have already seen, there are a good number of similar well-attested cases in the history of the saints (see pp.271). It is conceivable that paranormal powers rather than direct divine intervention were involved, although we have little understanding of what these powers would consist in such a case.

From the various accounts of the story in the four gospels, we may piece together what actually happened, once we have uncovered the theological overtones in which the story has been given in the early Church. A huge crowd went out into the countryside after Jesus and they hoped to persuade him to lead them in revolt against the Romans. Instead, he spoke to them, as was his custom, about the Kingdom of God. He absolutely refused the role of king which they had planned for him. By now it was getting late and he made them sit down in their paramilitary formations, and despite the small amount of food that he had available, Jesus gave them all more than enough to eat, and sent them home, he himself making his way alone into the hills, not even fully trusting his own disciples after this unsuccessful attempt at an uprising. That seems to be the story, rid of overtones. If Jesus did have paranormal powers, why should it be out of the question that there was a paranormal increase in the amount of food available?

There is an account in the synoptic gospels of Jesus apparently walking on the water as the disciples were rowing on the Sea of Galilee at night in rough weather. I write 'apparently walking on the water' because one possible translation of the Greek is that Jesus appeared by the seashore (*epi tes thalasses*). It is possible to understand the story as *haggadah*, a story told to illustrate the power of Jesus to give heart to his disciples in difficult conditions. But it is not out of the question that there is a paranormal explanation. Bilocation among a few of the saints is not unknown (see p.264).

The resuscitation of the widow's son at Nain (Luke 7:11ff.) and the return to life of Lazarus after he had been dead for four days (John 11:39), if these were historical events, can hardly be explained as paranormal. It is true that people can return to full consciousness after they have been certified as clinically dead, without suffering brain damage caused by anoxia. While this might just conceivably have been the case at Nain (among Jews, funerals had to take place speedily after death has been pronounced), it could not have happened in the case of Lazarus after four days in the tomb. But then, on critical grounds, commentators have held that the details of Lazarus's resuscitation have been modified so that it forms, in the structure of St John's Gospel, the last 'sign' that Jesus carried out before the culminating sign of his own death and resurrection.

The Resurrection of Jesus

Can the resurrection appearances of Jesus be explained in paranormal terms? Certain parallels can be adduced (Perry, 1959). A well-known phenomenon, often recorded in the annals of the SPR, is a 'crisis appearance' when a loved one may appear to (or a voice be heard by) a spouse or close relative around the time of death (see p.61ff.). It is perhaps the most common kind of hallucination, so-called 'veridical' because what is seen is not fantasy, but the appearance of a loved one. Usually the phenomenon takes place either to make contact at the moment of death, or to reassure the experient that the dead person is really still living. (My own grandfather, who never appeared to me to be in any way a psychic person, heard his son shout, 'Daddy, Daddy,' just at the very time that he subsequently learnt that his son died in the battle of the Somme in the First World War.)

There are some convergences between the resurrection appearances and phantasms of the dead. The latter always appear to those who have emotional bonds with the dead person; and that was so in the case of Jesus. Again, phantasms rarely allow themselves to be touched, and although Jesus evidently appeared substantial enough to be touched, Jesus is reported to have said to Mary Magdalen, 'Touch me not' (John 20:17). It is true that we are told that the women took hold of his feet (Matthew 28:9), but this could be a Matthaean embellishment; and, although the risen Jesus invited Thomas to touch him, he did not in fact do so (John 20:27ff.). Phantasms of the dead pass through doors and other physical objects, as did the risen Jesus. They appear and disappear suddenly as in the resurrection appearances. Clearly, Jesus was resurrected not in his physical body but in a spiritual body. Another similarity is that appearances happen at or shortly after death.

I am not suggesting that the appearances of Jesus to his disciples after his death were the same as phantasms of the dead. In the first place, the visions of Jesus were not given to reassure his disciples, but to give them words of command. There are other differences. The resurrection appearances continued for far longer after the death of Jesus than is the case with phantasms of the dead. Again, there is extended conversation between Jesus and his disciples which is not characteristic of veridical hallucinations. The number of people to whom Jesus appeared at the same time is altogether exceptional. Even if a hallucination seen by a person in the company of others has a tendency to spread, the appearance of Jesus to 'five hundred brethren at once' (1 Corinthians 15:6) is altogether exceptional.

The differences noted above show that the resurrection appearances of Jesus are not the same as phantasms of the dead, but at the same time they do seem to have sufficient in common to be classed among paranormal phenomena. Once again, it must be repeated that the mode of God's revelation – natural, paranormal or supernatural – has no bearing on its authenticity. The appearances were a visible sign of Jesus's spiritual presence.

As for the resurrection of Jesus himself, the disappearance of Jesus's physical body and the finding of the empty tomb are unparalleled in psychic phenomena. I have argued elsewhere that the evidence points to these as historical occurrences (Montefiore, 1992, p.111ff.), and I think that they must therefore be accepted as truly supernatural.

The Paranormal in the Primitive Church

There are paranormal phenomena in other parts of the New Testament as well as the gospels. In the Acts of the Apostles there are visionary appearances. Stephen is said to have seen the heavens opened and the glory of God and Jesus at his right hand (Acts 8:5ff.). This vision may be compared to that of Jesus at his baptism. Peter had a triple vision of a very different kind, a 'contraption' coming down from heaven in which was a large sailcloth containing animals both kosher and un-kosher; and he heard the words: 'Rise, Peter, kill and eat' (Acts 10:11) – not a very encouraging remark for vegetarians! This was a hallucinatory vision that could not be called veridical. It was of seminal importance for the early Church for it enabled Gentiles who did not keep the Jewish food laws to be members. Cornelius, a Roman centurion, had a parallel vision at the same time, bidding him to go and find Simon Peter. This seems a clear instance of the paranormal being employed in the service of God.

The apostles were given power to heal in the early Church. There are accounts of the healings of several sick persons and the casting out of evil spirits (which, as we have seen from the gospels, were generally believed to be the cause of all illnesses). There is even an account of a person being raised from the dead, although whether Tabitha merely appeared to be clinically dead (Acts 10:37ff.) we cannot know. In addition, there is an account of glossolalia at the first Christian Pentecost, a phenomenon common in charismatic circles today. Whether it should be classed as abnormal or paranormal is disputed. Paul clearly regarded it as the latter (1 Corinthians 14:2) and it certainly is a remarkable phenomenon. It can give rise to singing of very great beauty.

In addition, there are no less than three accounts in Acts of extraordinary escapes from prison: the angel of the Lord opening the prison doors in Jerusalem and enabling the apostles to escape (Acts 8:18ff.); the angel of the Lord loosing the chains with which Peter was bound in Jerusalem, with the result that he too escaped (Acts 10:23ff.), and Paul and Silas escaping from their prison at Philippi on the occasion of an earthquake (Acts 12:7ff.). It is hard to believe that the author of Acts would have included three extraordinary escapes from prison if none had taken place. They are recounted as supernatural rather than paranormal occurrences. I know of no paranormal analogies for such miraculous escapes, although escapes, not from prison but from bondage, are alleged by some Indian fakirs.

The Paranormal and St Paul

There is much that seems to be paranormal in the life of St Paul as recorded in his own letters and in the accounts of him in Acts (and its author would have known him well, if we consider that the 'we' passages in Acts represent the period when he was accompanying Paul on his travels). Paul shared in the other apostles' gifts of healing. At Lystra, he healed a cripple (Acts 14:8ff.), and such were his powers, we are told, that at Ephesus clothes taken from his body were laid upon the sick and they recovered, suggesting that he possessed some paranormal power to heal. He also seems to have had the gift of precognition. He told the shipwrecked crew of his ship off Malta that not a hair of their heads would be forfeit (Acts 27:22); and this turned out to be the case.

Paul had many visions. When he was at Troas he had a vision of a man of Macedonia, bidding him to come over there and help (Acts 16:9); and he went. In Corinth Paul had a vision of Christ who told him not to be afraid (Acts 18:9), for he would be with him, and no harm would come to him; and it was so. The night after Paul had been put into protective custody in Jerusalem after addressing the Jerusalem Council, he had a vision of Christ telling him to take heart, for he must bear his testimony in Rome as well as in Jerusalem (Acts 23:11); and indeed he did.

These accounts of Paul's visions are taken from the Acts of the Apostles, and scholars are divided about their historical accuracy. When, however, we consider those letters of Paul that are generally considered to be authentic, there is no reason to doubt this. From these letters, we learn that Paul himself spoke in tongues (1 Corinthians 14:18). We learn that he bore in his body the marks of the Lord Jesus (Galatians 6:17), which are generally, but not universally, thought to be the stigmata. Paul also recorded what appears to be an out-of-body experience. When he wrote to the Corinthian church about visions and revelations of the Lord, he was obviously speaking about himself:

> I know a man in Christ who fourteen years ago was caught up into the third heaven – whether in the body or out of the body I do not know, God knows. And I know this man was caught up into Paradise – whether in the body or out of the body I do not know, God knows – and he heard things which cannot be told, which man may not utter.
>
> 2 Corinthians 12:2–4

Paul in the same passage recorded also a word which Christ spoke to him in answer to prayer:

> My grace is sufficient for you, for my strength is made perfect in weakness.
>
> 2 Corinthians 12:9

What status should we give these visions and auditory experience? Are they to be put on a par with other hallucinations that people have had? Or was God working through paranormal means? Visions, as we have noted (see p.213), are not uncommon. Of course, the most important vision that Paul had was at his conversion, if it may properly be called a vision, because in the three accounts of it which the author of Acts gives us (Acts 9:3–6, 26:13–5, 22:6–11) Paul did not actually see Christ, but he did see a light which blinded him (light being a common expression of the Divine) and he heard a voice. However, in his own description of his conversion, he put it somewhat differently:

> When it pleased God, who separated me from my mother's womb and called me by his grace, to reveal his Son in me.
>
> Galatians 1:15, 16

So he evidently regarded this as not merely an occasion when he heard the words of Christ, but also when he revealed himself to Paul. Scholars have argued about the status of this vision. A man could not be an apostle until he had seen the Lord. Paul on his own confession was 'born out of due time' (1 Corinthians 15:8) and he was clear that he had been given apostolic status (2 Corinthians 1:1). It seems likely that all he saw was blinding light and that, together with the voice which told him not to kick against the pricks, was sufficient to assure him of the power and presence of the risen Lord. Those who accompanied Paul saw nothing (Acts 9:7), and so we must presume that his vision of blinding light was hallucinatory. At the same time, it seems impossible to doubt that God was using this paranormal means to make known to Paul the risen Christ (see p.283).

The Church's Record

In the light of this study of the paranormal in the New Testament, it is amazing to me that Christian theologians have tended to ignore it. Strange phenomena have either been regarded as due to the direct intervention of God, or as pious myths which express some spiritual truth.

The record of the Church of England over the paranormal has been lamentable. There have been few individuals who have been interested, despite the 'Churches' Fellowship for Psychical and Spiritual Studies' with its regular publications. The Church's bishops and theological professors, with very few exceptions, turn their backs on it. Way back in 1920, the Anglican Communion's Lambeth Conference received a report on Spiritualism, which was very positive on the subject of psychic powers 'which are as real as, through less general, than our physical powers' (*Lambeth Conferences*, 1948, p.107), and its authors were 'able wholeheartedly and without shrinking, to welcome research, criticism and scientific investigation' (ibid., p.108). Unfortunately, this enthusiasm drained away over the years. A further report, commissioned by the Archbishop of Canterbury, which reported in 1939, was actually suppressed for forty years! I was a member in the 1960s and 1970s of the Archbishops' Commission on Christian Doctrine, and I well remember the discussions that led to our report on prayers for the dead. I managed to persuade the Commission to include an appendix on psychic research. After recounting some striking cases of automatic writing and mediums, and after commenting on references to spiritual embodiment and to allusions to spiritual progress in the afterlife, the appendix ended with the words:

> The whole subject is full of uncertainties and alternative explanations, and we have no criteria for distinguishing true information from false. We ought therefore to say that those who are searching for certain knowledge of the world to come are unlikely to find it through psychical investigation.
>
> *Prayer and the Departed*, p.63ff.

This carefully worded statement did not deny that there may be probable knowledge of the world to come!

There was one further attempt to get the Church of England interested in the subject. I was present in the 1980s at the House of Bishops when it was asked to consider setting up a commission to look further into these matters. I well remember the silence – the shocked silence – with which this proposal was greeted. According to the minutes, the bishops, in the well-worn phrase 'did not think that the time was ripe'.

The Church of Scotland has been no more successful in these matters. Its General Assembly acknowledged that there were Christians with psychic gifts, and that these should be encouraged (*Report on Supernormal Psychic Phenomena*, 1922). In 1976, the Assembly received and actually published an inconclusive *Report of the Working Party on Parapsychology*. It decided, in another well-worn phrase 'to keep the matter under review'. Nothing further has happened.

The Roman Catholic Church has been less inactive. There is an annual meeting of parapsychologists, but there are no official statements or publications on the subject.

Reasons for the Churches' Lack of Interest

One reason for the lack of interest in the paranormal among theologians is the effect of the Enlightenment on Christian theology. Biblical scholars have tended to fight shy of it in dealing with biblical texts because it seems to them irrational to posit phenomena that cannot be rationally explained. Just as they have tended to discount miracles in the Scriptures, so also they tended to ignore the paranormal.

If theologians tend to play down the existence of evil spirits, a fear of becoming involved with them provides a further reason for the mistrust of the paranormal by ordinary Christians. Indeed, it *is* dangerous to meddle with the occult out of curiosity or for amusement, or for personal gain. The practice of using Ouija boards or a planchette in order to make contact with the spirit world can lead and has led to nervous breakdowns and worse. Exorcism should only very rarely be used in exceptional cases: in inexpert hands it has led to mental breakdown or even suicide.

Dr Anton-Stevens, formerly a psychiatric consultant in Birmingham, has written in connection with his medical work:

> The writer has had experience of dealing with a girl of fifteen, who, having experimented with an Ouija board at school, ended up with a barrage of voices shouting foul obscenities at her; he has had the experience of trying to deal with a young man who literally vomited with fear when, during some black magic rites, he found his legs and arms being moved without any control on his part, but with the hallucinatory experience of someone touching them.
>
> Anton-Stevens, 1992, pp.42–6

Of course, it is always dangerous to be in touch with evil of any kind, because one can be contaminated by it. But psychic evil, like other kinds of evil, needs to be confronted and overcome. In expert hands, it can safely be dealt with.

Those who have been given psychic gifts, whether in healing or deliverance, should not bury their talents in the earth, but they should be encouraged by the Church to use them; and those of us who have not been given such gifts should welcome those who have them. In any case, paranormal phenomena deserve to be investigated. The object of such research is not to gain power through the occult, but to increase our knowledge and understanding of God's universe. How can it be wrong to investigate an aspect of God's creation? Do we not have a duty to do this? I am not suggesting that the paranormal should be at the centre of the Church's concerns. These should be focused on worship, belief and behaviour. Nor should Christians accept the paranormal uncritically. This seems to be the characteristics of the heresy of 'Christian Spiritualism'. But if the mainstream churches choose to ignore the paranormal, it should heed the words of an American Episcopal priest:

> Clairvoyance, telepathy, precognition, psychokinesis and healing have been observed in and around the life of many religious leaders and nearly all Christian saints. If these phenomena are not accepted and given a legitimate place in religious life, they will be sought outside the Church and for other than religious reasons...

ESP is a natural phenomenon of the human psyche. It can be used for the glory of God and the enrichment of human life when it is understood and placed in the service of divine love, the love expressed through Jesus Christ.

Kelsey, p.143

Biblical Objections to the Paranormal

A major reason for the Churches' mistrust of the paranormal is to be found in some Old Testament passages. To understand these, it is necessary to see them in their biblical context.

One of these concerns Saul. In the earlier days of Israel, after the era of the Judges, the prophet Samuel anointed Saul to be the leader of Israel. But Saul did not seem to be up to the job. He constantly got things wrong in the lifetime of Samuel. Samuel had been his guide and adviser. But Samuel had died, and Saul desperately needed his counsel in the face of a huge army of Philistines who opposed him. Saul could get no message from dreams, nor from prophecy, nor from the Jewish form of divination known as Urim and Thummim. So he went in disguise to Endor to visit a medium. The medium did indeed consult the dead Samuel on his behalf. She is said to have brought back Samuel's spirit from the dead, and he spoke to Saul.

He did not pull his punches. He told Saul that he would die the very next day at the battle of Gilboa; and he did. In the earlier version of the story, the reason for his death is given:

> You have not obeyed the Lord or executed the fury of his judge-ment on the Amalekites: that is why he has done this to you this day.

1 Samuel 28:18

In other words, Saul had been too soft. But a later version of the story puts a different complexion on it. It is said that Saul died, not because he had been too soft, but because he had consulted a medium when he should have consulted the Lord (1 Chronicles 10:13). Evidently, by the time that the Books of Chronicles were compiled, mediums were rejected because they were considered to be part of pagan religion, whereas in Yahwism, divination was carried out by Urim and Thummim.

It seems that it was the evil king, Manasseh, who reintroduced pagan practices with ghosts and mediums into Jerusalem.

> He made his son pass through the fire, he practised soothsaying and divination, and dealt with ghosts and spirits.
>
> 2 Kings 21:6

The later King Josiah cleaned up the Temple, and it was in his reign that a book was 'discovered' in the Temple that reads suspiciously like our present Deuteronomy. It is not surprising that it contains a blanket prohibition on all pagan practices:

> Let no one be found among you who makes his son or daughter pass through the fire, no augur or soothsayer or diviner or sorcerer, no one who casts spells or traffics with ghosts or spirits, and no necromancer. Those who do these things are abominable to the Lord, and it is because of these abominable practices that the Lord your God is driving them out before you. You shall be wholehearted in the service of the Lord your God.
>
> Deuteronomy 18:10–13

Evidently the priestly editor of the Pentateuch agreed with Josiah's legislation against such practices. It should be remembered that, at that period, Jews did not believe in life after death: the dead went down to Sheol where they had a shadowy ghostlike existence and could be of no use to the living. They were outside the sphere of God's rule. So it is not surprising that the editor of Leviticus tersely commanded:

> Do not resort to ghosts or spirits, nor make yourselves unclean by seeking them. I am the Lord your God.
>
> Leviticus 19:31

And again:

> I will set my face against the man who wantonly resorts to ghosts and spirits, and I will cut that person off from his people. Hallow yourselves and be holy, because I the Lord your God am holy.

You shall keep my rules and obey them: I am the Lord who hallows you.

Leviticus 20:6

These rules should be seen in context. Resort to the dead was a mark of pagan religions. It is indeed dangerous to meddle with pagan occult religious practices, and it is against these that the biblical writers were inveighing. The idea of psychic research never entered their heads, nor were they condemning paranormal gifts that could be used in God's service.

Old Testament Evidence in Favour of the Paranormal

There is plenty of evidence for the paranormal in the Old Testament. (I continue to use the word paranormal to describe that which cannot be understood by natural causation, but which need not be seen as due to the direct intervention of God.) For example, Elijah and Elisha were two great figures of Israel's early days, prophets who appeared to be gifted with paranormal powers. When the king of Aram complained that the king of Israel had extraordinary intelligence about his battle plans, he was told that the prophet Elijah actually knew the very words he spoke in his bedroom (2 Kings 6:18) (It is not surprising that during the Second World War attempts were made to enlist the aid of parapsychology for military intelligence.) Elijah combined paranormal powers with a great zeal for God. He is even said to have been transported to heaven in a chariot of fire (2 Kings 2:11).

The canonical prophets of the Old Testament were concerned not merely with foretelling the future, but also with speaking the Word of God to their generation, condemning immorality and idolatry. Much of what they spoke was poetic in form, but the phrase 'The Word of the Lord came to me' is not to be dismissed as mere metaphor. The prophets heard with their inner ear what they believed to be divinely inspired words. Although their context was entirely different – they were speaking under divine inspiration – the idea of a message from another sphere of existence can also be found in such paranormal phenomena as speaking through a medium or automatic writing (see p.52). Whereas the content of what is spoken or written is quite dissimilar, their *modus operandi* seems to have some similarities with that of the canonical prophets.

Ezekiel, one of the major canonical prophets, was a complex character. His ecstasies and prophetic symbolism (including his 'acted symbols') have been variously dismissed as due to catalepsy, schizophrenia or hysteria. He has been described as abnormal; but no commentator, to my knowledge, has yet called him paranormal. Yet he seemed clearly to have paranormal powers. He was vouchsafed visions of the glory of the Lord, and he saw the heavens opened: but of course, his vision of God's glory was clothed in the imagery of his day, centring on the divine chariot and the cherubim (Ezekiel 1:3ff.). On more than one occasion, out-of-body experiences are recorded, as when the Spirit lifted him up from the land of the Chaldeans where he was living among the Jewish exiles in Babylon, and he was brought to the Jewish temple in Jerusalem, where he is reported to have seen the wickedness that was taking place there (Ezekiel 8:3ff.). On another occasion, he had a further out-of-body experience when he was taken to a high mountain before going for a second time to the Jewish temple (Ezekiel 40:2). These paranormal powers in no way interfered with his vocation as a prophet of God: on the contrary, they added strength to his prophetic witness.

These positive indications in the Old Testament outweigh the more negative passages which have been considered above; and it follows that there is no biblical obstacle to the investigation of the paranormal. Indeed, any objective analysis of the Old and the New Testaments seems to favour this. There is, therefore, little excuse for the Church's reluctance on Scriptural grounds, or indeed on any other grounds, to examine this aspect of God's creation.

CONCLUSION

I have now completed my investigation of the paranormal. It is, of course, by no means exhaustive; but the most important paranormal phenomena have been considered. In earlier chapters I have usually attempted to be impartial. In this last chapter I give my own conclusions.

Paranormal phenomena are certainly very strange; but so are many, many other aspects of existence. We have become so accustomed to the world that we seldom reflect how strange it all is. It is strange that the world exists at all, and that we exist within it. Life continues with its customary regularities so that, until some mishap occurs, we usually take things for granted. Yet the fact that human beings do exist is really very extraordinary. Only a minute difference in the relationships between the fundamental forces of the universe, and there would have been no universe at all. Further minute differences would have resulted in galaxies (and the stars within them) being unable to form. It all seems to stem from the singularity in which the universe began. What is the probability that, by chance, the universe had an initial singularity looking remotely similar? The probability is less than $10^{10^{123}}$ (Penrose, p.47).

The Big Bang, it is generally thought, occurred when time began some fifteen billion years ago (or, perhaps to be more accurate, just 'before' time began). No one knows for certain how, in the expanding universe, planet Earth appeared some five and a half million years ago, circling the sun (Taylor, pp.332–35). Its carbon content was formed by an improbably complex process in some star of an earlier generation, whose debris (after it had exploded) was swept up by the orbiting proto-earth and forms the basis of all our life systems. How life appeared on the earth some four billion years ago is also not known for certain. Dr Francis Crick has described it as 'almost a miracle' (Crick, 1981, p.88), so strange that he and other scientific gurus have explored the possibility of it being brought to earth from elsewhere in the universe (not that that would explain its origin). No one can explain how the primitive prokaryote cell came about, with its ability to reproduce itself; but it happened. The complexity of the living cell is as mysterious as the complexity of the living organisms that comprise millions of such cells.

It is almost universally agreed nowadays that all life has evolved from protozoa to the present day, although not all the steps of evolution are known to us, and even the precise way that evolution took place is controversial. Species have proliferated. Some thirty billion of them have come into being and passed away. Today, there are probably some thirty million species, although they are rapidly diminishing in what is their sixth (and the only man-made) great extinction. This vast variety of species is as much a subject for wonder as the amazing evolution of the cosmos. We human beings, alone among living things, can appreciate not only their beauty, but also their wonderful adaptation to function, whether within the body (for example, the immune system and the control of automatic functions) or in the outward aspects of the body (for example, the shape and form of the avian wing, or the 'lateral line' of fish which enables them to sense their environment). We have even learnt to regard the world (or rather the biosphere) as a kind of superorganism which evolves cybernetic mechanisms as a result of which it is optimal for life (Lovelock, 1979, p.9ff.).

Placental mammals evolved some sixty-three million years ago. The emergence of hominids is comparatively recent, and human beings evolved, we are told, far more recently, so that their history is to be measured in mere tens of thousands of years. More than 90 per cent of their genes are similar to those of chimpanzees. It follows that animal consciousness has much in common with human consciousness.

The exact make-up of each individual is as improbable as the existence of the rest of the universe. The average male contribution to the process of every conception is some four hundred million sperm, each sperm being unique in the genetic code it carries. So, simply on the basis of genetic inheritance, it is highly improbable that each one of us should exist with our precise genetic make-up. But we do all exist, and we have made phenomenal advances in intelligence, imagination and relationships, partly through our ability to speak and partly through cortical development. In addition to technical abilities, mankind has developed music, poetry, art and many intellectual disciplines, to say nothing of spiritual and moral insights and psychic powers.

To sketch in the whole panorama of evolution in this way may seem an odd way to begin an overview of man's psychic nature, but it is a necessary background if these psychic powers are to be seen in proper perspective. The fact that scientists have made such huge advances in understanding the history and nature of the natural world is amazing; but it should not obscure the truth that there is much that is still puzzling and mysterious in the development of the universe and the evolution of the planet. Scientists usually write about what they know, but just occasionally they can be persuaded to write about what they do not know. They did so in *The Encyclopaedia of Ignorance* (1977). Although some of the puzzles outlined there will have been solved during the last quarter century, others have not. As yet the final and efficient causes of sleep are unknown.

Naturally, psychic phenomena are not among the puzzles found in that encyclopaedia. Yet, these are even more mysterious than many of the remaining physical puzzles about the material universe. Just as it is hard to reconcile classical physics with quantum theory, so the psychic faculties of human personality cannot easily be reconciled with the phenomena of normal consciousness. Nonetheless, these psychic factors seem to me as undeniable as the realities of quantum physics. Just as scientists are beginning to realise that the natural world is far stranger than they thought (with the smallest elements of matter seemingly not material at all), so we have hardly begun to plumb the depths and scale the heights of human personality, which is far, far richer than had earlier been imagined.

Some psychic factors seem to have emerged in the course of evolution among non-human species. Domesticated animals, such as dogs and horses, show some evidence of telepathy. These powers are probably more developed in animals in the wild, about which it has not been possible as yet to conduct similar research. While it is always possible to dismiss all telepathy on the ground of coincidence, that seems to me to be far more improbable than the fact of telepathy itself. Telepathy would have been useful to a wild animal in giving warning of the approach of a predator, or in searching for a member of its group that was lost. It may even have originated among those groups of living creatures that form a superorganism, with differing functions within the group. We do not know what the basis of telepathy is and how it functions. We do not know why some human beings seem open to telepathy while others are not, but it seems likely that it is inherited by human beings from animal forebears, although with human beings it seems to be more articulated in the sense that what is communicated is not just emotion, but has some verbal or visual content.

Precognition is probably a further refinement of telepathy, although an important new factor is likely to be involved here. That there is a connection between the two seems probable because it was laboratory tests in connection with telepathy that revealed evidence of precognition. In my view, it is impossible to dismiss precognition by explaining it all as mere coincidence: the instances I have cited (and many, many more could be given) show this to be less credible than accepting it as a fact. Precognition cannot be a faculty of the brain, because the brain only processes information and retrieves it from its memory bank. In order to be aware of the future, a person must have some transcendental faculty, capable in some sense of existing outside time and therefore able to foresee something that will happen before it has actually happened. If this is not a faculty of the brain, it must be a faculty of the soul, which in a sense does exist outside time, as well as being anchored to a brain during a person's lifetime. Being immaterial, the soul is not confined to the spatio-temporal sphere. In order to explain precognition, therefore, it is necessary to assume that the soul can be distinguished from the brain. Although, as I have tried to demonstrate, this is a reasonable assumption, it is one of the reasons for many scientists' dislike of parapsychology, for if souls exist, they are not accessible to scientific analysis. It is easier for those who believe that the mind is identical with the brain to omit all mention of such an awkward subject like parapsychology (Blakemore, 1988; Cotterill, 1989).

Dowsing is a faculty with which many people in various countries have been endowed. In view of the satisfied customers of water diviners who have found underground supplies (among whom I count myself when a diviner found water supplies some years ago for our isolated holiday home), it seems foolish to dismiss this faculty on *a priori* grounds, on the mere grounds of improbability. It appears that some people can use the same dowsing faculty for the discovery of minerals or oil fields underground. Professor Dawkins seems to want such people to face criminal prosecution (Dawkins, p.121), but presumably hard-headed oil tycoons would not employ dowsers unless they felt that they were getting their money's worth. It is noteworthy that the extension of dowsing to minerals has been practised in Eastern Europe as well as in Western Europe. There is no explanation of the mode by which dowsing functions. Doctors in the past have found herbal remedies for the relief of sickness without knowing how they work, and no one objects to such pragmatism. Similarly, we can accept pragmatically that dowsing works, without knowing how it works.

As for the sense of being stared at from behind, without seeing the person concerned in a mirror or using any of our other senses, that is such a common phenomenon that it hardly seems to need comment, except to make the crucial point that it shows that extrasensory perception does exist.

Mediums present a difficult problem, because so many cases of fraud have been uncovered. But the fact that some are fraudulent should not prejudice us into thinking that *all* mediums are frauds. There is, in my judgement, good reason to believe that they are not. However, it is far from clear what is actually happening. Sceptics will say that a medium's 'control', if not fraudulent, is really a sign of 'multiple personality' akin to what can found in some who suffer from hysteria. Or they may say that a trancelike condition gives rise to hallucinatory phenomena, or that the knowledge of mediums is obtained telepathically from other people. They may be right in some cases. On the other hand, there is, in my judgement, genuine communication with the dead in other cases. To Christians, this should cause no surprise. They believe in 'the communion of saints', that is, that the living are linked in fellowship with the dead, so it should not seem incredible to them that some gifted souls are able to communicate with those with whom they already believe themselves to be in fellowship. If a person's soul is immaterial, and not confined to the spatio-temporal sphere, this eases the problem of how communication with discarnate souls may be possible. As Montague Keen, Secretary of the Survival Committee of SPR wrote to *The Times* in December 1997:

> Critics are confronted by an inescapable dilemma which they resolutely refuse to face: the huge number of recorded communications which give correct and precise information that could not have been known to the medium come indeed from spirit sources or are acquired paranormally by the medium's subliminal mind.

It seems incredible that mediums should be able to describe the owners of objects simply by holding their objects in their hands, and also should be able to foretell by this means a person's future, or recount the past. There is no known way by which this could happen. But the fact remains that it does happen. Maybe the object focuses the attention of a medium on its owner as if she or he is present. There are some paranormal phenomena that seem utterly inexplicable in our present state of knowledge.

Automatic writing is also extremely well attested. Those who attempt to explain it by means of the concept of 'multiple personality', in which the subconscious takes control of a person's hand, cannot really account for the phenomenon, especially in the case of 'cross correspondences' – a series of messages to different mediums in different parts of the world each of which on their own would mean nothing, but when put together make sense. Again, it hardly accounts for writing in languages not understood by the writer, nor for the kind of drawings made by Matthew Manning. If the writings do not originate in the subconscious of the writer, they must emanate from elsewhere. Telepathic communication is an insufficient explanation in cases when, for example, messages appear from a former owner of a house, long dead. The conclusion must be that these emanate in some way from spirits of the dead.

Again, psychokinesis at first sight seems most improbable. How can anyone have the ability to move objects at a distance without the use of physical force? The answer is that, in our present state of knowledge, we do not know. We are in a sphere where the normal rules of physics do not apply. At the same time, the comparatively common phenomenon of poltergeist activity leads to the inevitable conclusion that psychokinesis does occur. The evidence, once examined, is far too strong to be dismissed. It is ridiculous to set aside as rubbish well-documented evidence of objects flying across the room merely on the ground that it seems improbable. Again, we are in the sphere of mystery. To say that poltergeists are usually connected with the frustrations of a teenager or the release of psychic energy around the time of puberty does not explain how the phenomena occur: at best, it describes why they occur.

Astrology seems to belong to the era of superstition and satisfies an urge for fortune telling rather than the search for truth; and yet there now exist data that suggest there have been special influences at work on those who are pre-eminent in their professions. There will be those who will dispute the evidence and put the conclusions down to coincidences rather than the influence of planets; but, at the same time, the evidence of thousands of horoscopes is hard to refute.

When we turn to those paranormal phenomena that are related to religion, we have to beware lest religious prejudices cloud our judgement. With near-death experiences, it is difficult to decide whether they have a physical explanation or whether they do indeed represent an incipient journey from this world to the next. I have given reasons for dissatisfaction with all the attempted physical explanations and, on the whole, it seems to me more probable that they are indeed genuine experiences of a transcendental kind which give a fore glimpse of what awaits us when we die. They hang on the genuineness of the out-of-body experience as part of the near-death experience. It has to be remembered that OBEs can happen to people in many situations when the probability is that they are not out of their bodies. But this does not prove that this is the case with NDEs. It will be easier to be more certain of the genuineness of OBEs when experiments have been concluded over objects placed out of sight of a person in a hospital bed, similar to the successful experiments that are said to have taken place in the University of Nevada with people who experience OBEs during sleep. At the same time, it must be admitted that there is some subjective input, if only because we are bound to express transcendental experiences in language and imagery of this world.

Electronic voice phenomena are inexplicable, unless we suppose that thought can in some unknown way impose itself on tape. Raudive's book, *Breakthrough*, is sold with a record of some of the voices of the dead cited in his book. Speech is usually in German or Latvian (which I cannot understand); and short bilingual remarks, especially when one of the languages is Latvian, strain my credulity. The speed of speech and its indistinct nature against the background noise make it easy to imagine that there is a voice where there is none. But the more you listen, the more credible the voices become: the ear gets attuned. The Scole Report seems to corroborate EVP. I am left with an open mind about them. If the alleged voices are genuine, the terseness and speed of the messages and the faintness of the voices suggest that this is a very difficult medium for spirit communication. As for the Scole Report, the jury is still out about the strange phenomena that were encountered. While it would have been desirable for more safeguards to have been permitted during the meetings of the group, nonetheless the reports of what was seen and heard are very remarkable, and it is difficult to regard them as all elaborately contrived to deceive, especially as the Scole group did not, in the first place, ask to be investigated.

As for reincarnation, there are difficulties to be overcome in understanding the union of a reincarnated spirit with genetic inheritance from the two natural parents. There is no proof of reincarnation to be found in lives allegedly recalled under hypnotic trance, and in other cases the possibility of telepathic knowledge of allegedly 'earlier' lives cannot be dismissed. On the other hand there is the remarkable information gathered by Professor Ian Stevenson about children's memories of former lives (and their birthmarks and birth defects) in cultures where reincarnation is generally accepted. Despite objections to his work, it seems to me to have been meticulously documented. The evidence seems strong and presented in an objective manner, but perhaps not quite strong enough to be totally convincing. People from a Christian tradition may reject it *a priori* because it is not part of their tradition, but I have argued that it is not incompatible with Christian belief. I believe that an open verdict must be accepted until there is more conclusive evidence and certain difficulties have been cleared up; but the evidence is already robust.

Christian visions are difficult to evaluate and no doubt for this reason the Roman Catholic Church does not require acceptance of particular visions by its theologians who dissent for good reason, and this openness extends even to those visions officially approved by the Church. Many visions that people have are merely hallucinatory, the result of physiological or psychological pressures, and in some cases of serious mental disorder. But not all religious visions are necessarily of this kind, especially when they occur to people of sound health and mind. There are some criteria by which genuine religious visions can be distinguished from mere hallucinations, but the distinction can be difficult, for genuine visions can be mixed up with subjective elements. Genuine religious visions are 'imaginative' in the sense that, although the vision seems real to the person concerned, it is not visible to others, and therefore the product of their brain. A genuine vision is the result of divine grace working on the visual cortex of the brain.

The most striking paranormal phenomena within the Christian tradition are to be found in the lives of mystics and saints. They are often very well attested in sworn depositions. Even allowing for hagiographical exaggeration, very strange things have happened. For example, there can be little doubt that some saints have levitated, and no natural cause can be found for such a phenomenon. Although inexplicable in terms of physics, it seems to show that the soul is so closely integrated with the body that when the soul soars heavenward, the body is raised in the air. The same kind of psychosomatic explanation should be given for the stigmata, and to the light that can illuminate a holy person, and also to the odour of sanctity. The beauty and fragrance of the soul result in fragrant odours from the body. Other paranormal phenomena are far less explicable, such as the paranormal provision of bread (which seems more like a response to prayer): on the other hand, these are very well attested, and I accept them. In some cases, parallels for apparently paranormal behaviour can be found in hysterical behaviour (for example, in very long abstinence from food and drink), but the fact that there are parallels should not mean that the phenomena should always be regarded as hysterical. Because there are similarities, there is not necessarily identity. Those parts of the cortex and other elements of the brain that give rise to hysterical symptoms may well be the same as those that enable paranormal phenomena to be manifested.

Some healings achieved through the saints are inexplicable in medical terms. In the same way, incorruption of corpses and their retention of blood long after this could be expected are equally inexplicable: yet these occur. We accept that these are paranormal without any idea how they take place.

From the saints we move easily to the gospels and the Pauline epistles. Those who take the gospels seriously cannot afford to neglect the paranormal, even though the very idea will be strange to many. I have even suggested that some events which are usually regarded as miraculous interventions by God (or dismissed by critics as mere myths) may have a paranormal explanation. Such a possibility needs to be taken seriously.

Such a view entails no belittlement of the inspired Scriptures nor of Jesus Christ. In his case they are often signs of full humanity. It may well be that the divine can use the paranormal, as in Jesus's mighty works; and to say so in no way denies the possibility in some cases of direct divine intervention. Jesus never asked to be believed because of his miracles: he spoke against those people who wanted signs and wonders. Pope Leo was wrong when he wrote in his famous letter to Flavian, that 'to satisfy five thousand men with bread, to calm a tempest and to walk on water without sinking is without ambiguity divine' (Leo, A.D. 449). Jesus's divine nature is not shown by miracles: it shines out of his character and is attested to by his resurrection. In a not dissimilar way, the saints never claimed sanctity because of paranormal gifts: on the contrary, in the pursuit of the vision of God they found them somewhat embarrassing and usually tried to keep them from the common gaze. It is the spiritual nature of their lives, not outward paranormal phenomena, that attests to their sanctity. The appearance of the paranormal in the Scriptures and in the lives of saints and, of course, in Jesus does raise the question of the relation of the paranormal to the spiritual. They are not to be equated, but there must be some connection, but it is difficult to know just what it is. Without doubt the paranormal can be used as a channel of grace, just as the natural world can too.

I do not understand how people can refuse to admit that ghosts exist. There is testimony to their existence in every culture. There are many contemporary references. Recently, people buying a house asked that the price be reduced when they found that it was haunted. The evidence for apparitions of the living is strong: perhaps they are telepathic messages transcribed into living images: we do not know. Cases of apparitions, which appear to those closely related to a person at the moment of the death of that person, are far too numerous to be dismissed out of hand. Perhaps these apparitions at the moment of death are telepathic in character; perhaps they represent a spiritual being; we cannot be sure. But they happen, and they cannot be accounted for, other than by regarding them as paranormal. Similarly, evidence of hauntings cannot be dismissed on the grounds that people are superstitious and they see what they expect to see, for many happen to people who have had no previous knowledge of a haunting in that particular locality. Lord Rees-Mogg not long ago wrote about ghosts.

> I do believe in them, simply on the weight of evidence. I have never seen a ghost but I know many honest and sane people who have. A cousin discussed rare beetles with a British Museum entomologist in the New Forest: the entomologist had died ten years before. The same cousin frequently saw C Aubrey Smith's terrier in the family drawing room; the dog was long dead. Two ladies saw the Ston Easton ghost in what used to be our bed-room: in the attic room above, the upstairs maid had been murdered in the 1970s.

I even knew someone when she was alive who was seen after her death as a spirit. A cousin by marriage owned a house near Stratford-on-Avon. She spent her last years as an invalid, sitting in a garden summerhouse which had been built by her first husband in 1910. I used to sit and talk to her there. I went back to see the house in the 1980s, and was told by the owner, a widow, that the garden house was haunted by an old lady who left a great feeling of happiness and peace. The widow had no idea who that might be.

My grandmother's first cousin, who was knighted for being a successful Victorian Commissioner at the Metropolitan Police, was invited to stay at Longleat. As he came into the drawing room the company was called into dinner; he asked Lady Bath whether they should wait for the lady dressed in grey on the stairs. The grey lady is the most celebrated of the Longleat ghosts.

So the stories go on. Some no doubt are embellished, or become so. Any individual story may have been made up, or may have a natural explanation. Yet there are so many of them, and so many of the witnesses are so good, that it is sheer superstition to refuse to look at the evidence. Something happens, if we do not know what.

Rees-Mogg, 1997

We do not know what happens, but at least we can speculate. One speculation has been that, when death occurs, the body begins immediately to degenerate, but the self may take longer to disintegrate, and there may remain for a time a psychic husk, a 'psychic factor'. Professor Broad speculated along these lines.

If I may stick my neck out, I would say that I find it useful to picture a psi component of a highly complex and persistent vortex in the old-fashioned ether; associated (as a kind of 'field') with a living brain and nervous system, and with events and processes in the latter; having imposed upon it, by those events and processes, certain characteristics and more or less persistent 'modulations'; and capable of persisting (at any rate for a longer or shorter period), as a vortex on the surface of a pond may persist after the dropping of a stone into the water. The notion of a psi component does not of course presuppose this, or any other, concrete specification. But I find it convenient to have one, and this is the one I use.

Broad, p.419

Professor Broad was a self-confessed agnostic. Indeed, he ended his lectures on psychic research by affirming that:

> I would be slightly more annoyed than surprised to find myself persisting after the death of my present body.

I suspect that his prejudices made him unwilling to envisage for himself a future spiritual soul rather than a mere psychic husk. I can see no reason why the soul should not be substantial and enduring, although we know too little about our eternal destiny to know whether or not it will be everlasting. At the very least, we can say that a person persists after death, and that ghosts are not merely hallucinations. Christians believe that a person outlives death, so that God's purposes may be perfected in her or him. Christians, however, are somewhat wedded to the doctrine of the resurrection of the body rather than to the persistence of the soul, and they do not, alas, take kindly to the notion that the former refers to the same process as the latter, described in terms of a different tradition and culture.

If souls do survive death, it is not surprising that some of them should wish to help people who are still alive on earth, and that one form of such help should be concerned with healing, in terms of both diagnosis and therapy. Presumably, it would be those who knew something about healing during their earthly lifespan who would wish thereafter to continue a ministry of healing among people on earth. How does the process of healing occur through departed spirits? We cannot pretend to knowledge that we do not possess. We do not even know how spiritual healing takes place through the ministry of living people who have the gift of healing through the laying on of hands, so how we can we know how it occurs through the ministry of departed spirits? When people speak of draughts of hot or cold air over the affected parts, they are speaking only of their own subjective impressions, not necessarily about what is actually happening. The notion that some people have a superfluity of life force or exude radiation of a kind undetectable by modern medical technology is purely suppositional. It is better to admit ignorance.

An extension of the Christian ministry of healing is the

Christian ministry of deliverance. It has a twofold aim: to help to send on their way to the Light those lost souls who have become earthbound, perhaps without even realising this; and to deliver people on earth from the influence of evil spirits and malicious souls.

So far as earthbound spirits of the dead are concerned, it would perhaps not be surprising that some have lost their spiritual way at death, when one considers how easy it is for people to lose their spiritual way during their earthly life. Materialism is often (and rightly) condemned on the grounds that it is deadening to the soul, and the same is (again rightly) said of all forms of evil and wickedness. It is understandable, therefore, that some souls are so convinced that their material existence is the only form of existence that they cannot realise that they are dead, and that some others are so bound up with their work on earth that their one wish is to continue it. Those who suffer from sudden death may not realise that they are no longer alive. Such souls are in need not of banishment and condemnation, but of help and assistance; and those who are especially gifted so as to be in communication with these earthbound souls can give them the help that they need (providing they are willing to receive it), just as pastors can give people living on earth the help and assistance that they need.

Most of us are a mixture of good and bad, with only a few that are saintly and a few who are really evil. There is no good reason to imagine that we are the only spiritual beings in all creation. If there are other forms of spiritual beings, it is likely that some will be good and helpful (among whom I would include guardian angels), while others will be evil and destructive. We know that evil people on earth have an evil influence on other people, and in rare cases they can so dominate them that these people have no will of their own. It follows, therefore, that people can also come under the influence of evil spirits and in very rare cases may even be taken over or 'possessed' by them. In the early Church, one of the chief reasons why Christianity spread so fast was that it became evident that Christ had power over the demons which were believed by people to oppress them. It remains true for all time that Christ has conquered evil and he is therefore supreme over evil spirits. It follows that it is effective to invoke the power of Christ to make evil spirits depart to their own place, and to stop them polluting a locality and influencing (and on rare occasions possessing) human beings. Naturally, this invocation of the power of Christ is a special ministry that requires special aptitudes, special training and deep commitment to Christ. Those licensed to undertake this ministry can testify to its extraordinary effectiveness.

In conclusion, I repeat what I have written elsewhere in this book, that the scientific method can seldom be applied to most paranormal phenomena; that there is a psychic sphere of reality in which it is dangerous for an untrained person to meddle; that extrasensory perception does occur; that some kind of non-physical causality does exist; that the mind (and the soul) is not confined to the physical brain; that life extends beyond death; that communication between the living and dead is possible; that there is a very close connection between the human spirit and our physical body, and this is manifested particularly in the lives of saints and mystics; that many of the so-called miracles of Jesus are in fact a manifestation of the paranormal powers with which his full humanity was endowed, in support of his ministry to inaugurate God's Kingdom on earth. These are important conclusions, and they run counter to contemporary scientific assumptions.

It is surely prejudice that causes a distinguished philosopher of religion to write that belief in the paranormal is 'superstitious' (Cupitt, p.25). On the contrary, it is superstitious not to accept such things in the face of the evidence, on the grounds that they do not fit in with one's presuppositions. There are forces and powers in the universe that we do not understand. One of our foremost mathematicians has written about physics:

> My own view is that, to understand quantum non-locality, we shall require a radically new theory. This new theory will not just be a modification of quantum mechanics, but something as different from quantum mechanics as General Relativity is different from Newtonian gravity. It would have to be something which has a completely different conceptual framework.
>
> Penrose, p.137

If physicists are looking for an entirely new conceptual framework to explain physical phenomena, it seems reasonable that those investigating psychic phenomena should need an entirely new conceptual framework to explain psychic phenomena.

Professor Dawkins has recently stated that belief in the paranormal is an abuse. He strongly disapproves. He has expressed disbelief in poltergeist activity and he writes that he regards dowsing as a confidence trick. In the adult world, he says,

> There are no devils, no hellfire, no wicked witches, no haunted houses, no daemonic possession, no bogeymen or ogres.
>
> Dawkins, p.137

No, no, Dr Dawkins! I do not know about ogres or bogeymen, because I am not sure what they are. But I am sure about psychic realities, and I have given evidence about them in this book. It is only right and proper that a Professor of the Public Understanding of Science should be concerned about the public understanding of science. But why must this involve running down paranormal phenomena? They badly need further investigation. I believe that we are deeply impoverished if we turn our backs on the evidence of psychic realities and reject the paranormal. It needs further investigation among scientists. I also regret the reluctance of the Church to investigate paranormal phenomena as part of God's creation, especially in the interface of the psychic and the spiritual; and it is my hope that this book may contribute to a renaissance of interest.

Appendices

Appendix I
THE SOUL AND THE BRAIN

In the main chapters of this book, there has been a discussion of phenomena, culled from the actual experiences of real people, for which normal explanations do not seem to suffice, and which are regarded by many people as paranormal. A good many of these experiences assume the existence of a discarnate spirit or entity – call it what you like – which is connected with a dead person. Near-death experiences, visions of dead people, ghosts and reincarnation, if any one of these be accepted as genuine, presume some kind of continuance of a person after death, and exorcism presupposes the existence of discarnate spirits.

Is this credible in the light of science and philosophy? Does not the idea of a soul or a mind which is not dependent on the brain belong to a past pre-scientific age, before people had knowledge about the functioning of the brain and its close connection with mind states? Dualism has even been called a 'scientific heresy'. This is the assumption of many thinkers today, scientists and philosophers. There is, it is claimed, 'overwhelming evidence that the mind is the activity of the brain' (Pinker, p.129). Many rule out of court the very idea of these paranormal phenomena because of their assumption that when the brain dies, so also do the mind and the soul. There even seems to be a foretaste of this in some biblical texts.

> The Lord God formed man from the dust of the ground and breathed into his nostrils the breath of life, and man became a living being.
>
> Genesis 2:7

If man is wholly made of matter, and if the breath of life is removed, it follows that his mind and soul disintegrate with his body when he dies. There are, of course, other texts that could be adduced to the contrary, such as:

> Do not fear those that can kill the body and not the soul; rather fear him who can destroy both body and soul in hell.
>
> Matthew 10:28

But this important matter requires not textual proofs, but philosophical and scientific consideration. I am including this appendix on the relationship of brain and mind because there would be no point in investigating alleged paranormal phenomena if they made no sense on scientific or philosophical grounds.

It is not my object to prove that the mind is not dependent on the brain. Substantial volumes have already been written on this subject from various viewpoints (Foster, 1991; Chalmers, 1996; Swinburne, 1986). I doubt whether proof one way or the other can ever be achieved. All that will be attempted here is to show that it is reasonable to hold that the mind is not identical with the brain, and that there are grave difficulties in holding a contrary view. It is possible to argue the problem from a scientific or from a philosophical stance, or to combine both.

Scientific Views of the Mind/Body Relationship

A scientist naturally looks for answers in scientific terms. Francis Crick has entitled his work on this subject, *The Astonishing Hypothesis*. He begins his book thus:

> The Astonishing Hypothesis is that 'You', your joys and your sorrows, your sense of personal identity and free will, are in fact no more than the behaviour of a vast assembly of nerve cells and their associated molecules. As Lewis Carroll's Alice might have put it: 'You're nothing but a pack of neurons.' The idea is so alien to most people who are alive today that it can truly be called astonishing.
>
> Crick, 1982, p.3

It is, of course, perfectly proper for a scientist to approach the question of the mind/body relationship in this way, and if he thinks fit, to examine a hypothesis of this kind to see whether he can vindicate it on scientific grounds. The crux is to find an objective scientific explanation for the subjective experience of consciousness. It is interesting that Crick, for all his scientific expertise, cannot achieve this. He does, indeed, sketch out as a rough guide to a solution some kind of overall scheme about the origin of consciousness involving cortical connections with the thalamus. But he is very cautious indeed about putting weight on it. He comments thus on his own hypothesis:

> So much for a plausible model. I hope no one will call it the Crick (or the Crick-Koch) Theory of Consciousness. While writing it down, my mind was constantly assailed by reservations and qualifications. If anyone else produced it, I would unhesitatingly condemn it as a pack of cards. Touch it and it collapses. This is because it has been carpentered together, with not enough crucial experimental evidence to support its various parts. Its only virtue is that it may prod scientists and philosophers to think about these problems in neural terms, and so accelerate the experimental attack on consciousness.
>
> Crick, 1982, p.252

The fact that Crick has not found a solution to the phenomenon of consciousness that is tenable in scientific terms does not in itself imply that no such explanation can exist. It does, however, enable someone to hold with perfect propriety that the mind – and the soul – cannot be explained (or explained away) in material terms.

Crick, of course, is not the only person to attempt a scientific solution to the problem. The neurobiology of the brain, with its multiple circuits, has been used in the attempt to explain consciousness. Such theories bring in the various elements of the brain: the hippocampus, amygdala, septum, Broca's and Wernicke's areas, as well as various regions of the cortex. But an objective study of brain mechanism cannot explain the subjective experience of awareness any more than an analysis of an ulcerous condition of the stomach can explain a subjective feeling of postprandial pain. Such an approach may well explain the way in which our mental states function, but it does nothing to explain the fact of consciousness itself.

Nor does it help to invoke evolution as an explanation. It may be generally agreed that cultural evolution as well as natural selection accounts for the development of the brain from that of a primitive hominid to that of Homo sapiens. But consciousness does not seem to have functional value for survival or for propagation. A zombie (a creature that would be our identical twin except that it would have no consciousness) could function as well as Homo sapiens, even though it would lack any consciousness.

Dennett prefers an explanation along the lines of cognitive modelling. He replaces the Cartesian metaphors of consciousness with such words as software, virtual machines, multiple paths, etc. Emphasising their plasticity, he uses the model of parallel computers, which are enormously more powerful than an ordinary computer.

> There is no single definitive 'stream of consciousness' because there is no central Headquarters, no Cartesian Theatre where 'it all comes together' for the perusal of a Central Meaner. Instead of such a single stream (however wide) there are multiple channels in which specialist circuits try, in parallel pandemoniums, to do their various things...
>
> Dennett, p.254

An argument like this may well illuminate some of the somewhat chaotic contents of consciousness; but it accounts neither for the unconscious, nor for the subjective experience of consciousness arising from the objective functioning of the brain.

A different scientific approach to consciousness makes use of quantum theory to explain the phenomenon. Penrose has argued that Gödel's Theory shows that mathematical theory is not computational, because it cannot be coded in the form of some computation that we know to be correct (that is to say, any particular calculation depends upon axioms unprovable within the terms of the calculation). So if it is non-computational, it must be something else. Since it is unreasonable to separate mathematical understanding from other forms of understanding, it follows that all understanding is non-computational; so it cannot be satisfactorily explained after the model of a computer. Penrose believes that quantum gravity may also be non-computational and that there may be higher order types of quantum gravity. It may exist in the microtubules of the human brain. If this be so, it would account for the non-computational nature of human judgement, common sense, insight, aesthetic sensibility and morality, and also for the human values of truth, goodness and beauty. In this way, Penrose hopes to make the higher functions of the brain accessible to the natural sciences (Penrose, pp.112–33). He may have found their physical basis (I do not know), but they still need, in the words of Popper, which I shall quote later, the self which can play on the brain as the pianist plays on the piano, or a driver on the controls of a car; and quantum gravity cannot give any explanation of the subjective experience of consciousness.

It has been suggested that the existence of the self has been disproved by scientific measurement. If volunteers decide to move one of their limbs in some way, it is possible for them to note from a clock the precise moment when they make this decision. It is also possible, by fixing an electrode to the place on their bodies where the movement takes place, to record the exact time when this occurs, and also by fixing an electrode to the scalp, to record the exact time when a particular brain pattern known as 'the readiness potential' takes place. The latter occurs just before a complex action takes place, and is thought to be associated with what happens in the brain when the next move is being planned. Benjamin Libet of the University of California in San Francisco persuaded volunteers to carry out this experiment. He found that the decision to move comes not before but after the electrode attached to the scalp records 'the readiness potential'. Even if this is the case, it does not disprove the existence of the self. It only shows that the self may be more complex than is generally thought. One perfectly adequate explanation of this phenomenon could be that a decision is made unconsciously by the self just before a person becomes conscious of this decision.

It used to be thought that the centre of consciousness was associated with a characteristic frequency in a particular part of the brain, such as the thalamus with its amplifying loops. Certainly, Positron Emission Topography (PET) shows which parts of the brain have to work hardest when a person is having thoughts. Functional Magnetic Imaging (FMIRI) is even more sophisticated.

By means of this, the actual oxygen levels of blood can be measured as they flow through the brain. Similarly, MEG (magnetoencephalography) measures the electrical activity of different parts of the brain. The result of these technologies, however, is to show that the brain works in a holistic way. Reductionism is no longer seen to be appropriate. While certain aspects of the brain may be compared to a computer, the brain as a whole functions dynamically, with many interconnections and feedbacks from its different parts.

These technologies may shed light on how the brain functions, but they shed no light at all on the subjective aspect of consciousness. There are evident difficulties in the scientific approach to the mind/brain relationship. Science has been unable to prove that mind is the activity of the brain.

Philosophical Approaches

There are those who hold that the mind is to be equated with the brain. This is sometimes called 'hard materialism'. At first sight, it seems ridiculous to equate a physical organism with a non-physical mental state. But highly intelligent people have made this equation. Professor Gilbert Ryle felt very strongly on the subject, referring to dualism by the phrase 'ghost in the machine':

> I shall often speak of it with deliberate abusiveness, as the 'dogma' of the 'Ghost in the Machine'. I hope to prove that it is entirely false not only in detail but also in principle. It is not merely an assemblage of particular mistakes. It is one mistake, and a mistake of a particular kind. It is a category mistake...
>
> Ryle, p.17

The phrase 'ghost in the machine' is a caricature. No dualist thinks of the mind or the soul as a ghost. Ghost implies an entity that is not merely invisible for most of the time, but also passive and insubstantial. Far from being insubstantial, the self is at the centre of human personality; nor is it passive, since it is actively searching and it can actually modify neuronal systems in the brain.

In the place of dualism, Ryle substituted behaviourism, the theory that all statements about the mind are in the last analysis to be understood in behavioural terms. At first sight, this seems absurd, but the word 'behaviour' is used by him in an extended sense to include behavioural dispositions. Even then, it hardly copes with the situation when I am conscious of a pain, but this pain in no way affects my behaviour. The difficulty about behaviourism is that is not able to explain conscious experience. I do not mean the content of experience – it is able usually to give some sort of explanation of that – but the fact of consciousness itself. The same objection applies to a similar theory called functionalism, which attempts to explain apparent mental events in terms of their causes and effects.

There is a further type of materialism, which might be called 'soft materialism'. According to this way of thinking, matter can have both physical properties and mental properties, and the two are distinct. The brain has both. Without the material brain there could be no mental properties. As matter becomes more complex, it evolves new states of being. At the simplest level, there is physics. More complex physical structures give rise to chemical structures, with their own laws. Again, more complex chemical structures give rise to life, and hence biological structures. These structures are composed of simpler elements, but they exist in such complex forms that new kinds of structures are produced with new kinds of laws. According to this theory, very complex forms of biological structures in the brain give rise to mind, with its own mental laws. Without the simpler elements of which it is composed, mind could not exist. There is no separate entity, mind or soul or self. Mind has evolved on the basis of brain, and cannot exist without it. This is the form of materialism that is most common today. But there is a problem, because mind is entirely different from brain. If a brain is dissected, it can be reduced to chemical and physical properties. But you cannot reduce mind to brain. They are entirely different in kind. The brain, a biological organism, obeys the laws of physics and chemistry and biology. But mind in no sense obeys the laws of physics, chemistry, or biology. It does not function according to any of the laws of matter. How then can it be a property of the material brain? This is the great difficulty that soft materialism has to face.

There is another form of materialism that seeks to evade this difficulty called 'naturalistic materialism'. Consciousness is thought to be a property that arises from a physical basis, but which is governed, not by the fundamental laws of physics, but by a natural law that is psychophysical in nature. Although it is 'ontologically independent of physical properties' it is not itself a physical substance (Chalmers, p.125). This view is not unlike soft materialism, in as much as it holds that physical matter can produce mental states as well as brain states, with the proviso that the former is not reducible to the latter.

The advantage of naturalistic dualism is that it leaves intact the causally closed world of physics. No 'ghost' can in any way influence the 'machine' of the brain, for consciousness is envisaged as entirely passive, leaving the individual to have conscious experiences, but in no way able to order, interpret or initiate conscious experience. On the one hand, it insists that consciousness, although derived from a physical base, is itself something entirely non-physical. On the other hand, it in no way upsets the materialist assumptions of contemporary science, for it retains the causally closed world of physics.

The difficulty of this theory (and it is only a theory) is that it seems to treat consciousness like a surd, something that appears for no apparent reason from the physical world, but is not part of it. Since it is entirely non-physical (according to this theory), it is difficult to see how it could be produced by the random mutation of physical entities such as genes. So the theory cannot give a satisfactory reason for the emergence of consciousness.

This is the basic difficulty that besets all scientific explanations and materialistic theories of consciousness. Of course, increasingly sophisticated reductive 'explanations' of consciousness will be put forward, but these will produce only increasingly sophisticated explanations of cognitive functions. Even such 'revolutionary' developments as the invocation of connectionist networks, non-linear dynamics, artificial life and quantum mechanics will provide only more powerful functional explanations. This may make very interesting cognitive science, but the mystery of consciousness will not be removed.

Dualist Theories of the Mind/Body Relationship

The alternative is to posit not just one organism with different properties, but two different entities – the brain and the mind. Scientists and philosophers have held and do hold this view (for example, Koestler, 1972; Swinburne 1986). Sir Karl Popper was an eminent philosopher and Sir John Eccles a very distinguished brain scientist. Here is a quotation from a dialogue between them, when they were discussing materialistic theories of consciousness:

ECCLES: We can now turn to other aspects of the basis for our strong dualistic hypothesis. I want to mention just briefly that our self-conscious mind has some coherence with the neuronal operations of the brain, but we have furthermore to recognise that it is not in a passive relationship. It is an active relationship searching and modifying the neuronal operations. So this is a very strong dualism, and it separates our views from any parallelistic views where the self-conscious mind is passive. That is the essence of the parallelistic hypothesis. All varieties of identity theories imply that the mind's conscious experiences have a merely passive relationship as a spin-off of the neuronal machinery, which themselves are self-sufficient. These operations give the whole motor performance, and in addition give all conscious experiences and all memory retrievals. Thus on the parallelistic hypotheses the operations of the neuronal machinery provide a necessary and sufficient explanation of all human actions.

POPPER: That is exactly what I tried to express when, with a feeling of despair, I said in Oxford in 1950 that I believed in the ghost in the machine. That is to say, I think that the self plays on the brain, as a pianist plays on the piano or a driver on the controls of a car.

Popper and Eccles, p.484

When Eccles speaks here of neuronal activity, he is referring to the functioning of the brain, and when he refers to parallelistic views, he is speaking of materialist theories which we have briefly examined, and which equate the brain with the mind, and thereby eliminate the concept of the self.

Memory, Mind and Brain

If we hold that there is a self as well as the brain, what are we to make of the memory and the unconscious?

There are various kinds of memory. The simplest are the unconscious memories of skills that have been learnt. These are to be found almost everywhere in the animal kingdom. Research suggests that these memories are stored through modification of nerve cells in an animal's brain as a result of incoming messages, and are probably connected with the hippocampus, which lies beneath the temporal lobe of the brain, and may reside in the cerebellum, which lies close to the brainstem.

Human beings have developed two further types of memory, both of them conscious. Short-term memories are probably the result of circuits of cortical nerve cells in the brain forming closed loops, causing memories to last for a short time as they reverberate, rather like the fading resonance of a tolling bell. In order to make sense of these neuronal circuits, consciousness is needed. As consciousness cannot be fully explained in purely materialist terms, the self is needed for the short-term memory to operate.

There is also the long-term memory which stores a person's everyday experience. How this long-term memory comes about is not known, nor is how it is stored. It is thought that signals are sent that modify the hippocampus, and that 'signals sent back to the cerebellum from the hippocampus result in a permanent change in a distributed network of cortical cells' (Blakemore, p.61). The change that takes place is probably in the shapes and sizes of the synaptic contacts in many parts of the cortex. Experience of parallel computers suggests that by this means vast amounts of information can be stored. No one knows how we can recall memories into consciousness.

This is an extremely abbreviated account of a very complex and mysterious subject, namely, how memories function. Neither the short-term nor the long-term memory would be of any use whatsoever to mankind without consciousness. We have already maintained that there can be no materialist explanation of consciousness. It belongs, not to the brain, but to the mind, which is in a very close relationship with the brain. In ways unknown to us, this close embrace of soul and brain enables memories, which consciousness brings into experience from synaptic modifications in the cortical networks, to be imprinted on the mind also. How this happens we do not know, and probably we cannot know. In such a view, the mind, even when sundered from the body by death, can still retain memories of its past life on earth.

Long-term memories seem to be stored in a memory bank, and hypnosis has shown that many memories are stored at a level below consciousness. What is stored is not merely physical memories, but also so called 'qualia' such as intentionality, etc. Since a brain is a purely physical entity, it has been argued that it cannot store representations that are not physical in themselves (Rivas, p.34). Thus there is posited a mental memory bank that is able to contain such 'qualia'.

The Soul

The mind is the part of human personality that is connected with mental states. It makes possible the consciousness of human sensations and feelings, attitudes and purposes and decisions. It is sometimes referred to as the self, in so much as it is in control of the conscious processes of the mind (although not of its unconscious processes, which it can however suppress). The soul is a somewhat broader concept, which includes the mind, but refers in particular to a self in relationship to God and to other people. Those who believe in the psychic world hold that the soul has access to that world with its paranormal characteristics. Since the life of those animals high in the scale of nature enjoy more than mere sensation and share to a greater or lesser degree in consciousness, they also have souls appropriate to their stage of mental development. Such a view of animal souls, which takes its origin from Aristotle, has been held in orthodox Christian circles for centuries.

Some Christians hold that, as evolution is active throughout the universe, it is appropriate to hold that God so ordered things that the soul evolves together with the body in accordance with the natural law of its being. In this view, the soul gradually evolves from embryo to foetus to infant (Mahoney, p.21). Again, there are Christians who hold a 'materialist' view of the soul, believing that it dies on the death of the body, and then at the resurrection it is recreated when God provides the dead with a new spiritual body. According to traditional Christian doctrine, each soul is specifically linked to a human body, although there is a difference of opinion about when this takes place. According to St Thomas Aquinas, it was sixty days after conception for a male and ninety for a female; according to Pope John Paul II, the soul is joined to the body at the moment of conception, a somewhat difficult concept as conception is not instantaneous. According to Plato, the soul is eternal, but (whether or not a person believes that reincarnation can take place) the eternity of the soul is not a Christian doctrine, because God alone is eternal, and everything else is his creation.

Whatever view about the soul is held, it is not simply the passive bearer of consciousness. It is in the driving seat at the centre of human personality, enabling a person to have conscious experiences and so to feel, think and decide to act. It enables a person to have free will. In a materialist view, our thinking and therefore all actions that we take (not merely those that are spontaneous) are either random or physically determined. In a dualist view, actions that are not spontaneous are freely decided by the self.

Although there are marks of similarity here with Descartes' view of the soul, there are also profound differences. From the Cartesian viewpoint, there are two elements in a human being: *res cogitans*, immaterial substance where thinking and experience take place; and *res extensa*, concrete inanimate matter. The two, according to Descartes, are joined together at the pineal gland. The view of the soul put forward here is different. There are certainly two elements, but *res cogitans* is hardly a suitable description of a soul, for this includes relationships with God and with other human beings, and above all it includes consciousness.

It has been objected that Alzheimer's Disease shows the preposterousness of a dualist view.

> A person who can no longer read or write, whose memory has disappeared, whose speech is incoherent and who is totally indifferent to his environment has in effect lost all or most of what we normally call his mind. The relevance of this to our discussion is obvious. While still alive, an Alzheimer patient's brain is severely damaged and most of his mind has disappeared. After his death his brain is not merely damaged but completely destroyed. It is surely logical to conclude that his mind has also gone. It seems preposterous to assume that, when the brain is completely destroyed, the mind suddenly returns intact, with its emotional and intellectual content, including its memory, intact.

> Edwards, p.282

This is a matter about which I have had long personal acquaintance, since my wife suffered from Alzheimer's Disease for fourteen years, and for several years was in the situation described above. I do not believe that her mind had been destroyed. Certainly, her brain was scarcely functioning, but that is different. It was rather like a computer whose software is intact, but whose computer terminal is in increasingly bad repair and may soon cease to function at all; or, to use Professor Swinburne's analogy cited below, there is a fault in the light socket that is increasingly preventing the bulb from illuminating. I have no reason to doubt that in another sphere with another kind of computer terminal her mind and her memory now function again. We have no evidence that this is not the case, nor can there be such evidence, because we can never observe a mind being extinguished at death, whereas there is alleged to be evidence from psychic research that it is not so extinguished. Even if this evidence is not accepted, there still remains no evidence that mind is annihilated at death. This point is made by Bishop Butler (1907), J S Mill (1969), and A C Ewing (1968).

A dualist view of the soul and the body certainly involves difficulties, which may perhaps be more aptly described as mysteries. We have no idea how the soul is joined to the physical body. It seems to function as a kind of field. We have no idea of the relationship of the soul to the brain, except that there is a very close interaction, and (if paranormal phenomena be accepted) it seems that the soul can store memories, etc. which originate in the brain. The soul or the self or the mind is able to direct the brain, to un-code its computations and to receive its non-computational inputs, if there be such. The soul seems to be endowed with its own motive power which directs the functioning of the brain (except, of course, during sleep, although there seems to be then the possibility of communication with others through dreams). The energy of the soul is not derived from the body, and it is not material energy: it is a mystery and we do not know what it is.

These difficulties or mysteries are anathema to some people.

> The fundamental unscientific stance of dualism is, to my mind, its most disqualifying feature, and is the reason why in this book I adopt the apparently dogmatic line that dualism is to be avoided at all costs. It is not, I think, that I can give a knockdown proof that dualism in all its forms, is false or incoherent, but that, given the way dualism wallows in mystery, accepting dualism is giving up.
>
> Dennett, p.37

But the phenomenon of consciousness is, as we have shown, equally mysterious for those who hold a materialist stance, because they can give no explanation of it; so there can be no ground for their rejection of the dualist position on this account. Since the soul lies outside the sphere of physics, it does not interfere or contradict the laws of nature discovered through the natural sciences, which are autonomous within their own sphere; but at the same time, it does explain the phenomenon of consciousness and the conviction that we have free will and that we are in control of our minds as much as we are of our bodies.

The relationship of the soul to the brain has been described as follows:

> The soul is like a light bulb and the brain is like an electric socket. If you plug the bulb into the socket and turn the current on, the light will shine. If the socket is damaged, or the current turned off, the light will not shine. So too the soul will function (have a

mental life) if it is plugged into a functioning brain. Destroy the brain or cut off the nutriment supplied by the blood, and the soul will cease to function, remaining inert... Human beings can move light bulbs and put them into entirely different sockets. But no human being knows how to move a soul from one body to another, nor does any natural force do this. Yet the task is one involving no contradiction, and an omnipotent God could achieve it; or maybe there are other processes which will do so. And just as light bulbs do not have to be plugged into sockets in order to shine (loose wires can be attached to them) maybe there are other ways of getting souls to function other than by plugging them into brains.

Swinburne, 1986, p.311

As I wrote earlier, it is not the purpose of this appendix to *prove* that the soul is not dependent on the brain. It is possible, indeed probable, that no such proof exists. I personally believe that the soul is not to be equated with the brain: otherwise I could not have written this book. But I have tried to disregard this conviction in writing this appendix. I have attempted to set out in summary form as fairly as I can various scientific and philosophical positions that are held on this subject, and I have tried to point out the difficulties involved in all these various viewpoints. Since there is no valid argument that can prove that the soul is dependent on the brain, I feel justified in holding a dualist position. While this in no way proves that paranormal phenomena exist, it does allow me to investigate those paranormal phenomena that point to the soul continuing after death, since there is no compelling scientific or philosophical reason why this should not be the case.

Appendix II

PRELIMINARY REPORT ON MATTHEW MANNING'S PHYSICAL PHENOMENA

PHYSICAL PHENOMENA OF MATTHEW MANNING ARE BRIEFLY DESCRIBED

A R G OWEN, MA, PHD

Matthew Manning visited the New Horizons Research Foundation from 18 June to 5 July to participate in both formal and informal sessions of the First Canadian Conference on Psychokinesis.

On 18 and 19 June he gave informal demonstrations of an ability to move a compass needle by passing his hand to and fro at a distance of nine to twelve inches above it. These demonstrations were recorded on film and videotape, and though not sufficiently formal to prove the point with full scientific rigour were striking enough to suggest to the witnesses that Matthew has this unusual power.

On the same days Matthew bent several keys and forks in full view of witnesses. In one case a stainless steel knife held by someone else at about ten foot distance from Matthew was seen to be in process of bending, and did in fact become permanently bent.

During the days of plenary conference sessions (20–24 June) Matthew bent about thirty keys in the presence of several witnesses. Sometimes the key was held in his clenched hand but without any sign that he was applying appreciable muscular effort. On several occasions also Matthew only held the haft of the key, the shaft being visible, so that it could be seen in process of bending. Sometimes the key was held by a witness, and it bent while merely being touched lightly by Matthew.

On 28 June a professional film was made taking the form of an extended interview with Matthew in the presence of Dr Owen, Dr Tanous, Dr Whitton, Professor Josephson, Allen Spraggett, and William McQuestion. The record shows an uninterrupted view of Matthew's hands. The key is seen at the outset to be perfectly straight. After being held for about a minute in Matthew's lightly closed hand it is seen to be in the process of bending. It continues visibly to bend in full view of the camera, with the haft only being held by Matthew.

Dr Douglas Dean, of Newark College of Engineering, Newark, New Jersey, took a number of Kirlian photographs of Matthew's fingertips under two conditions: (a) mental relaxation, (b) in the same state of concentration Matthew usually is when he tries consciously to direct energy into his fingertips. In state (a) the fingertips in the photograph where normal. However, when Matthew was in state (b) the 'aureoles' or 'coronas' around the fingertips were much brighter. 'In addition,' writes Mr Dean, 'Matthew made the white part fill up right into the centre, giving a cloud of brilliant white. I have never seen that before.'

Matthew participated in an experiment which compared his electroencephalogram under conditions (a) and (b). It was found that, in state (b), whether actually bending a key or attempting to do so, his encephalogram contained a remarkable amount of low frequencies. This result has not yet been interpreted. We do not know if this is a concomitant of Matthew's psychic ability, or whether instead it relates to some peculiarity of his emotional or physiological state when carrying out the operation of metal bending by mind power.

6 July 1974
New Horizons Research Foundation
Toronto Society for Psychical Research

ACKNOWLEDGEMENTS

I have made every effort to contact copyright holders but I have not been successful in some cases. To them I offer my apologies. I gratefully acknowledge permission kindly given by the following authors and publishers to quote from their books.

Blackwell's Publishing for a quotation from S Zeki's *Visions of the Brain*;

Continuum for Wiesinger's *Occult Phenomena in the Light of Theology* (Burns Oates) and for J Beloff's *Parapsychology* (Athlone Press) and for R Williams's *St Theresa* (Chapman);

Darton Longman and Todd for D Walker's *The Ministry of Deliverance*;

Peter and Elisabeth Fenwick for their *The Truth in the Light* (Hodder Headline);

R Hale for R Petitpierre's *Exorcising Devils*;

Little Brown for C Sylvia and W Novak's *A Change of Heart*;

News International Syndication for Lord Rees-Mogg's 'Haunted by Evidence of a Spirit World' (*The Times*);

Orion Publishing Group for K Thomas's *Religion and the Decline of Magic* (Weidenfeld and Nicolson);

Oxford University Press for R Swinburne's *Evolution of the Soul*;

Palgrave Publishers for P and L Badham's *Immortality or Extinction?* (Macmillan);

Routledge for C D Broad's *Lectures on Psychical Research*;

SPCK for *Exorcism*, edited by R Petitpierre;

The Tablet for C O'Connell's 'An African Ministry'.

BOOKS CITED OR REFERRED TO IN THE TEXT

Acta Apostolicae Sedis, 1923

Anton-Stevens, D, 'Demons and Daemons', *The Christian Parapsychologist*, 1994

Anton-Stevens, D, 'Visions and Voices', *The Christian Psychiatrist*, 1992

Arndt, W, and Gingrich, F, *A Greek English Dictionary of the New Testament*, CUP, 1957

Aubrey, J, *Miscellanies*, Reeves and Turner, 1890

Bacci, *Life of St Philip Neri*, Antrobus (ed.), 1902, vol. I

Badham, P and L, *Immortality or Extinction?*, Macmillan, 1982

Balfour, R, *Seraphic Keepsake*

Bander, P, *Carry on Talking*, Colin Smythe, 1972

Baring-Gould, L, *The Lives of the Saints*, Longmans Green, 1898

Barker, J C, 'Premonitions of the Aberfan Disaster', *Journal of the Society for Psychical Research*, 1967

Barrow, J D, *The World Within the World*, OUP, 1988

Barrow, W and Westerman, T, *The Divine Road*, Methuen, 1926

Bede, *A History of the English Church and Nation*, translated by L Sherley-Price, Penguin, 1956, Book 5, Chapter 12

Beloff, J, *Parapsychology*, Athlone Press, 1993

Blackmore, S, *Dying to Live*, Grafton Books, 1993

Blake, H, *Talking with Horses*, Souvenir Press, 1972

Blakemore, C, *The Mind Machine*, BBC Books, 1988

Bretherton, D H and Haddon, A H, *The Paranormal in Holy Scripture*, Churches Fellowship for Psychical and Spiritual Studies, 1988

Broad, C D, *Lectures on Psychic Research*, Routledge and Kegan Paul, 1962

Bultmann, R, *Die Geschichte der Synoptischen Tradition*, Göttingen, 1931

Butler, J, *The Analogy of Religion*, Gladstone, W E (ed.), London, 1907

Calvin, J, *Comm. On St John's*, Gospel

Chalmers, D J, *The Conscious Mind*, OUP, 1996

Coffrey, J, *Politics, Religion and the British Revolution: The Mind of Samuel Rutherford*, CUP, 1997

Coghlan, A, 'A Midnight Watch', *New Scientist*, 19 February 1998

Cornwell, R, *Powers of Darkness, Powers of Light*, Viking, 1991

Cotterill, R, *No Ghost in the Machine*, Heinemann, 1989

Creed, J M, *The Gospel According to St Luke*, Macmillan, 1942

Crick, F, *Life Itself*, Simon and Schuster, 1981

Crick, F, *The Astonishing Hypothesis*, Simon and Schuster, 1982

Cupitt, D, *After God*, Weidenfeld and Nicholson, 1997

Cupitt, D, *The Revelation of Being*, SCM Press, 1998

Dalton, K, *et al.*, 'Comparison of Sender/No Sender in the Ganszfield', *Proceedings of the 38th Annual Convention of the Parapsychological Society*, 1995

Dawkins, R, *Unweaving the Rainbow*, Penguin Press, 1998

de Caussade, J P, *Self-Abandonment to Divine Providence*, Burnes Oates, 1959

de Scoraille, R, *Francois Suarez*, Paris, 1911

Dennett, D C, *Consciousness Explained*, Allen Lane, 1991

Dibelius, M, *From Tradition to Gospel*, London, 1934

Drane, A T, *Life of St Catherine*, 1918 edition

Duncan, R, and Weston Smith, M, (eds) *The Encyclopaedia of Ignorance*, Pergamum Press, 1977

Dunne, J W, *An Experiment with Time*, Faber, 1927

Duval, P, and Montredon, E, 'ESP Experiments with Mice',

Journal of Parapsychology, 1974

Edwards, D L, *After Death*, Mowbray, 1999

Edwards, P, *Reincarnation*, Prometheus Books, 1966

Ellis, D J, *The Mediumship of the Tape Recorder*, Ellis, 1978

Enright, D J (ed.), *The Oxford Book of the Supernatural*, Oxford University Press, 1995

Enright, D J (ed.), *The Oxford Book of the Supernatural*, Oxford University Press, 1995

Ertel, S and Irving, K, *The Tenacious Mars Effect*, Urania Trust, 1996

Eusebius, *Hist. Eccl.*

Evans-Wentz, W J, *The Tibetan Book of the Dead*, Oxford University Press, 1957

Ewing, A C, *Non-Linguistic Philosophy*, Allen and Unwin, 1968

Eysenk, H J and Nias, D K H, *Astrology: Science or Superstition?* Temple Smith, 1982

Fenwick P and E, *The Truth in the Light*, Hodder Headline, 1995

Feynman, R P, 'The Theory of Positrons', *Physical Review*, 1949

Foster, J, *The Immaterial Self*, Routledge, 1991

Gaskill, M, *Hellish Nell*, Fourth Estate, 2001

Gauld, A and Cornell, S D, *Poltergeists*, Routledge, 1979

Gheon, R, *The Secret of the Curé d'Ars*, Sheed and Ward, 1929

Goldie, *Story of St Stanislaus Koska*, 1873

Green, C and McCreery, C, *Apparitions*, Hamish Hamilton, 1975

Gregory, R (ed.), *The Oxford Companion to the Mind*, Oxford University Press, 1987

Grey, M, *Return from Death*, Arkana, 1985

Gurney, E, Myers, F W H, Podmore, F, *Phantasms of the Living*, Kegan Paul, 1889, abridged edition, 1918

Hearne, K, *Visions of the Future*, Aquarian Press, 1989

Hettlinger, J, *Exploring the Ultra-Perceptive Faculty*, Ryder, 1941

Hick, J, *Death and Eternal Life*, Collins, 1976

Holldobler, B and Wilson, E O, *Journey of the Ants*, Harvard University Press, 1994

Imbert-Gourbeyre, *La Stigmatisation*, 1

Inglis, B, *Trance*, Grafton Books, 1989

Ingram, J, *The Barmaid's Brain*, Aurum Press, 1999

Israel, M, *Exorcism: The Removal of Evil Influences*, 1997

Ivedell, D, *Journal of the Society for Psychical Research*, 2001

Iverson, J, *More Lives Than One*, Souvenir Press, 1976

James, W, *The Varieties of Religious Experience*, Longmans Green, 1919

Jaynes, J, *The Origin of Consciousness in the Breakdown of the Bicameral Mind*, University of Toronto Press, 1976

Johnson, R J, *The Imprisoned Splendour*, Hodder and Stoughton, 1953

Keen, M, Ellison, A and Fontana, D, 'The Scole Report', *Proceedings of the Society for Psychical Research*, 1999

Kelsey, M, *The Christian and the Supernatural*, Search Press, 1977

Kempis, Thomas à, *St Lidwina of Schiedam*, translated by Sculhy, V, 1912

Koestler, A, *The Roots of Coincidence*, Hutchinson, 1972

Lambertini, Prospero, *De Serv. Det Beatification*

Lambeth Conferences (1867–1930), SPCK, 1948

Leary, T, Metzner R and Alport, R, *The Psychedelic Experience*, Universal Books, 1964

Leggett, D M A, *The Sacred Quest*, Pilgrim Books, 1987

Lemoyne, G B, *Vita del B. Giovanni Bosco*, vol. II

Leo, *Epistola ad Flavianum*, 13 June 449

Lovelock, J, *Gaia*, Oxford University Press, 1979

Lovelock, J, *Healing Gaia*, Harmony Books, 1991

M, Perry (ed.), *Deliverance*, SPCK, 1996

Mackenzie, A, *Hauntings and Apparitions*, Heinemann, 1982

Mahoney, *Bioethics and Belief*, Sheed and Ward, 1981

Mahoney, M, *The Making of Moral Theology*, Clarendon Press, 1987

Manning, M, *The Link*, Corgi, 1974

Manning, M, *In the Minds of Millions*, Allen, 1977

Manning, M, *The Strangers*, Colin Smythe, 1978

Manning, M, *No Faith Required*, Eikstein Publications, 1995

Manning, M, *One Foot in the Stars*, Element Books, 1999

Markwick, B, 'The Establishment of Data Manipulation in the Soal/Shackleton Experiments', *Proceedings of the American Society for Pyschical Research*, 1974

Markwick, E, *Proceedings of the Society for Psychical Research*, 1978

Martyrdom of Polycarp, 15

Matthews, R, 'To Infinity and Beyond', *New Scientist*, 1998

McAll, K, *Healing the Family Tree*, Sheldon Press, 1982

McConnell, J V, 'Cannibalism and Memory in Flatworms', *New Scientist*, 1994

Memmi, G B, SJ, *Vita della Serva de Dio Suor Caterina Savelli*, Rome, 1883

Migne, *Patrologia Latina*, XIV

Mill, J S, *Three Essays on Religion*, Routledge and Kegan Paul, 1969

Mir, M, *Vida de Santa Teresa*, Madrid, 1912

Montefiore, H, *Credible Christianity*, Mowbray, 1993

Montefiore, H, *The Womb and the Tomb*, Fount, 1992

Moody, R A, *Life After Death*, Bantam, 1975

Morris, R, *et al.*, 'Security Measures in an Automatic Ganszfield System', *Proceedings of the 37th Convention of the Parapsychological Association*, 1994

Morris, R, 'What Parapsychologists Do', *The Christian Parapsychologist*, 2000

Morris, R, *New Scientist*, March 2001

Murphy, G, 'An Outline of Survival Evidence', *Journal of the American Society for Psychical Research*, 1945

Myers, F W H, *Human Personality and the Survival of Bodily Death*,

Longmans Green, 1919

Nineham, D E, *St Mark*, Penguin, 1963

O'Connell, G, 'An African Miracle', *The Tablet*, 28 February 1998

Oppenheim, J, *The Other World: Spiritualism and Psychic Research in England 1850–1914*, Cambridge University Press, 1985

Ostrander, S and Shroeder, L, *Psi: Psychical Research Behind the Iron Curtain*, Abacus, 1973

Owen, A R G, *New Horizon*, June 1974, vol. I, no.4

Owen, A, *The Darkened Room*, Virago, 1989

Owens, J E, Cook, E H and Stevenson, L, 'Features of the Near-Death Experience', *The Lancet*, 1990

Parnia, S *et al.*, 'A Qualitative and Quantitative Study of the Incidence, Features and Aetiology of Near-Death Experiences in Cardiac Arrest Survivors', *Resuscitation*, no.48, 2001

Pearce-Higgins, J D, 'Poltergeists, Hauntings and Possession', *Life and Psychical Research*, Rider, 1973

Peers, E A, *Complete Works of St Teresa*, Sheed and Ward, 1950, vol. I

Penrose, R, and Longair, M, *The Large, the Small and the Human Mind*, Cambridge University Press, 1997

Perry M, *The Easter Enigma*, Faber, 1959

Perry M, *Psychic Studies: A Christian's View*, Aquarian Press, 1984

Perry, M (ed.), *Deliverance*, SPCK, 1996

Petitpierre, Dom R, *Exorcising Devils*, Hale, 1976

Petitpierre, *Exorcism*, Dom R (ed.), SPCK, 1992

Pinker, S, *How the Mind Works*, Penguin, 1998

Polkinghorne, J, 'How the Resurrection Makes Sense', *The Tablet*, 7–10 April 1999

Popper, K, and Eccles, J, *The Self and Its Brain*, Springer, 1977

Pratt, J G, *Parapsychology*, Allen, 1964

Prayer and the Departed: Report of the Archbishops' Commission on Christian Doctrine, SPCK, 1971

Price, H H, 'Psychical Research and Human Personality', *Hibbert*

Journal, 1949

Price, H H, 'Regurgitation and the Duncan Mediumship', *National Laboratory Psychical Research, Bulletin 1*, 1931

Price, H H, *Poltergeist: Tales of the Supernatural*, Senate, 1945

Prince W F, *The Case of Patience Worth*, Boston Society for Psychical Research, 1971

Radin, B, *The Conscious Universe*, USA, Harper Collins, 1997

Rahner, K, *Quaestiones Disputatae: Visions and Prophecies*, Herder and Herder, 1963

Ramsey, A M, *The Glory of God and the Transfiguration of Christ*, Longmans Green, 1949

Raudive, K, *Breakthrough: An Amazing Experiment in Electronic Communication with the Dead*, Colin Smythe, 1971

Rawlinson, A E, *The Gospel According to St Mark*, Methuen, 1925

Rees-Mogg, W, 'Haunted by Evidence of a Spirit World', *The Times*, 22 December 1997

Report of the Working Party on Parapsychology, a Paper of the General Assembly of the Church of Scotland, 1976

Report on Occult and Psychic Activities, adopted by the 188th General Assembly of the United Presbyterian Church of the USA, 1922

Report on Supranormal Psychic Phenomena, a Report of the General Assembly of the Church of Scotland, 1976

Rhead, G, 'Evidence for Milli-Meter Wave Radiation Associated with Paranormal Activity', *Journal of the Society for Psychical Research*, 2001

Rhine, J B, 'A New Case of Experimental Unreliability', *Journal of Parapsychology*, 1974

Rhine, J B, *et al.*, *Extrasensory Perception after Sixty Years*, Boston, Bruce Humphries, 1940

Rhine, J B, *Extrasensory Perception*, Boston Society for Psychical Research, 1932

Rhine, L E, 'Frequencies of Types of Experiences in Spontaneous Precognition', *Journal of Parapsychology*, 1954

Rhine, L E, 'Precognition and Intervention', *Journal of Parapsychology*, 1955

Ring, K, *Life At Death*, MacCann and Geoghegan, 1982

Rinpoche, S, *The Tibetan Book of Living and Dying*, Ryder, 1992

Rivaldini, 'Tony Blair and the Last English Witch', Luce e Ombra, 1988

Rivas, T, 'The Efficacy of Mind in General', *Paranormal Review*, 1999

Roll, W G and Pratt, J G, *Journal of the American Society for Psychical Research*, 1971

Ryall, E, *Born Twice: Total Recall of a 17th Century Life*, Harper and Row, 1974

Ryle, G, *The Concept of Mind*, Peregrine Press, 1976

Sabom, M B, *Recollection of Death*, Corgi, 1982

Seymour, P A H, *The Paranormal*, Arkana, 1992

Sguillante, and Pagani, *Vita della Serafina de Dio*, Rome, 1948

Sheargold, R J, *Hints on Receiving the Voice Phenomenon*, Colin Smythe, 1973

Sheldrake, R, 'The Sense of Being Stared At in Schools', *Journal for Psychic Research*, no.851, 1998

Sheldrake, R, Correspondence in *The Journal of the Society for Psychical Research*, no.859, 2000

Sheldrake, R, *Dogs That Know When Their Owners Are Coming Home*, Hutchinson, 1999

Sheldrake, R, *Seven Experiments That Can Change The World*, Fourth Estate, 1994

Sheldrake, R, *The Rebirth of Nature*, Century, 1990

Soal, S G and Bateman, F, *Modern Experiments in Telepathy*, Faber, 1959

Spedding, F, 'Physical Phenomena and Psychical Research', *Life, Death and Psychical Research*, Pearce-Higgins, J D (ed.), Ryder, 1973

St Gregory, *Dialogues*

St Teresa of Avila, *Foundations*

Stemman, R, 'The Druse and Reincarnation: Research in Lebanon', *Reincarnation International*, no.15, 1998

Stevenson, I, *20 Cases Suggestive of Reincarnation*, ASPR, 1966

Stevenson, I, *Cases of the Reincarnation Type in India*, University of Virginia, 1975

Stevenson, I, *Cases of the Reincarnation Type, vol. I India, 1975; vol. II Sri Lanka, 1977; vol. III Lebanon and Turkey 1980; vol. IV Thailand and Burma 1983*, USA, University of Virginia Press

Stevenson, I, *Children Who Remember Previous Lives*, USA, University of Virginia Press, 1987, revised edition 2001

Stevenson, I, *Where Reincarnation and Biology Intersect*, Newport and Connecticut, Praeger, 1997

Stevenson, I, *Where Reincarnation and Biology Intersect*, USA, Praeger, 1986

Summarium super dubio an sit signanda Commissio Introductionis Causae Servi Dei Andrei Huberi Fournet

Summarium super Virtutibus

Sutter, P, *Satans Macht und Mirken in zwei besessenen Kindern*, Germany, Eckman, 1921

Swinburne, R, *The Evolution of the Soul*, Oxford University Press, 1986

Sylvia, G K, and Novak, W, *A Change of Heart*, Little Brown, 1997

Taylor, S R, 'On the Difficulties of Making Earthlike Planets', *Meteoric and Planetary Sciences*, 1999, 34

Taylor, V, *The Gospel According to St Mark*, Macmillan, 1953

The Encyclopaedia of the Lutheran Church, Augsburg Publishing House, 1965

Thiery, *Nouvelle Biographie*, vol. II

Thomas, K, *Religion and the Decline of Magic*, Penguin Books, 1991

Thurston, S, SJ, *The Physical Phenomenon of Mysticism*, Burnes Oates, 1952

Tyrrell, G N M, *The Personality of Man*, Penguin Books, 1947

Underhill, E, *Mysticism*, Methuen, 1923

Veillot, *Ste Germaine Cousin*, 1904

Vita e Dottrina di Santa Caterina da Genova, Genova, 1847

Von Hugel, F, *The Mystical Element in Religion*

Walker, D, *The Ministry of Deliverance*, Longman, Barton and Todd, 1997

Weber, B, *La V Jeanne Marie de la della Croce of Roveredo*

Whitaker, T, *Yorkshire's Ghosts and Legends*, Collins, 1983

Whyte, H A Maxwell, *Demons and Deliverance*, Whitaker House, 1989

Wiebe P H, *Visions of Jesus*, USA, OUP, 1997

Wiesinger, Abbot A D, *Occult Phenomena in the Light of Theology*, Burnes Gates, E.T., 1957

Williams, R, *St Theresa*, Chapman, 1991

Wilson, I, *Reincarnation*, Penguin Books, 1982

Wilson, I, *The After-Death Experience*, Sidgwick and Jackson, 1987

Wilson, J Dover, *What Happens in Hamlet*, OUP, 1959

Yepes, *Vida, Virtudes y Milagros*

Zammit, D, *A Lawyer Argues for the Afterlife*, Sydney, Association for the Investigation of the Afterlife, no date

Zeki, S, *Vision of the Brain*, Blackwell, 1993

Printed in the United Kingdom
by Lightning Source UK Ltd.
125906UK00001B/7/A